IMAGES of America

SAVANNAH'S HISTORIC NEIGHBORHOODS

ARDSLEY PARK, CHATHAM CRESCENT, ARDMORE

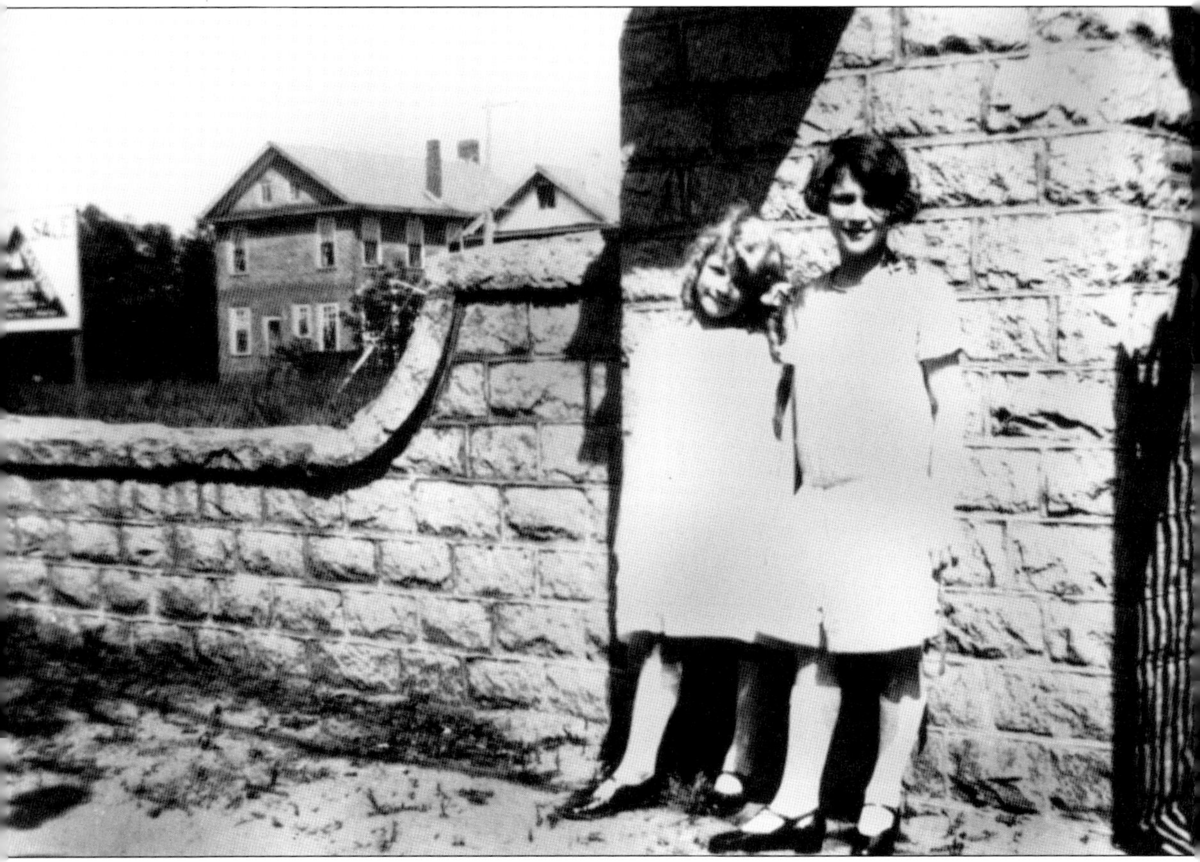

The Belgian-block wall and columns marking an entrance to Ardsley Park provide the perfect backdrop for an Easter 1927 snapshot of sisters Pauline Cargill (Powers) and Ernestine Cargill (Cole). Some sections of the wall and the pillars still exist today, although most of the pillars have lost their orange tile roofs. In 2001 Omar El-Khalidi, a building contractor who lives in Ardsley Park, offered to restore the pillars, a plan that received the endorsement of both the Ardsley Park Neighborhood Association and the Ardsley Park Garden Club, which offered support and assistance.

IMAGES
of America

SAVANNAH'S HISTORIC NEIGHBORHOODS

ARDSLEY PARK, CHATHAM CRESCENT, ARDMORE

Polly Powers Stramm

ARCADIA
PUBLISHING

ISBN 978-0-7385-1395-9

Published by Arcadia Publishing
Charleston, South Carolina

Printed in the United States of America

Library of Congress Catalog Card Number: 2001093049

For all general information contact Arcadia Publishing at:
Telephone 843-853-2070
Fax 843-853-0044
E-mail sales@arcadiapublishing.com
For customer service and orders:
Toll-Free 1-888-313-2665

Visit us on the Internet at www.arcadiapublishing.com

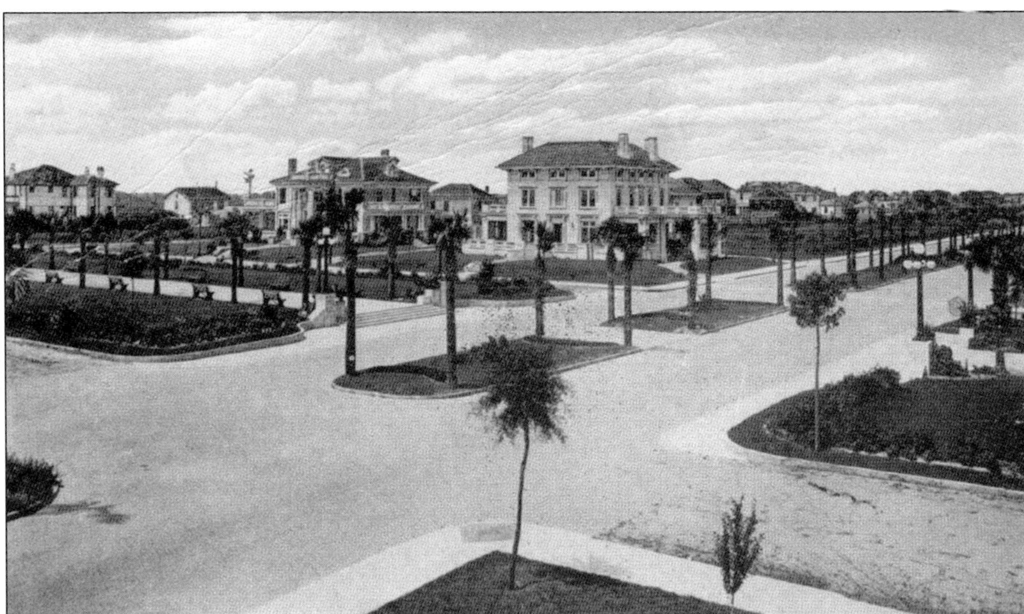

This vintage postcard of Estill Avenue (now Victory Drive) at the Atlantic Avenue mall shows the R.M. Hitch home. Hitch was mayor of Savannah in the 1930s. The house was designed by noted architect Hyman Witcover while he was in partnership with E. Lynn Drummond. Witcover practiced in Savannah from 1897 until 1923. Among his other designs are City Hall and the Bull Street branch of the main library.

Contents

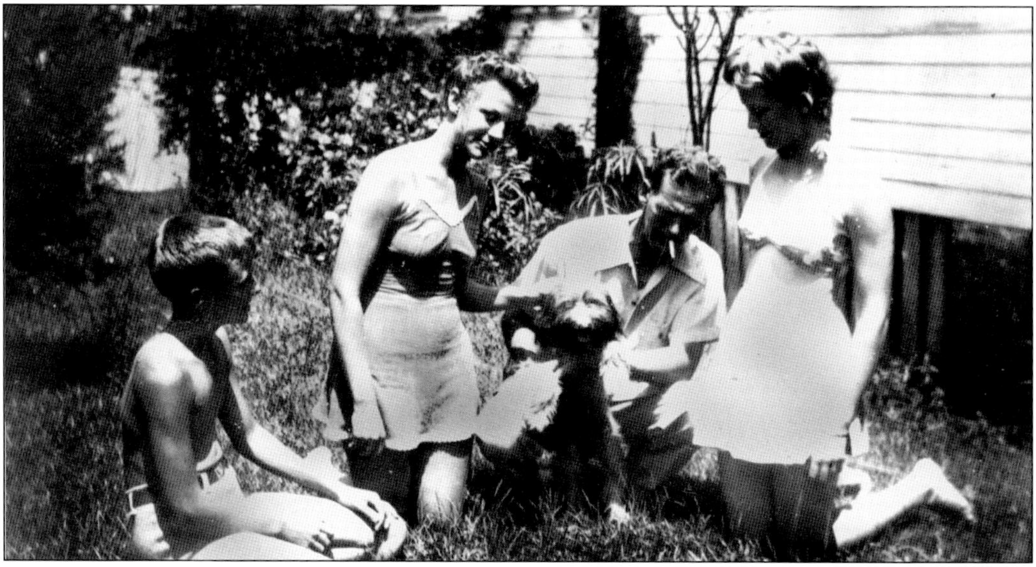

Members of the Martin family help wash Rusty the dog during the early 1940s. From left to right are Robert Martin, Sara Martin (Black), Capt. John Martin, and Ellen Martin (Mallory).

ACKNOWLEDGMENTS

This book would not have been possible without the help of dozens of current and former Ardsley Park, Chatham Crescent, and Ardmore residents who shared stories and opened treasured family scrapbooks. They generously offered to let me borrow their photos for this volume of memories. I appreciate their kindnesses.

I also applaud the research of Beth Lattimore Reiter, whose grandfather and great uncle were the developers of Ardsley Park. Beth did a yeoman's job of documenting the history of the neighborhoods for the Historic Savannah Foundation. Her documentation, which led to Ardsley Park and Chatham Crescent being named to the National Register of Historic Places, was a tremendous resource for the writing of this book. Another huge thank you goes to Harvey Granger, whose grandfather was the man behind Chatham Crescent. The 1910 marketing brochure for Chatham Crescent, with its maps and intriguing copy, which Mr. Granger shared with me, paints a fascinating picture of Savannah in those early days.

Much information also was gleaned from church archives and from papers written by Suzanne P. Johnson and Susie Meyers, W. Patrick Giglio and Douglas Scott, all former students at The Savannah College of Art and Design. SCAD Historic Preservation professor Marlborough Packard provided vintage postcards and offered valuable tips.

I couldn't have put together a book of photographs without turning to photographer (and good friend) Steve Bisson for advice. Steve is chief photographer for the *Savannah Morning News* and, obviously, has a sharp eye when it comes to selecting heartfelt images.

Last but not least I wish to thank my friends, off of whom I bounced ideas, and my dear family, including my two daughters, my husband, and my parents, Dr. and Mrs. Leander K. Powers, who taught me to appreciate the good things in life, like the opportunity to grow up in a wonderful neighborhood.

INTRODUCTION

For three years during the early part of the 20th century, thousands of Savannahians watched in awe as dozens of newfangled vehicles called automobiles zoomed along Estill Avenue (now Victory Drive) during the Great Savannah Races. During those years—1908, 1910, and 1911—plans already were taking shape for the construction of a handful of grand homes in Ardsley Park and Chatham Crescent, the city's first two automobile suburbs. These neighborhoods were developed simultaneously on open, boggy land on the fringes of the streetcar lines in what was then the southeastern part of Savannah.

Surprisingly, Ardsley Park was—and still is—a relatively small subdivision. The idea was the brainstorm of Harry Hays Lattimore, William Lattimore, and anonymous partners in the Ardsley Park Land Corporation. No one is certain how the Ardsley name evolved though some have theorized that it was borrowed from a British neighborhood. The area was laid out in grids with squares, similar to the plan used in downtown Savannah by Gen. James Edward Oglethorpe, founder of the Colony. The northern and western boundaries of Ardsley Park were marked at Estill Avenue and Bull Street by an impressive looking retaining wall made of Belgian block similar to those used as ballast on ships sailing from England. At key intersections stone pillars with Spanish-looking tile roofs marked the entrances to the park.

Adjacent to Ardsley Park was a much larger piece of acreage known as the Granger Tract. Owner Harvey Granger was something of a transportation visionary who is credited with paving the first concrete road in the state and finishing the Atlantic Coastal Highway, which ultimately connected the seaboard states with Florida. He also helped bring the auto races to the city and served on the Chatham County Commission.

Marketed as Chatham Crescent by Granger's Chatham Land and Hotel Company, the Granger Tract took its design from the Beaux Arts plan popular at the time. At various points in the neighborhood, city blocks were punctuated with one-acre circles (named for city and county officials), a crescent-shaped street, and a landscaped mall. At the end of the palmetto-lined mall stretching from Maupas Avenue to 47th Street was to be the centerpiece of Chatham Crescent—a magnificent tourist facility called the Georgia Hotel.

The Spanish Revival–style hotel was designed by noted architect Henrik Wallin, who assisted Henry Bacon with New York's Astor Hotel. Apparently, the developers hoped that wealthy Northerners would check into what was to be a luxurious hotel and decide to purchase a second home in Chatham Crescent. Unfortunately, the hotel encountered numerous problems and barely got off the ground. Eventually, Savannah High School (now the Savannah Arts Academy) was built on the nearly eight acres of land set aside for the hotel.

Despite the delay and ultimate abandonment of Chatham Crescent's hotel, both that neighborhood and Ardsley Park proved to be popular, not with Northerners, but with some of the city's most influential residents. One of the first houses built in Chatham Crescent was the beautiful home of William H. Robertson who served as chairman of the city's Park and Tree Commission for more than 50 years. Robert Hitch, who was elected mayor in the 1930s, constructed a Mediterranean-style home at the intersection of Atlantic and Estill Avenues in 1911, and Oliver Bacon, chairman of the county commission, built next door. Among the first Ardsley Park homeowners were the Lattimores, Emmersons, and Myricks.

Evidently prospective homeowners were impressed by amenities such as city sewers, water, gas, public transportation, electric streetlights, granite curbing, and cement sidewalks. No doubt, green space also was a factor in the popularity of both areas. The Ardsley Park squares were originally landscaped by the Berckman firm of Augusta. Botanist P.J. Berckman had established the Fruitlands Nursery in Augusta, which became Augusta National Golf Club, home of The Masters.

Ardsley Park was designed with tree-planting strips, or tree lawns, between the streets and the sidewalks, while Chatham Crescent featured large trees planted directly on the front lawns. More than 5,000 trees were planted in Chatham Crescent under the direction of Henri Bignault, a landscape architect trained at the Ecole De Beaux Arts.

These comfortable, attractive neighborhoods included architectural styles ranging from elaborate Greek Revival to simple Craftsman bungalows. The areas grew to include churches, schools, and a few small, but tasteful storefront businesses like Kleeman's Market on By the 1930s, for the most part, development of Ardsley Park and Chatham Crescent was complete. The Lattimores' next project was Ardmore, to the south of both Ardsley Park and Chatham Crescent. At the southern end of this new neighborhood was diamond-shaped Hull Park, which became a popular recreational site. Bordering one side of the park was the Gould Cottage for Children, funded by millionaire philanthropist Edwin Gould and designed by architect Cletus Bergen. All in all, the Lattimores developed and sold six residential subdivisions, involving more than 1,500 lots.

In 1985, Ardsley Park and Chatham Crescent were named to the National Register of Historic Places under the collective name of Ardsley Park. The Ardsley Park Neighborhood Association encompasses Ardsley Park, Chatham Crescent, Ardmore, and nearby streets.

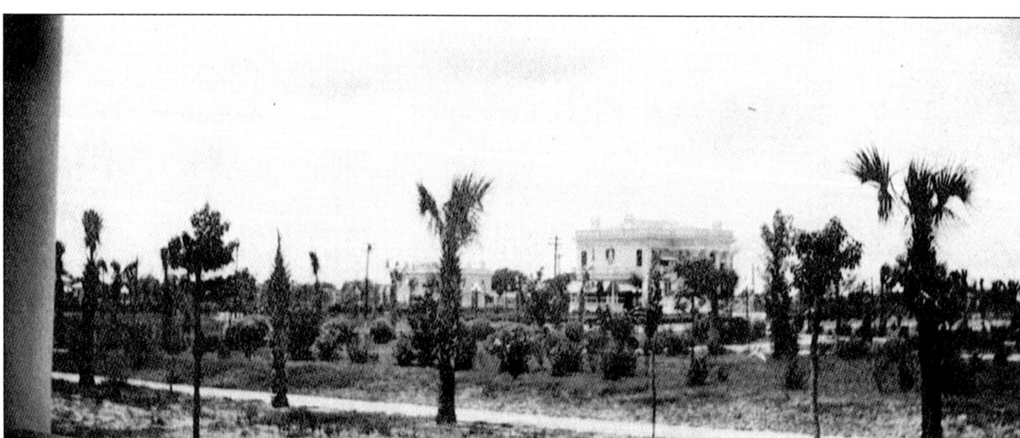

This view, taken around 1912 from the porch of an East 46th Street house, shows a desolate looking Kavanaugh Park and, in the distance, the Lattimore home at Washington Avenue and Abercorn Street, as well as the Emmerson home on East 49th Street. The Lattimore house was built in 1910 and the Emmerson house was constructed between 1911 and 1912. The Livingston family purchased the Emmerson home in 1916 and lived there until 1971. Mrs. Livingston, who enjoyed entertaining, added a huge ballroom to the Mediterranean-style home.

One

Ardsley Park

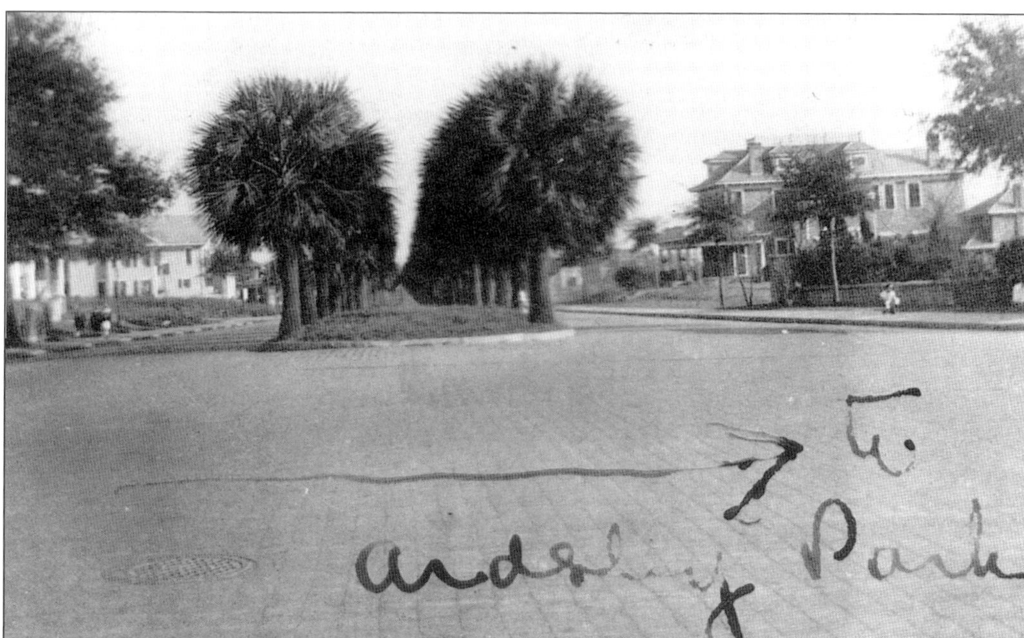

This photo of Estill Avenue (now Victory Drive) and Abercorn Street was taken around 1914 and borrowed from the Myrick family album. The handwriting obviously points to Ardsley Park.

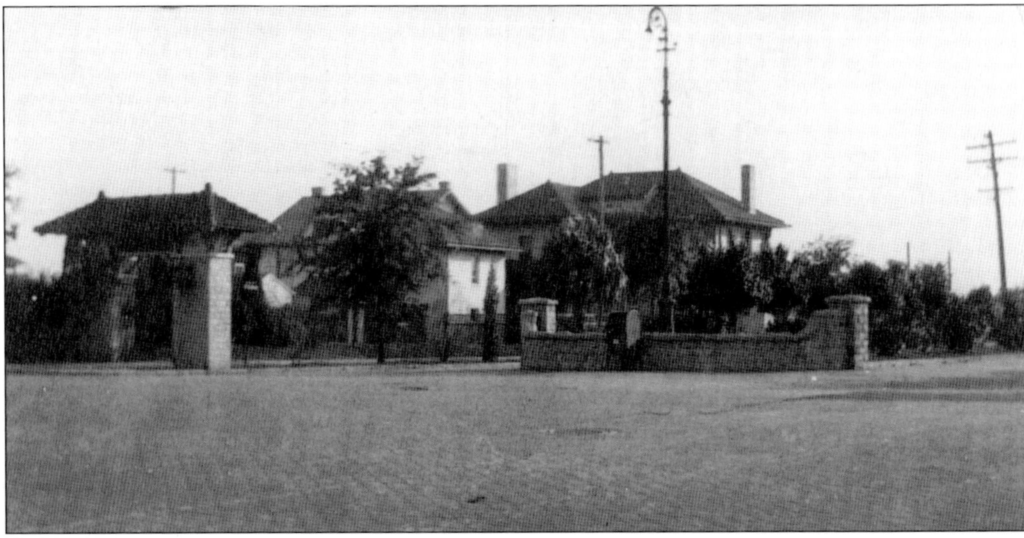

The Belgian-block gates at Estill Avenue (now Victory Drive) and Abercorn Street marked the dramatic entrance to Ardsley Park. Other pillars were situated at key entrances to the subdivision. Decorative iron gates were removed from the pillars to be used as scrap metal (for the cause) during World War I.

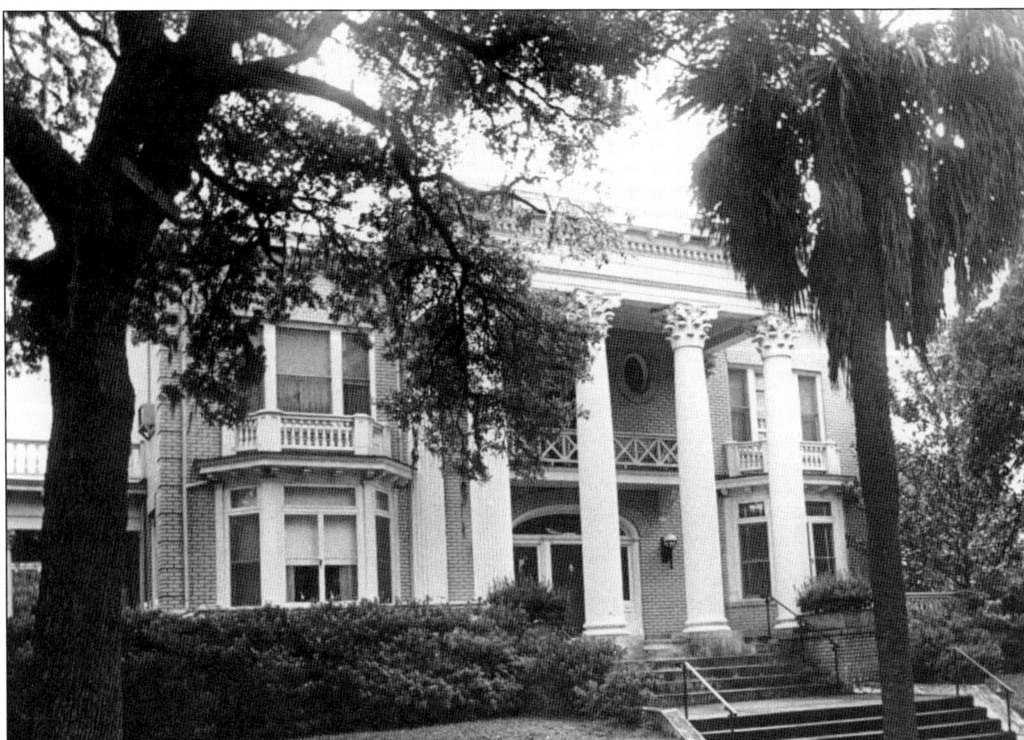

The Lattimore house at 39 Washington Avenue was designed in the Greek Revival style by architect Percy Sudgen. It was originally faced with terrazzo, which cracked, and then was refaced with yellow brick, which was popular at the time. Sudgen was born in England and by 1888 had arrived in Savannah. He was involved in the platting of Ardsley Park.

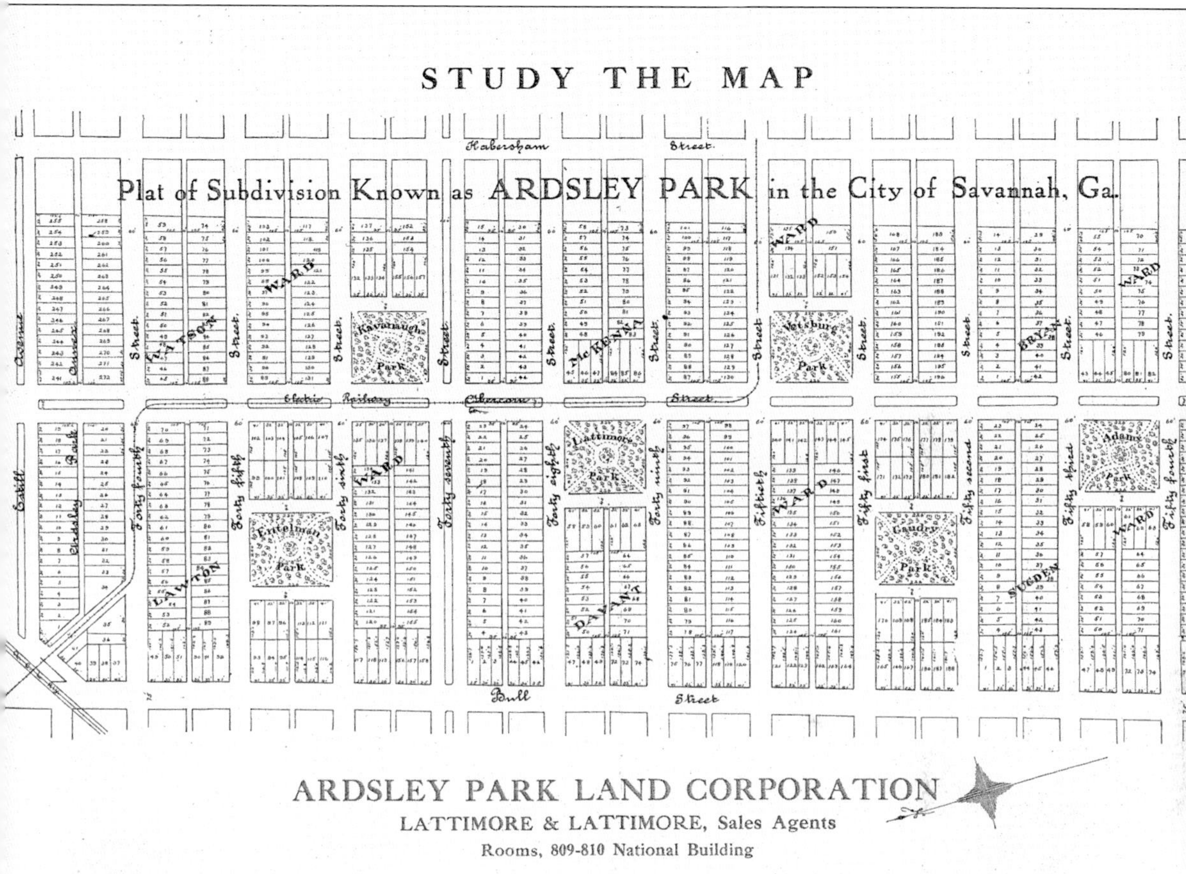

The map of Ardsley Park shows just how small the neighborhood is. The eastern boundary looks as if it stops just short of Habersham Street because it probably would have been where Lincoln Street would be if it had been extended south of Estill Avenue (now Victory Drive). A Belgian-block pillar still standing on the south side of Victory Drive between Abercorn and Habersham Streets apparently marked the eastern boundary of Ardsley Park.

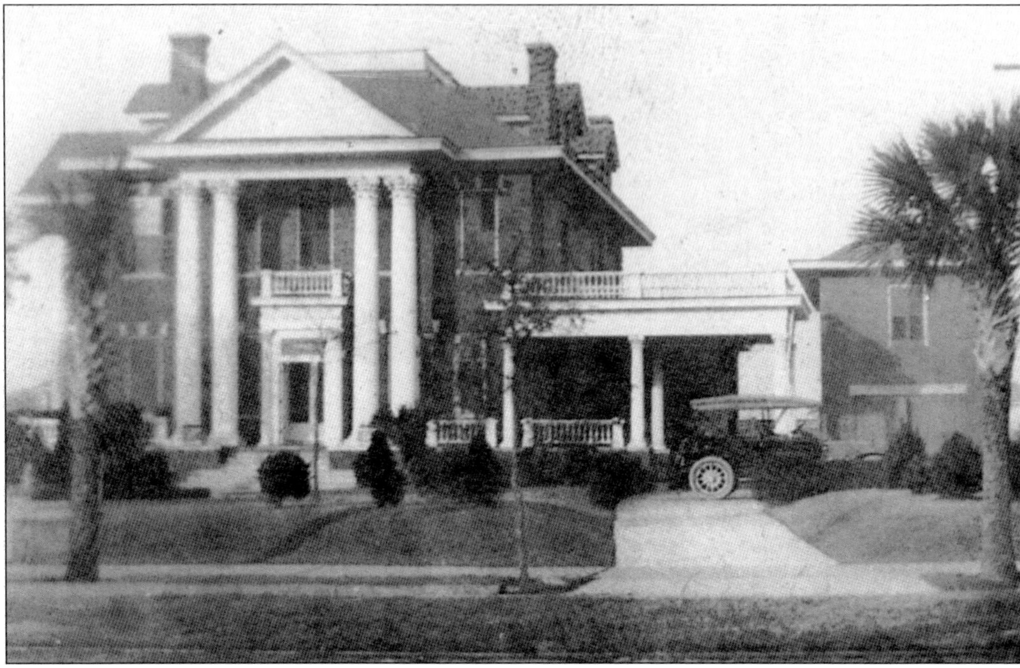

The Myrick house, built in 1914 at 2807 Abercorn Street, was one of the first Ardsley Park homes to face Abercorn. It was designed by engineer and architect Olaf Otto who immigrated to the United States from Norway. He moved to Savannah about 1912. Among his Savannah projects was the first steel bridge linking Savannah with South Carolina and the original Bay Street Viaduct.

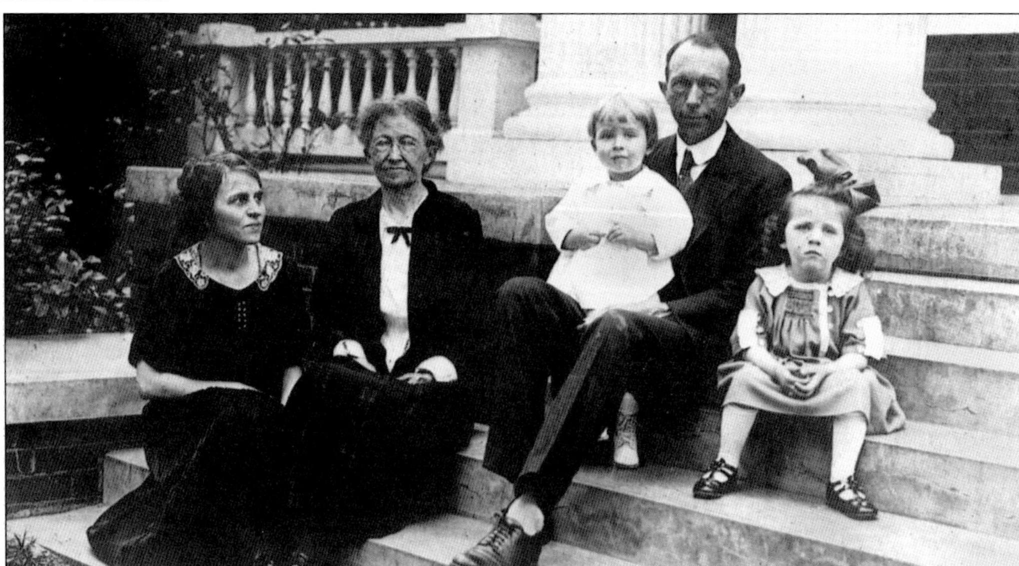

The Myrick family sat on the front steps of their house for this photograph. From left to right are Mary Robinson Myrick, Marie Louise Scudder Myrick, Shelby Myrick Sr. holding Shelby Myrick Jr., and Mary Myrick. After her husband died in 1895, Marie Louise Myrick took over as editor of the *Americus Times-Recorder* and became one of the most politically influential women in Georgia. She moved to Savannah around 1907 to be near her son Shelby and his family.

Otto's bill to Shelby Myrick totaled $18,780, including $425 for a concrete driveway and steps.

OFFICE PHONE 4201 — RESIDENCE PHONE 2821

OLAF OTTO
ENGINEER
ROOM 309
GERMANIA BANK BUILDING
BUILDING CONSTRUCTION — INDUSTRIAL PLANTS
CONTRACTS TAKEN FOR ALL CLASSES OF BUILDING
REINFORCED CONCRETE, STEEL CONSTRUCTION, ETC.

SAVANNAH, GA., May 12th, 1914

Col. Shelby Myrick,
National Building,
Savannah, Ga.

Dear Sir:-

I enclose herewith statement to cover cost of completion of your new residence in Ardsley Park.

-S T A T E M E N T-

Contract price on residence and garage	$16,750.00
Two granite door sills (East and South entrance)	50.00
Roof on garage changed and slate substituted for tin, Dec.26	175.00
Roof on kitchen changed from tin to slate " "	50.00
Promenade tile for entrance and South porch	82.50
Fences complete letter Jan. 14th.	258.00
Concrete driveway and steps according to plan furnished letter, Jan 14th.	425.00
Interior trim cahnged to hardwood, letter Jan 27th.	275.00
Interior Cornice, letter March 17th	65.64
Two screened porches, letter March 30th.	150.00
Extra on mantels, letter April 11th.	69.50
Work on garage, letter April 18th.	98.75
Work in kitchen, pantry and store room, letter April 24th.	69.00
Extra plumbing and wiring, letter May 4th.	91.52
Chicken coop, driveway etc, letter May 6th	67.50
W. G. & R. C. Harrison, paid on insurance	53.62
Shutters etc., letter May 12th.	48.97
TOTAL Cost of Residence	$18,780.00
Deduction for electric fixtures	100.00
TOTAL DUE	$3,555.00
Paid on contract December 1st, 1913	3,562.50
" " " January 1st, 1914	3,550.00
" " " February 1st, 1914	2,162.50
" " " March 1st, 1914	3,450.00
" " " April 1st, 1914	2,400.00
TOTAL PAID	$15,125.00

Received from Shelby Myrick the sum of $3505.00 on above statement which is the final statement of indebtedness of said Shelby Myrick to me on contract for building above house. The sum of fifty dollars is withheld by said Shelby Myrick pending an adjustment of some electrical bills and some

Yours very truly,
Olaf Otto

This was the bill for the Myrick's icebox, a forerunner of the refrigerator.

Estimates furnished and all work positively Guaranteed. Power work given proper attention. We install the latest and most up-to-date steam and hot-water systems. Especial attention to repairing unsatisfactory heating systems.

Savannah, Ga., May 1st 1914

Mr. Olaf Otto
City

TO **Peerless Plumbing and Heating Co.,** DR.
THE QUALITY SHOP
E. J. BRUTCHER, Prop.
108 Congress St., E. — Phone 4223

Ice box at Myrick Residence

April 2	To 10 ft 2" Soil pipe @ .10	1 00
"	10 lbs. caulking lead @ .06	60
"	1 - refrigerator drain	1 25
"	1 - 1½" 45° Ell	25
"	1 - 2" X ⅛ bend	16
"	1 - 2" - Cleanout	16
"	1 - 2" - Y	20
"	2 - 1½" X 6" Galvanized nipple	20
"	2 lbs. Oakum	10
"	6 hours labor for Plumber & Helper @	4 08
		8 00
"	20 %	1 60
		9 60

May 2-14 Paid Peerless Pl & Htg Co
E Brutcher

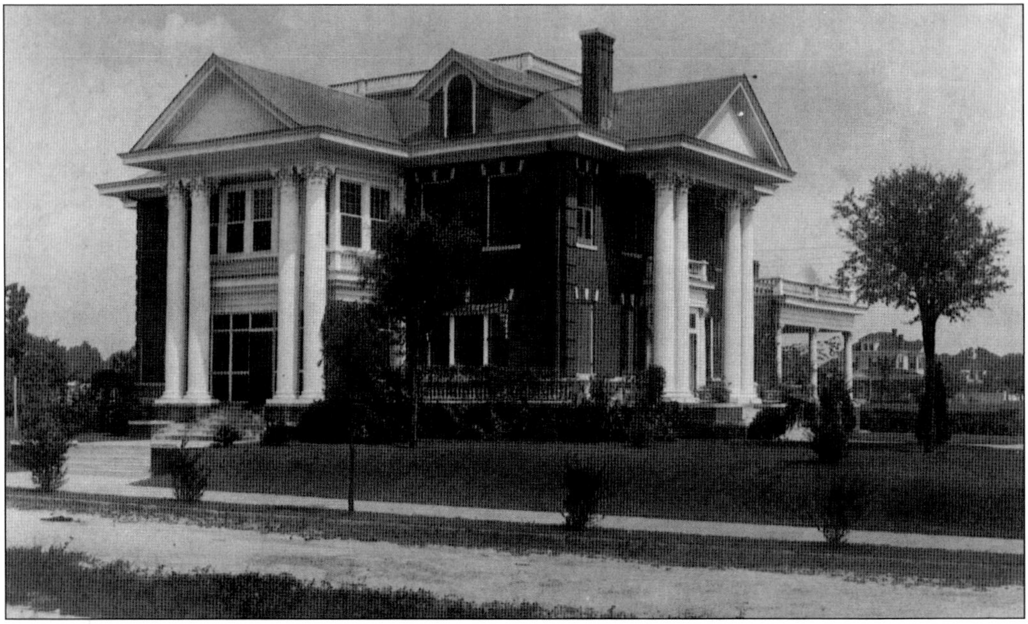

The side view of the Myrick residence shows an unpaved 46th Street.

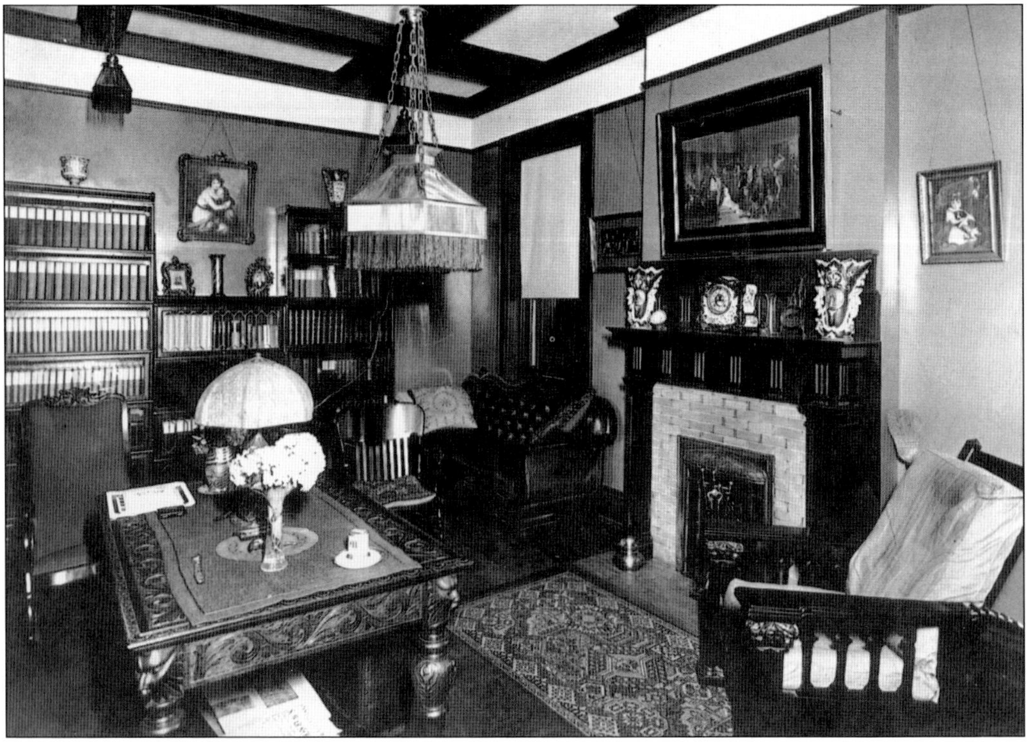

The interior of the Myrick home, showcasing the latest in Victorian décor, was featured in a national magazine.

The Craftsman-style home at 101 East 49th Street was built in 1912 as a spec house and possibly was the second residence in Ardsley Park. The current owners, the Ellis family, acquired this photograph from a man who rang their doorbell one day. He told them he had lived in the house as a child and was touring the country visiting all of his former homes. The Byron "Crook" Smith family lived in the house for many years. Mrs. Marion Smith taught at both Charles Ellis Elementary and Savannah High Schools.

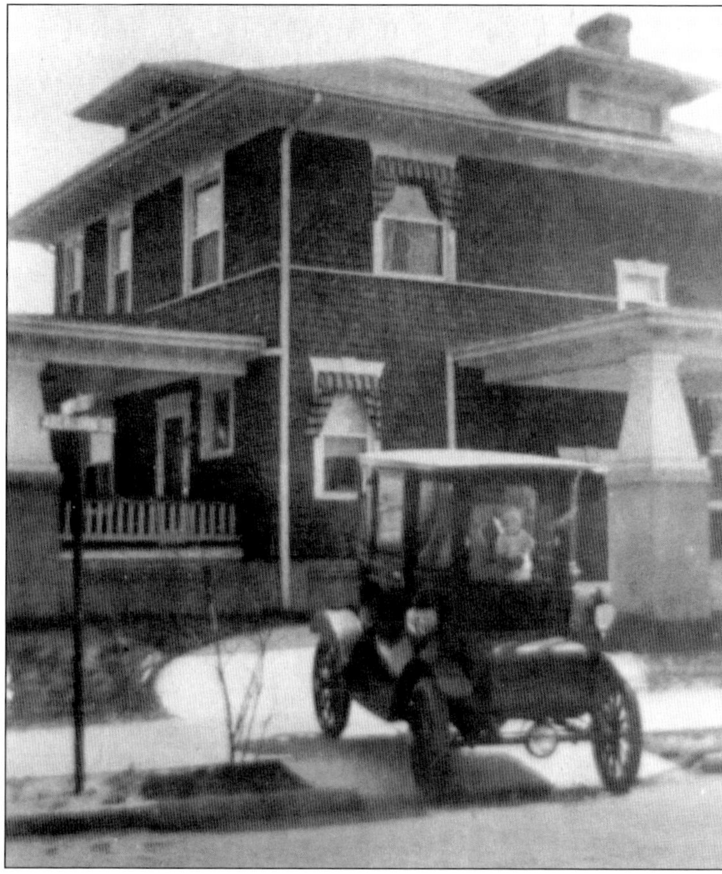

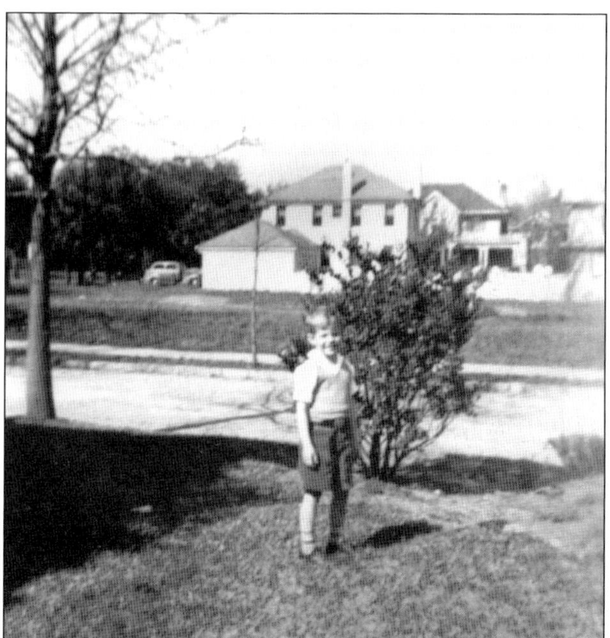

This little boy stands on the southeast corner of East 45th and Abercorn Streets during the 1930s. The house in the background is at 102 East 44th Street.

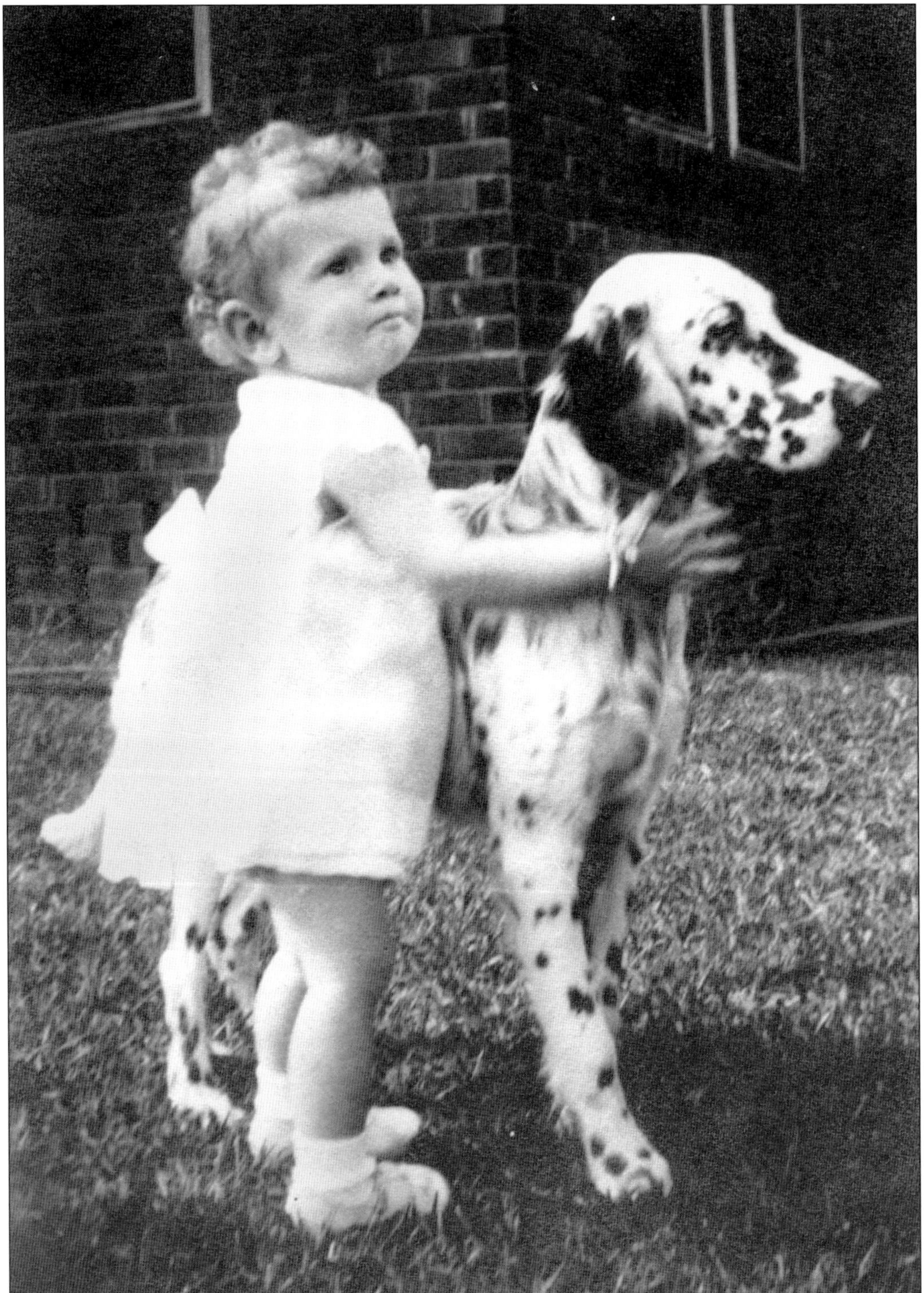

Beth Neville (Whelan) is pictured here with her dog, Joe. The Neville family lived on East 49th Street for years.

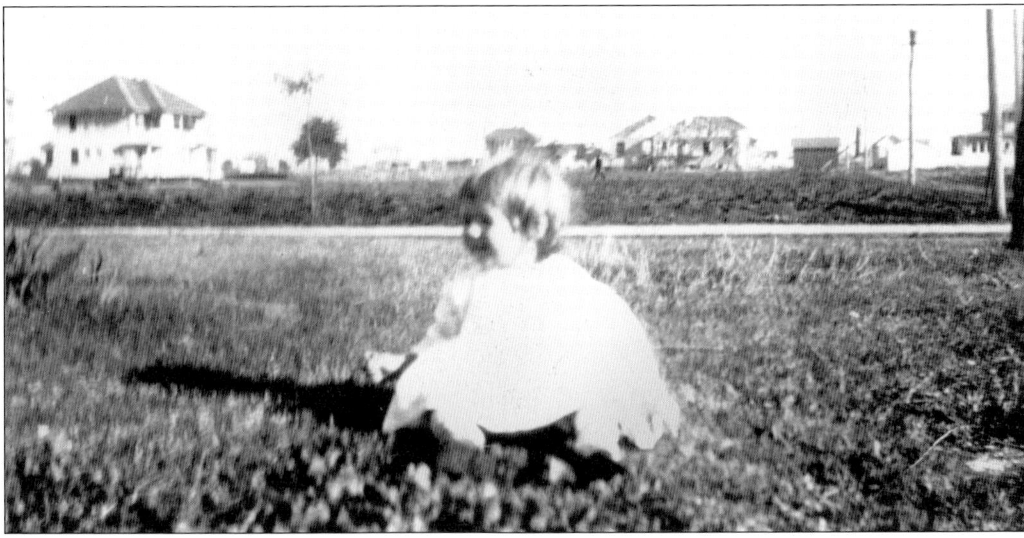

Little Virginia Arden's picture was taken in 1922 in the backyard of the Arden home at 137 East 49th Street. The house overlooked an unpaved Habersham Street with very few homes in the distance.

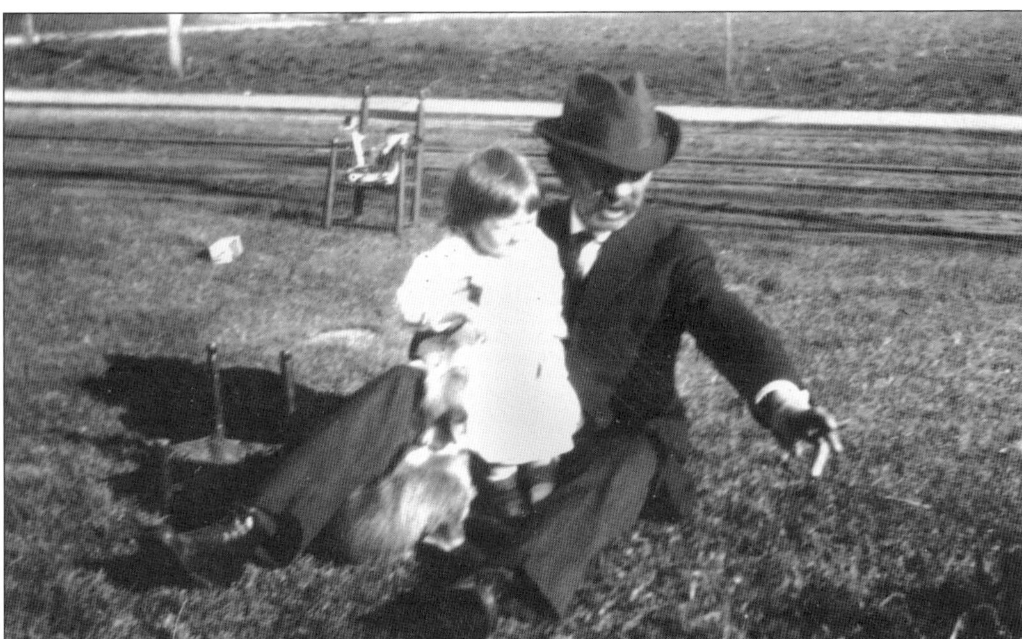

The photograph of Virginia and her father, Frank Arden Sr., offers a closer look at unpaved Habersham, including streetcar tracks.

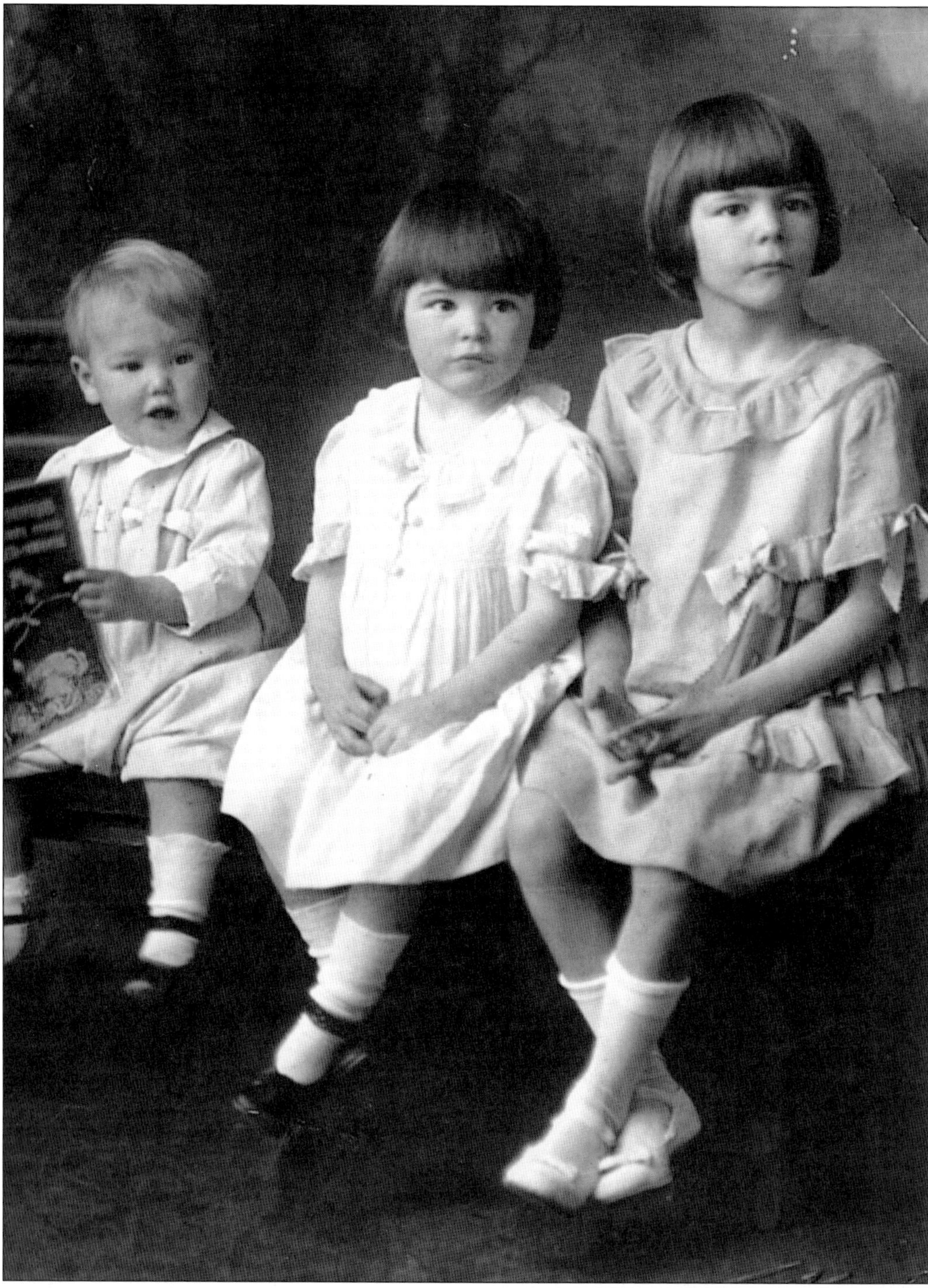

The Heyward children included (from left to right) George, Alice, and Marjory (Mingledorff).

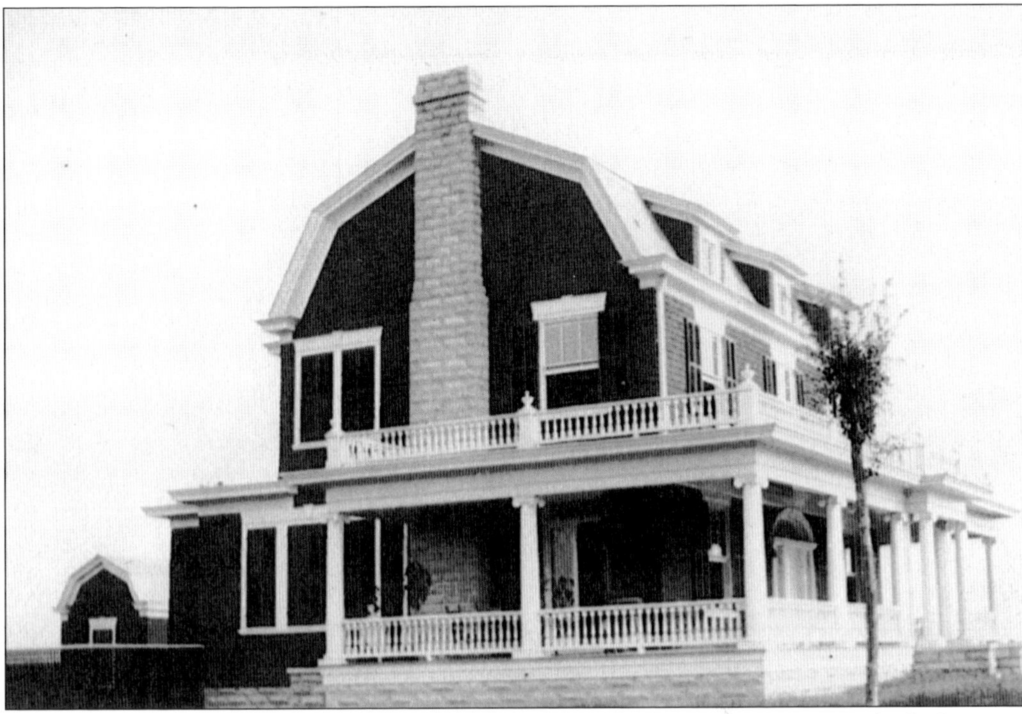

The George Heyward residence, built around 1912 at 123 East 46th Street, overlooked Kavanaugh Park and was constructed to resemble houses in Maine where Mrs. Heyward grew up. This photograph of the Heyward home was taken from the northwest. George Heyward was in charge of the Cotton Exchange and later practiced law.

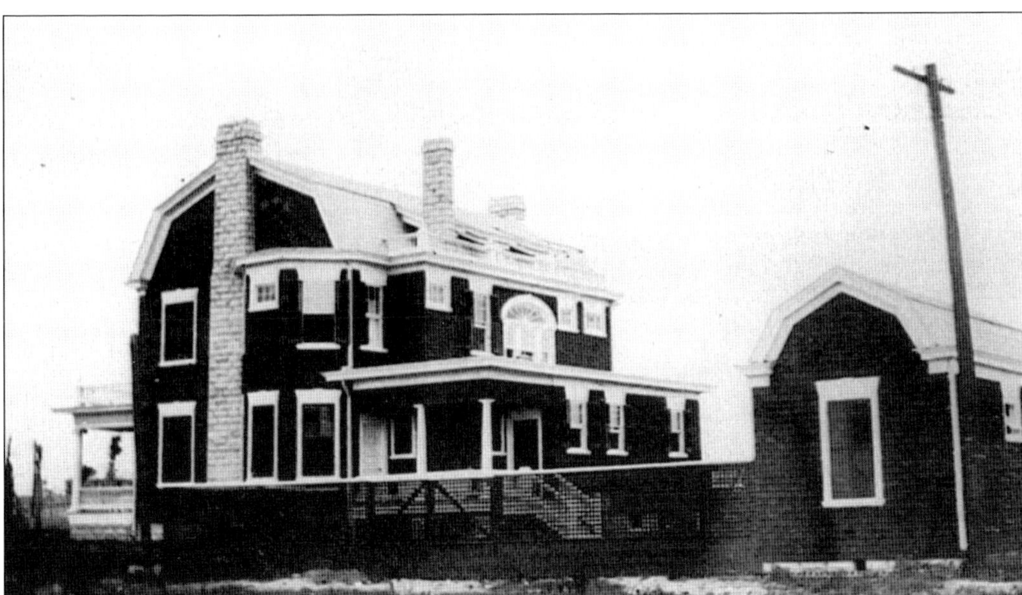

The Heywards moved from 46th Street around 1930. Later residents included the Calhoun family and the Hester family, which lived there for more than three decades.

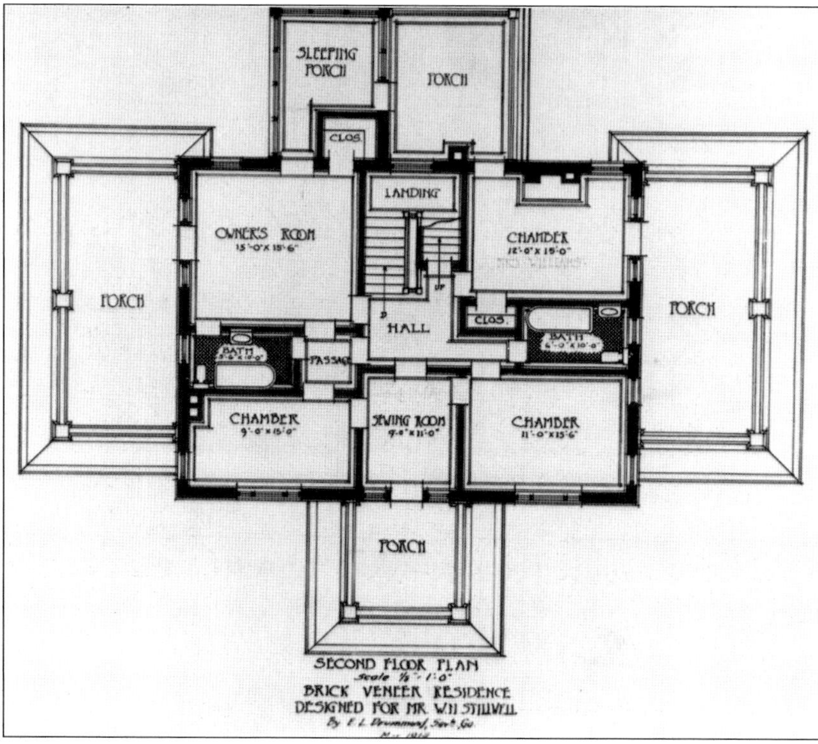

An architectural rendering shows the second floor of a Craftsman-style residence at 135 East 45th Street. The house was built for W.H. Stillwell in 1914 by E. Lynn Drummond, one of the most prolific architects to work in Ardsley Park and Chatham Crescent. He was only 21 when he designed this house.

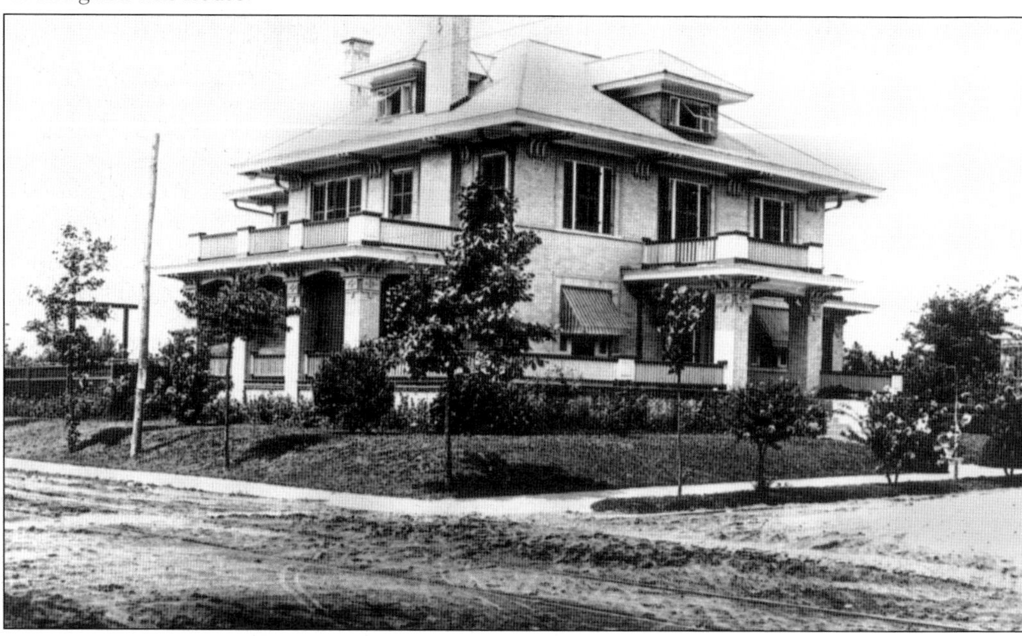

This view of the Stillwell home shows an unpaved Habersham Street, complete with streetcar tracks.

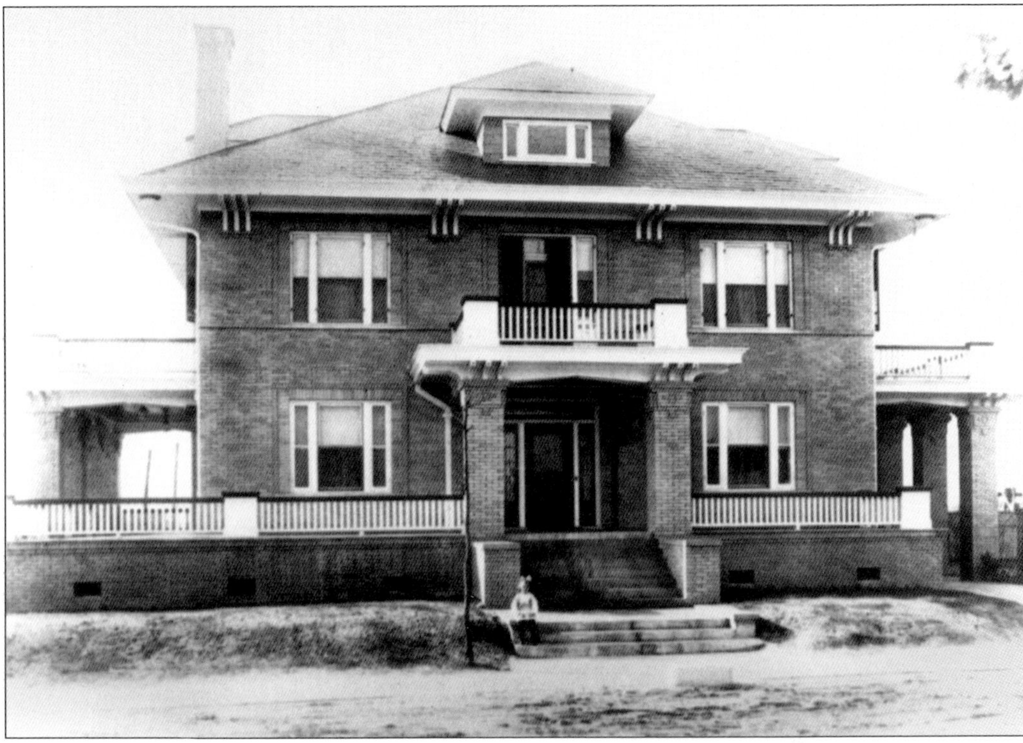

Apparently the Stillwells owned the house briefly before selling it to the Williams family. Daughter Bette Williams (Quinn) is the mother of journalist Sally Quinn.

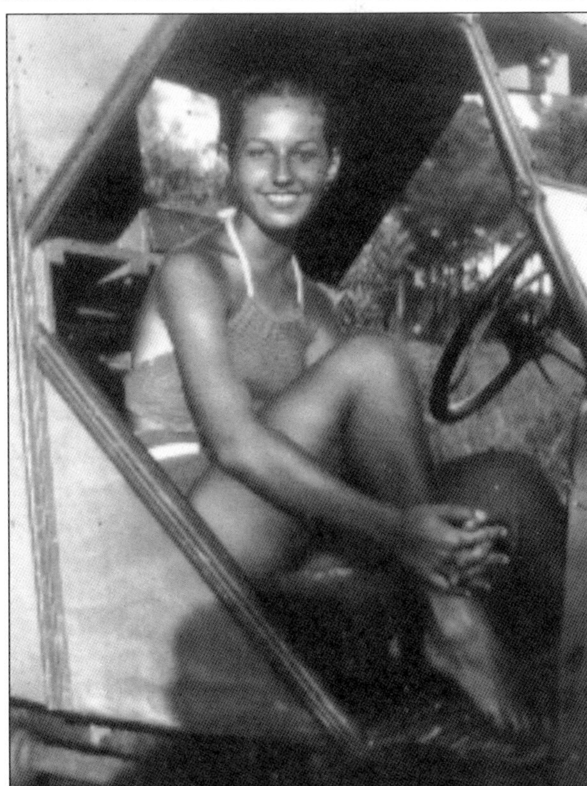

Bette Williams (Quinn) was photographed in 1934 by a friend.

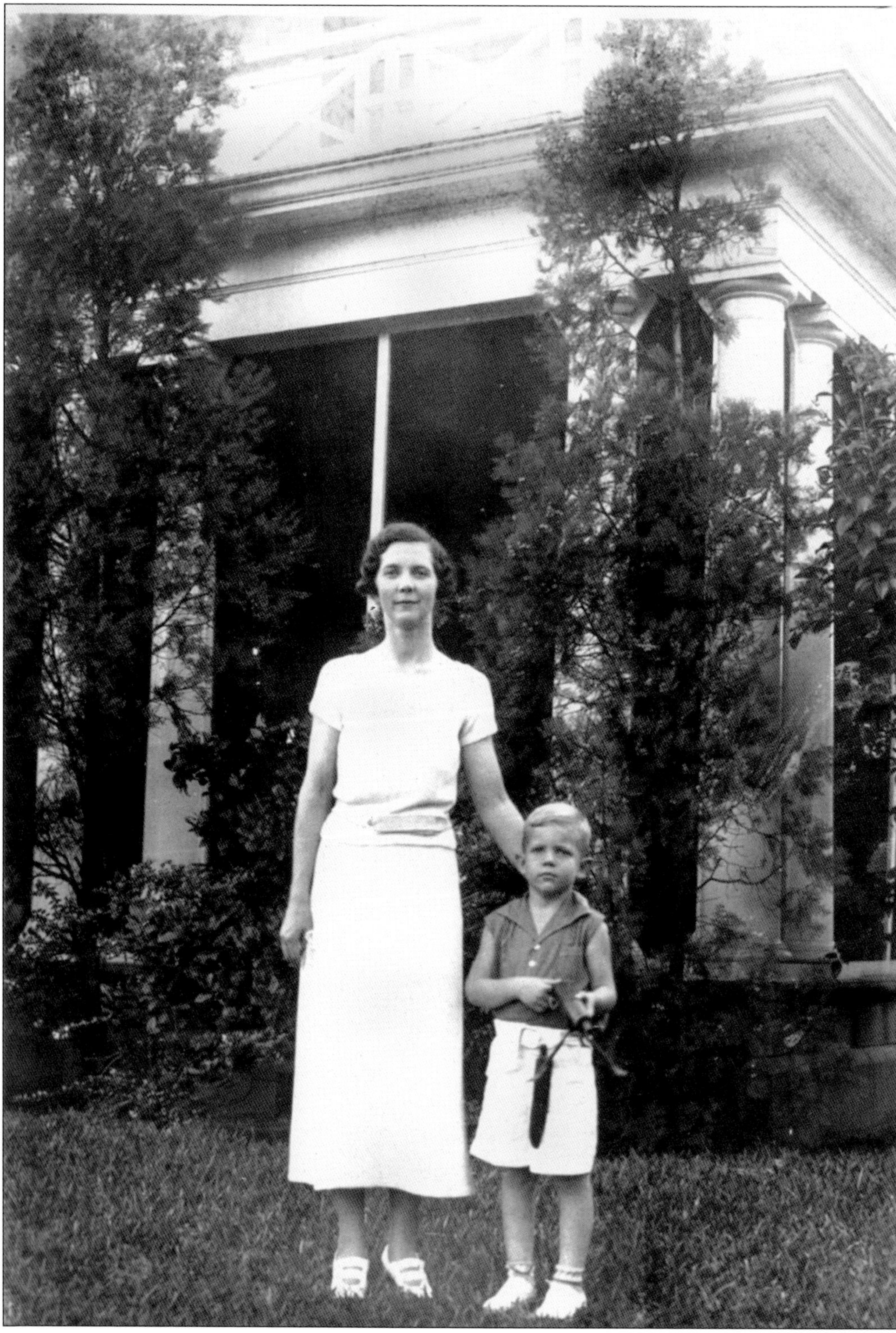
Deb Maner and his mother, Peg, stand in the yard of their home at 101 East 45th Street.

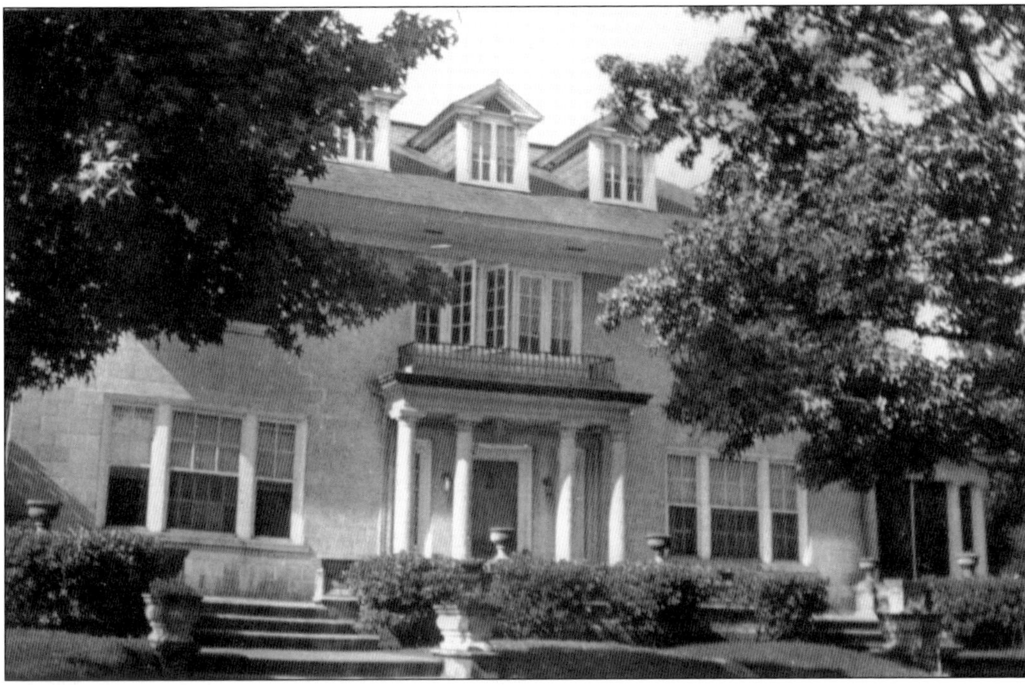

The Maner home was built in 1919 for C.S. Rowland.

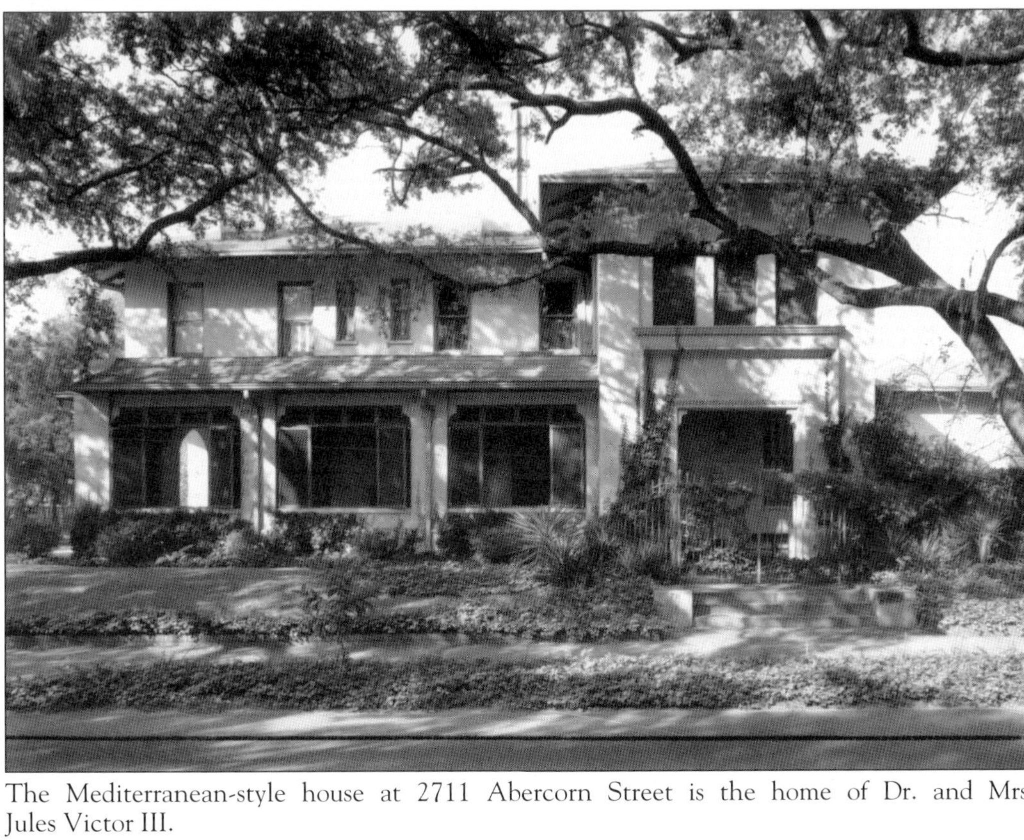

The Mediterranean-style house at 2711 Abercorn Street is the home of Dr. and Mrs. Jules Victor III.

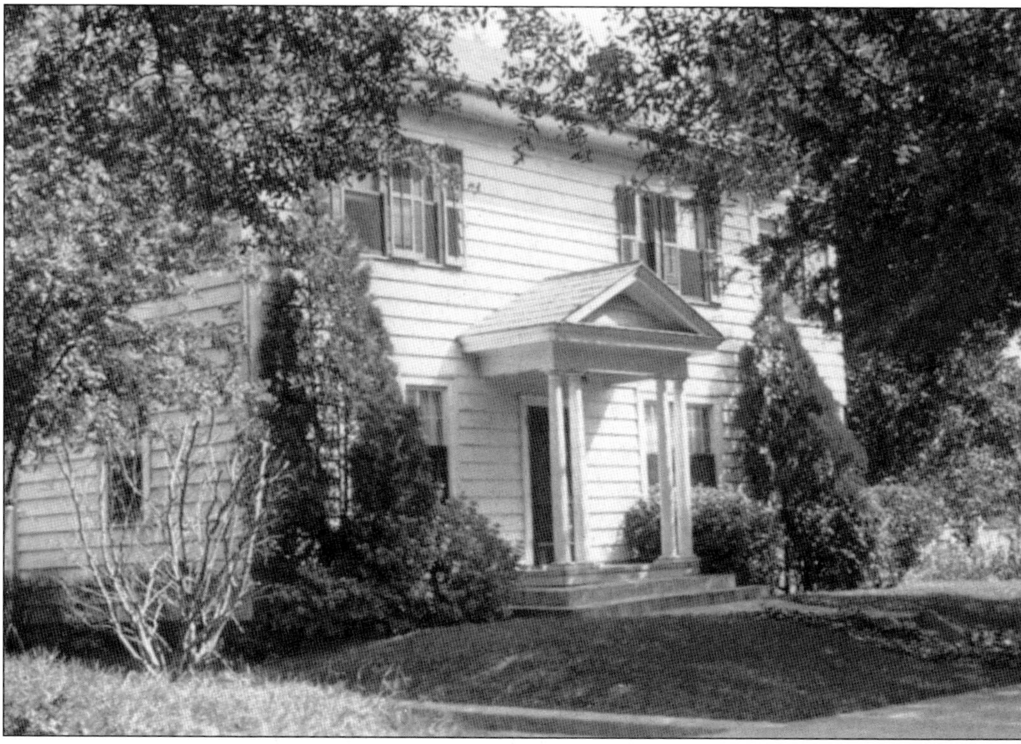

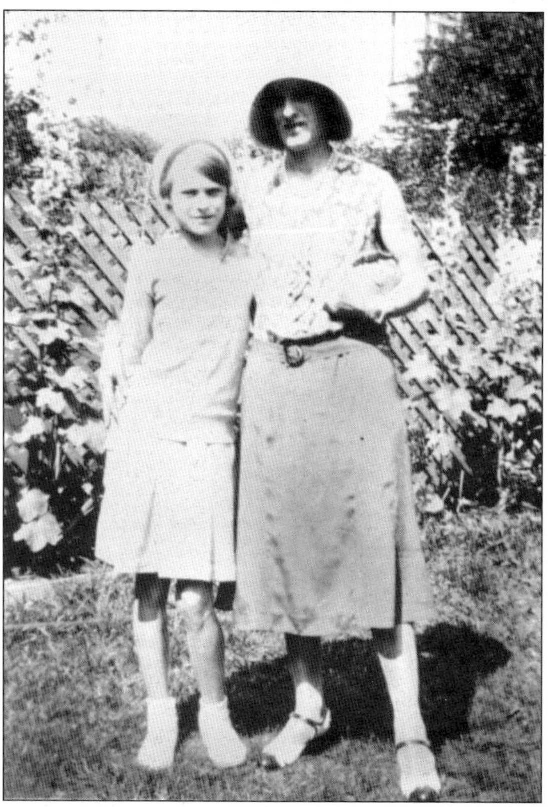

The two-story frame house at 116 Washington Avenue has been the home of Marian Beall (McIntosh) since 1936.

Marian Beall (McIntosh) and her mother, Myrta Beall, stand in their backyard.

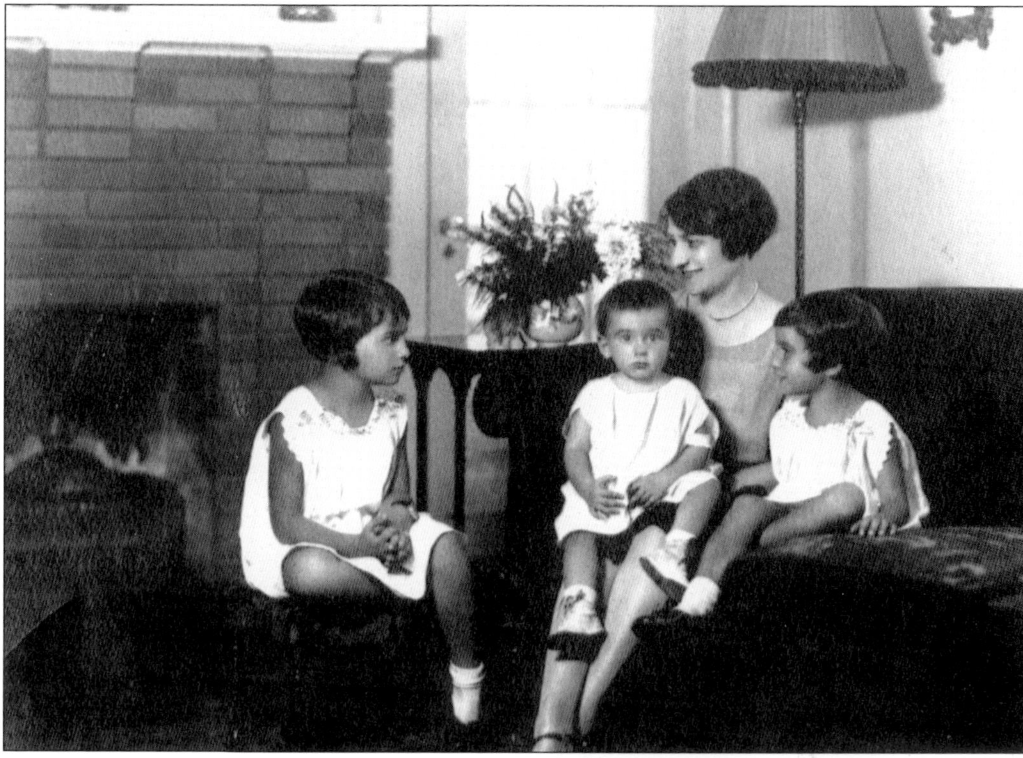

Louise Minis is shown with her daughters in the living room of their Ardsley Park home. Florance is on the stool, Caroline is on her lap, and Frances is on the sofa.

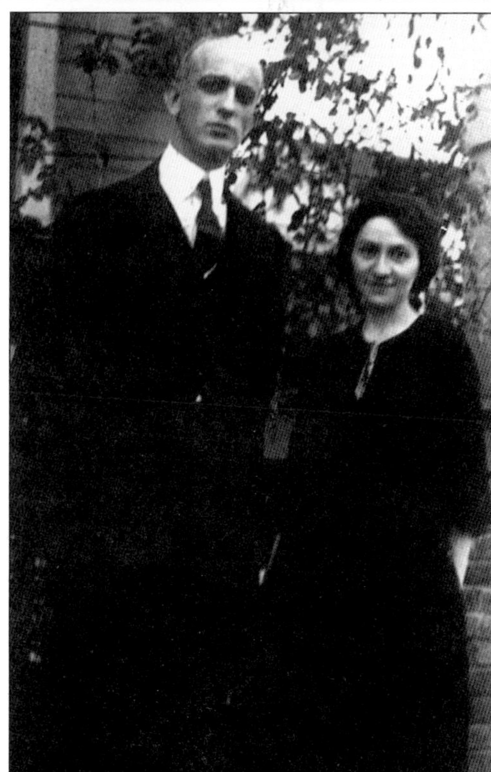

Mr. and Mrs. Isaac Minis lived at 137 East 51st Street. Mr. Minis owned a collection agency and Mrs. (Louise) Minis operated a real estate company.

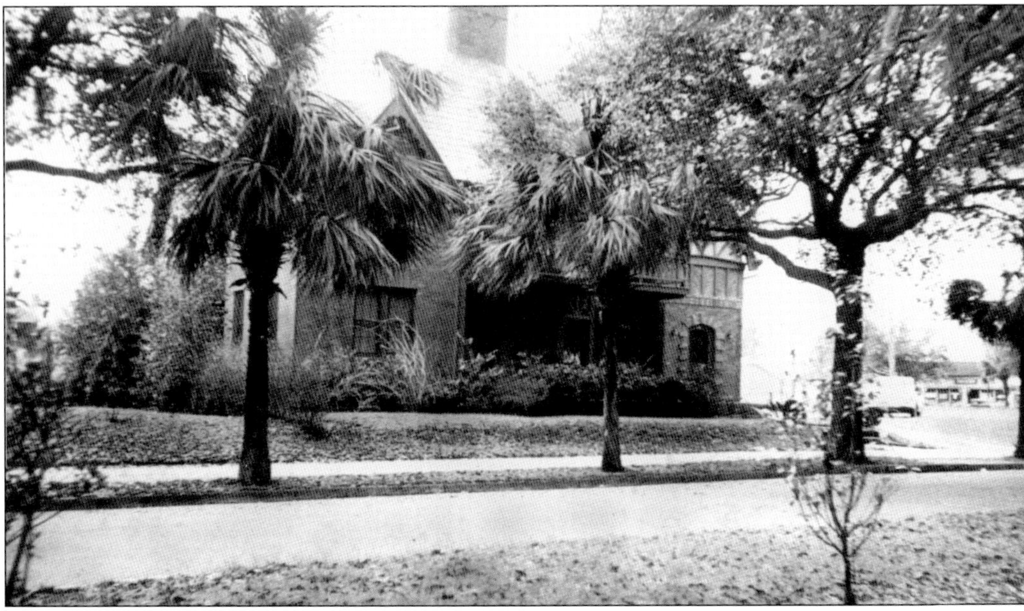

The Suddath home at 25 Washington Avenue was photographed for this vintage postcard.

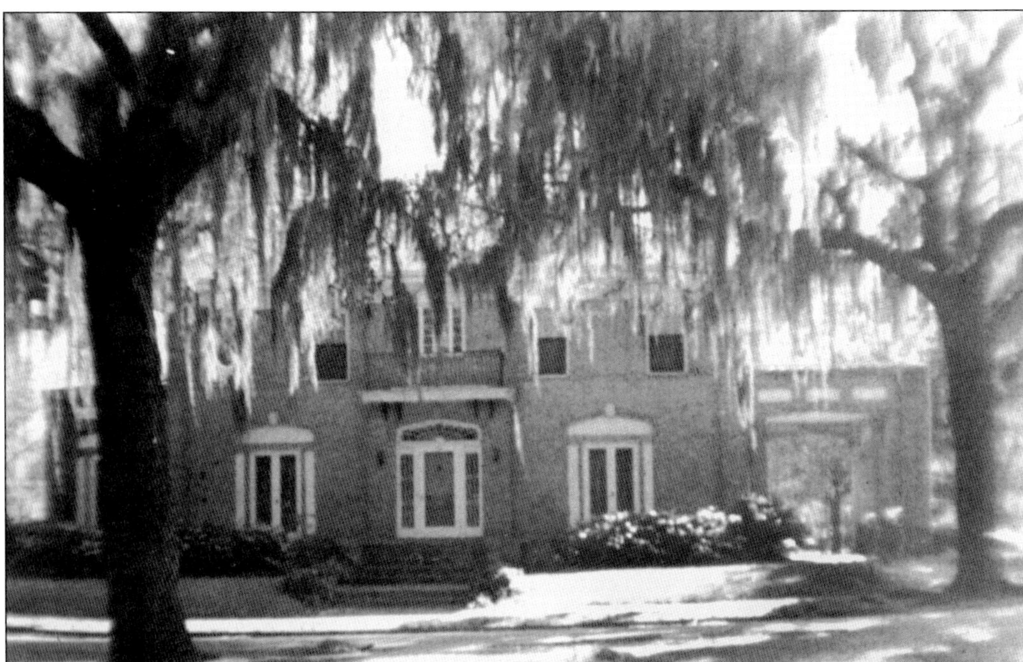

This is the Furse home at 101 Washington Avenue as it looked in the late 1920s. For years the brick Colonial-Revival style home was the manse for Independent Presbyterian Church. The home is now privately owned and has columns in the front.

Two

Chatham Crescent

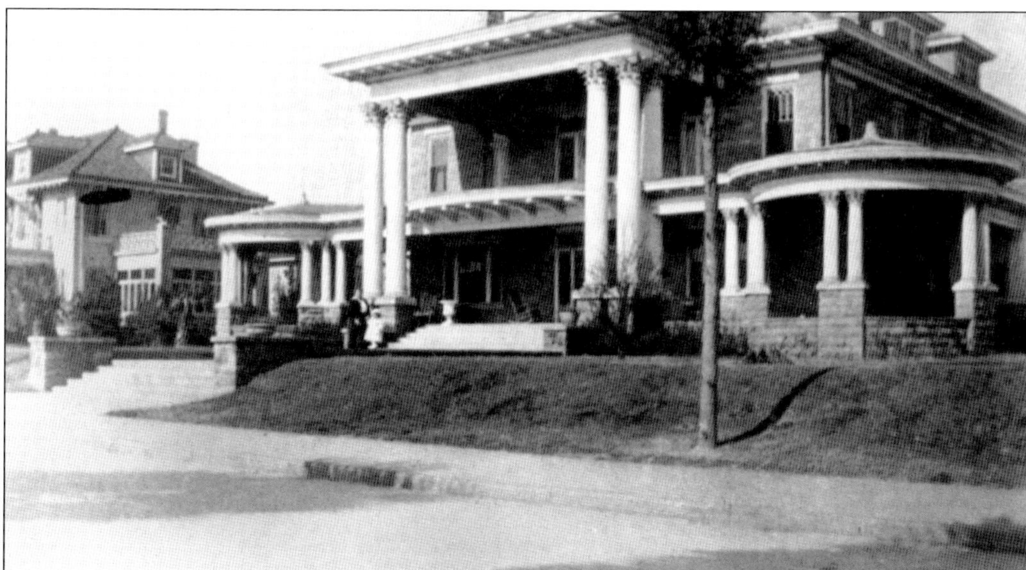

The Robertson home at 920 East Victory Drive, right, and the Pearce home at 910 East Victory Drive were the first two houses built in Chatham Crescent. The Pearce home was built in 1910 by William K. Pearce of Hunter, Pearce & Battey, cotton and naval stores factors. The Robertson home was built under the close supervision of Capt. William H. Robertson. The Robertson family owned the home for more than 80 years.

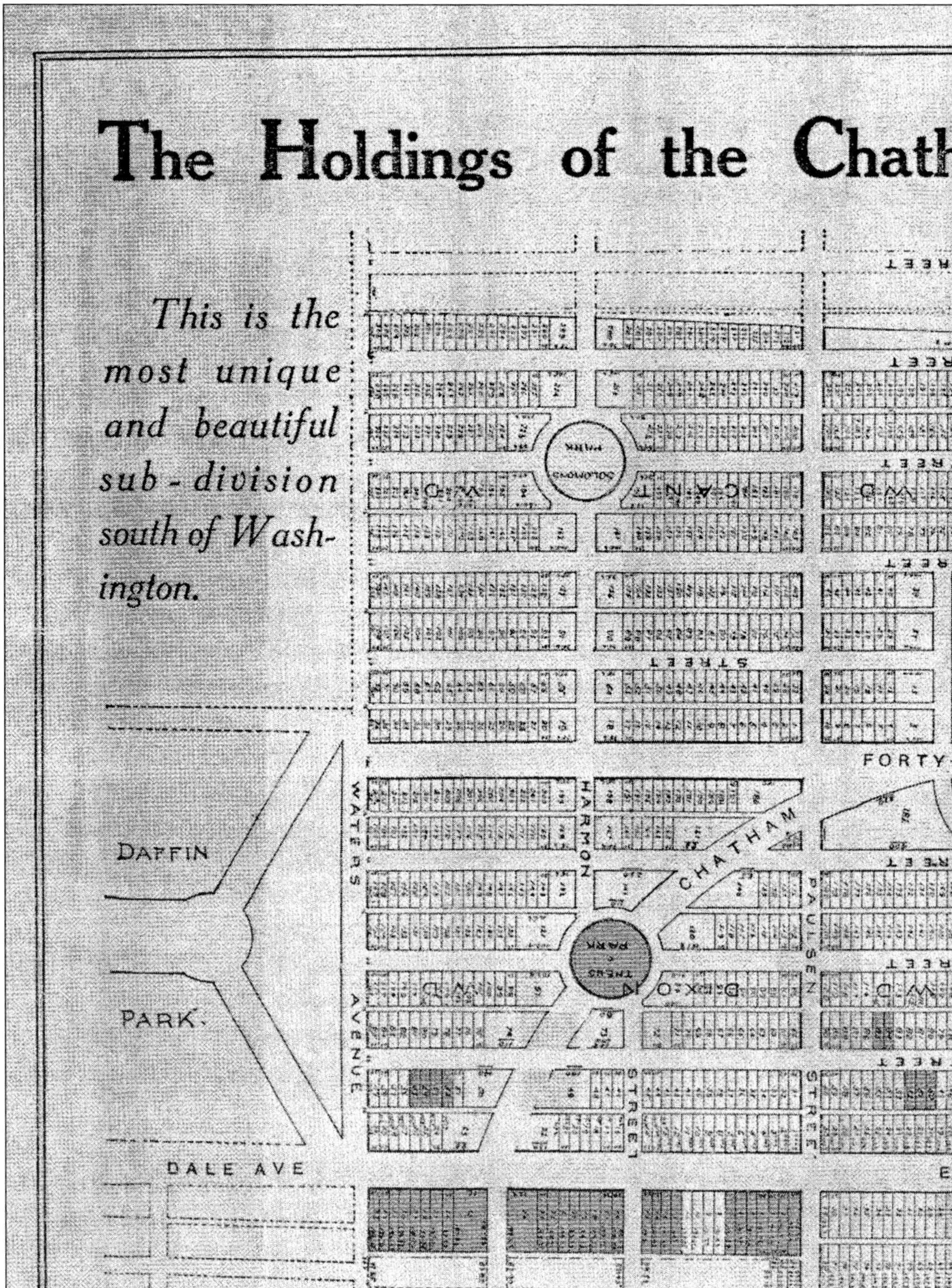

The 1910 map of Chatham Crescent, or the Granger Tract, indicates how large the neighborhood is—roughly 174 acres—extending north to Maupas Avenue and south to 51st Street. The map details the crescent-shaped streets and parks named for city officials. Tiedeman Park in front of the proposed hotel site was named for George

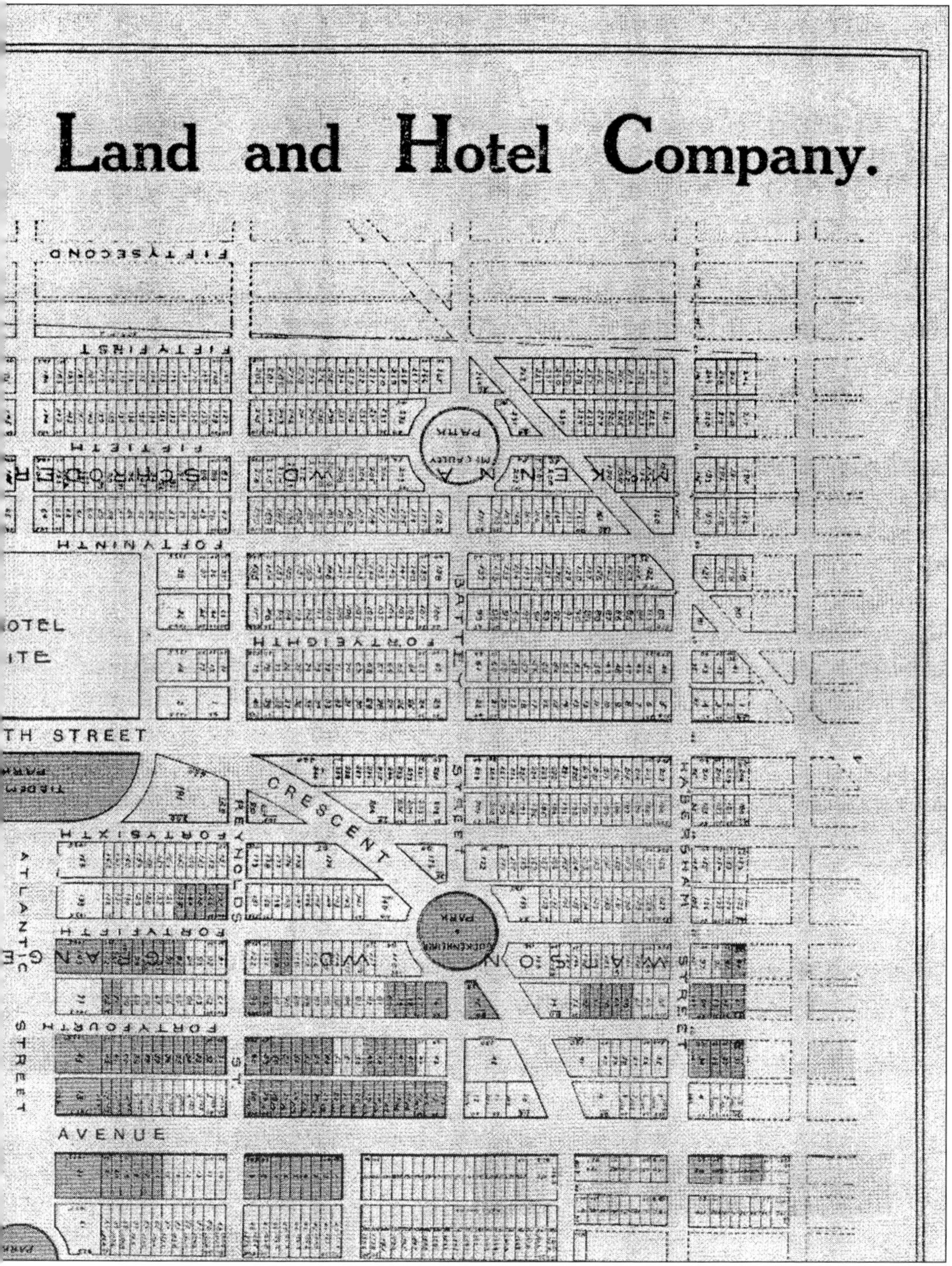

Tiedeman, who was Savannah's mayor in 1908. Abe S. Guckenheimer, George Baldwin, and W.F. McCauley were city aldermen, and S.E. Theus and I.A. Solomons were members of the Park and Tree Commission

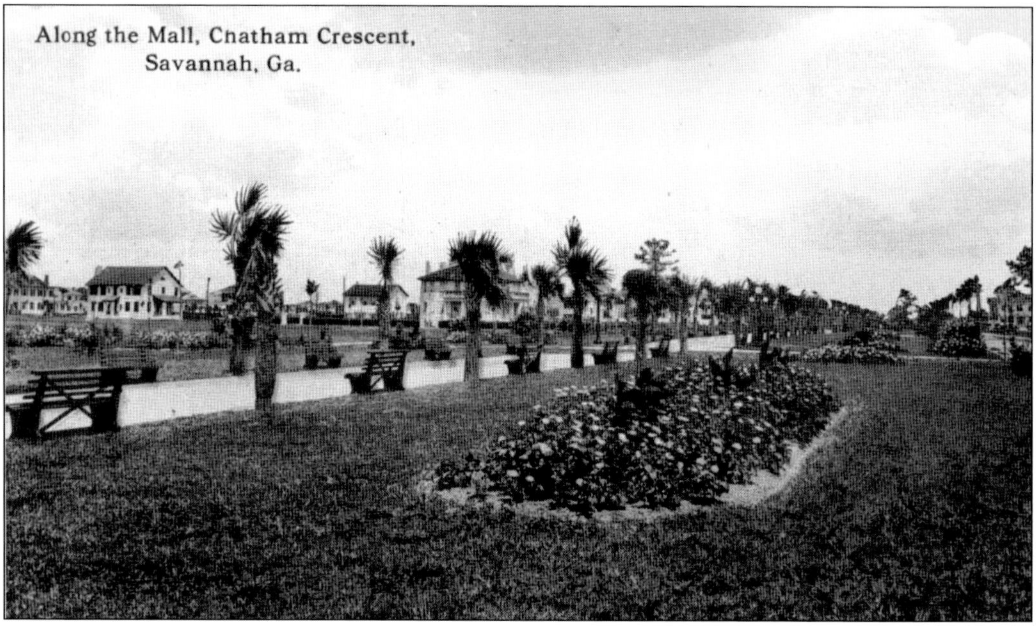

This vintage postcard is entitled "Along the Crescent" and depicts the Atlantic Avenue mall.

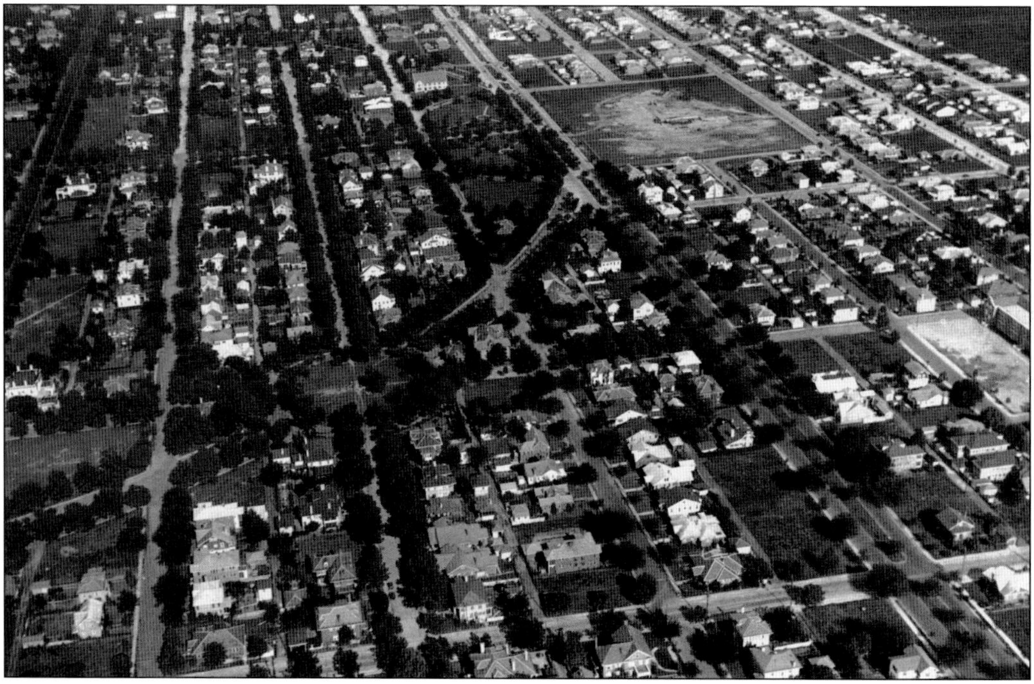

The large vacant lot in the right part of this aerial photograph is the site of the proposed Georgia Hotel, later Savannah High School and now the Savannah Arts Academy. This photograph was probably taken in the early 1930s because Charles Ellis Elementary School, which opened as Forty-Ninth Street School in 1929, is in the picture (at center right). Note the vacant areas on Washington Avenue and other streets.

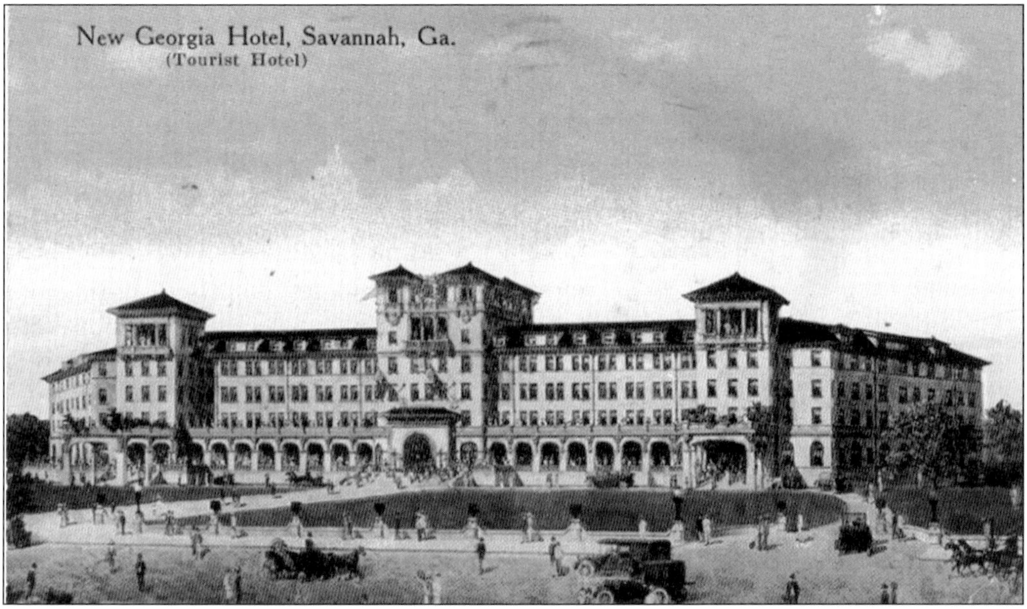

This vintage postcard shows the proposed Georgia Hotel in all its Spanish Revival architectural splendor. Ground was broken for the hotel in 1912. The basement was dug and a first floor was constructed but probably torn down soon after. No other work was done at the site for more than 20 years. Neighbors often complained to city officials about the unsanitary and unsafe conditions on the eight-acre tract. Rainwater would fill the basement hole and hooligans sometimes would throw baby alligators in the pit. Finally, the land was turned over to the board of education and Savannah High School was built.

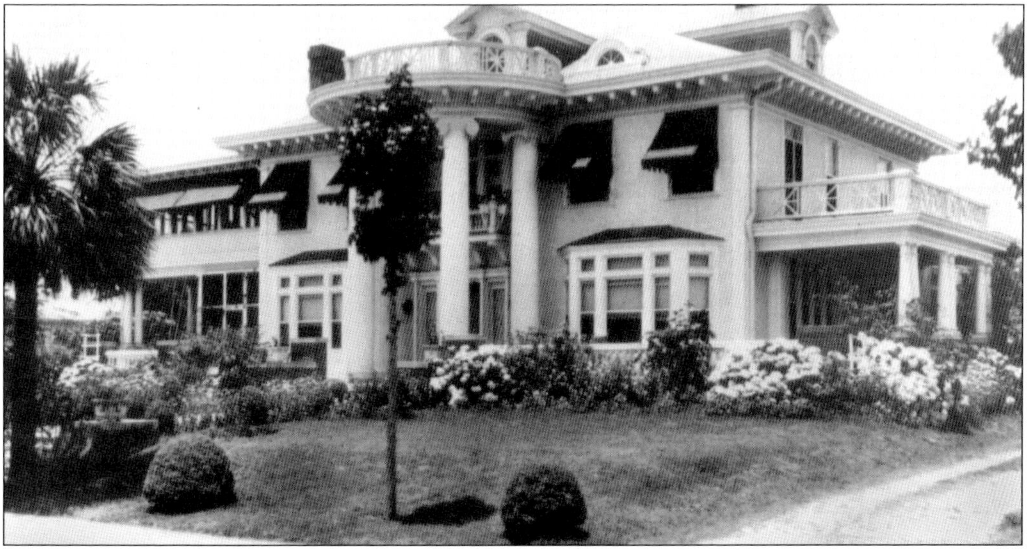

An article in the July 8, 1911 edition of the *Savannah Morning News* reported that "arrangements have been completed by Oliver T. Bacon for the building of a handsome home on the Chatham Land and Hotel Co. tract." The two-story frame Classical Revival–style home is at 2609 Atlantic Avenue. Bacon was elected to the Chatham County Commission in 1908 and named chair in 1913. He was chairman in the early 1920s when the road to Tybee Island opened. The land occupied by the municipal golf course is named in his honor.

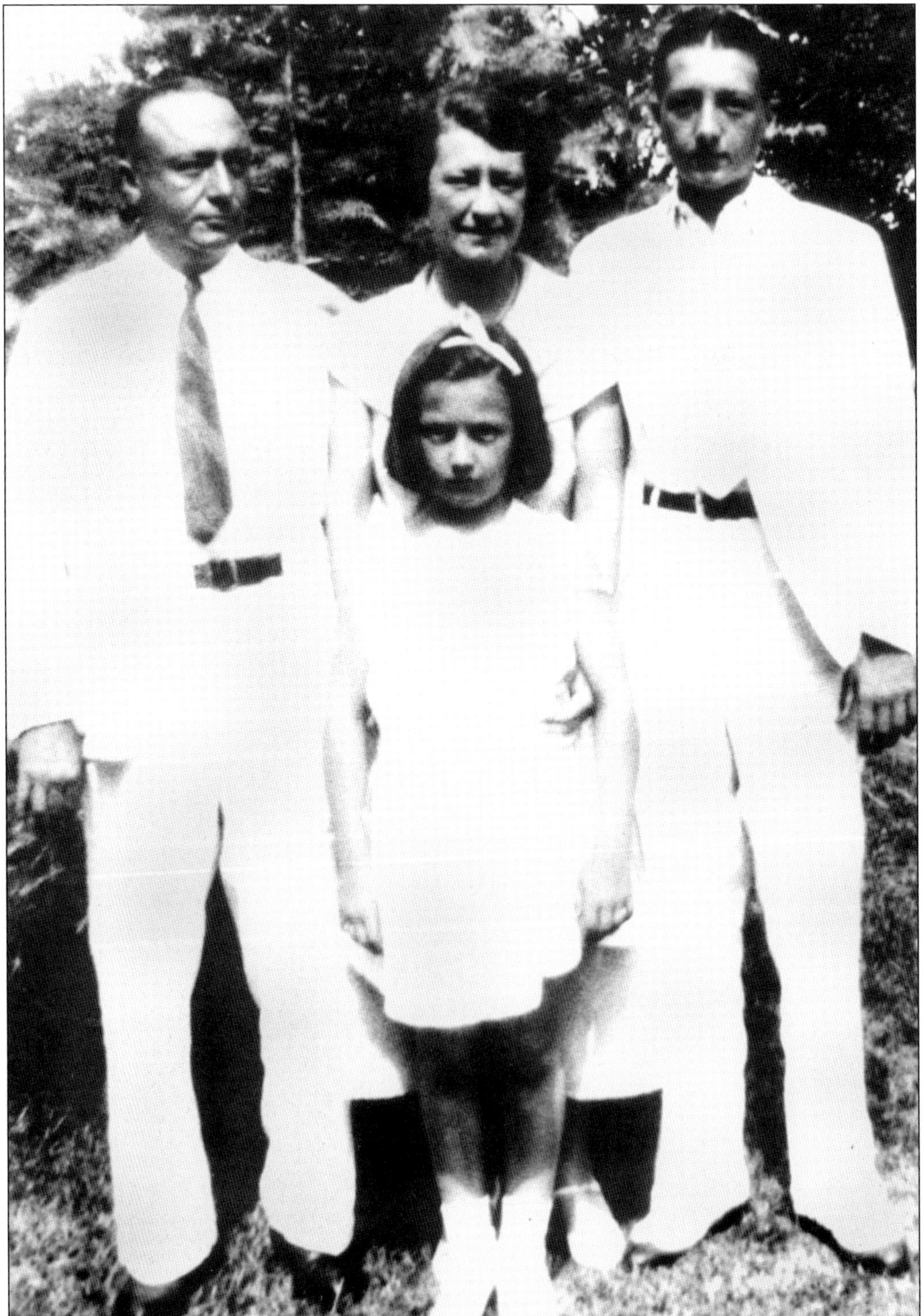

In the 1930s the Cay family included, from left to right, (back row) John Eugene Cay, Caroline Palmer Cay, and Jack Cay; (front row) Armin Cay (Chisholm).

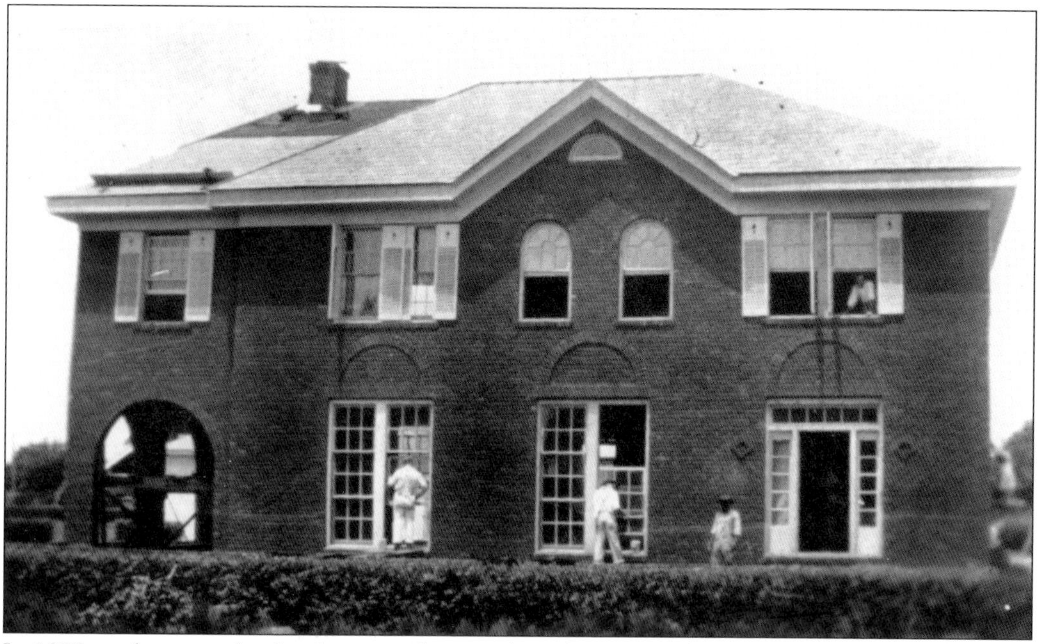

In 1923 workers put the finishing touches on the John Eugene Cay home on Atlantic Avenue.

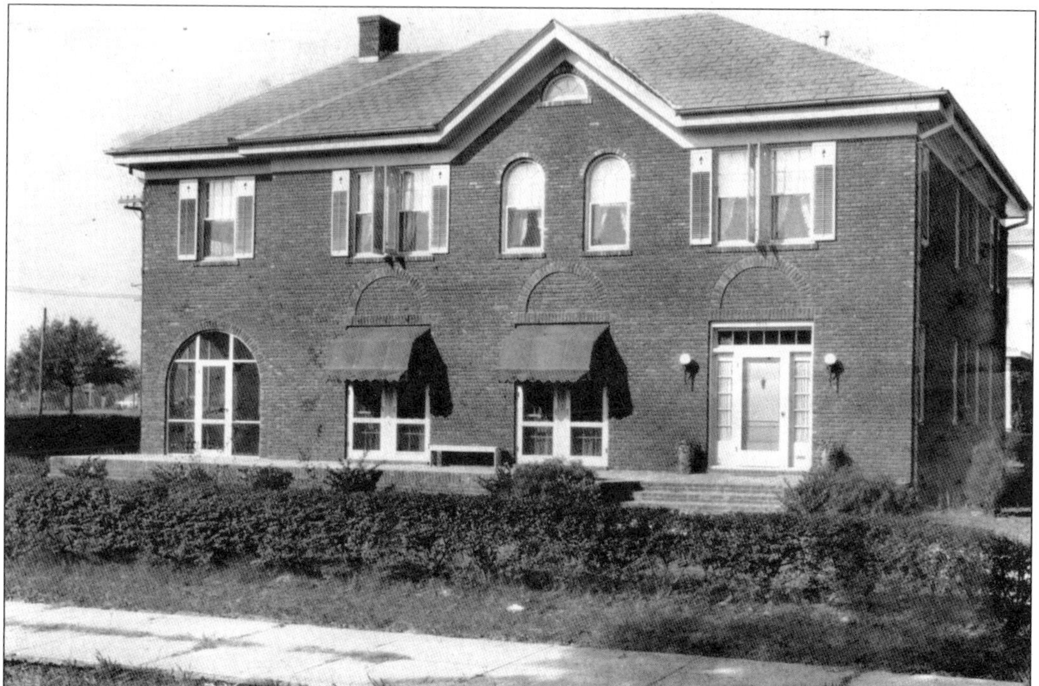

The Cay home was photographed just after completion.

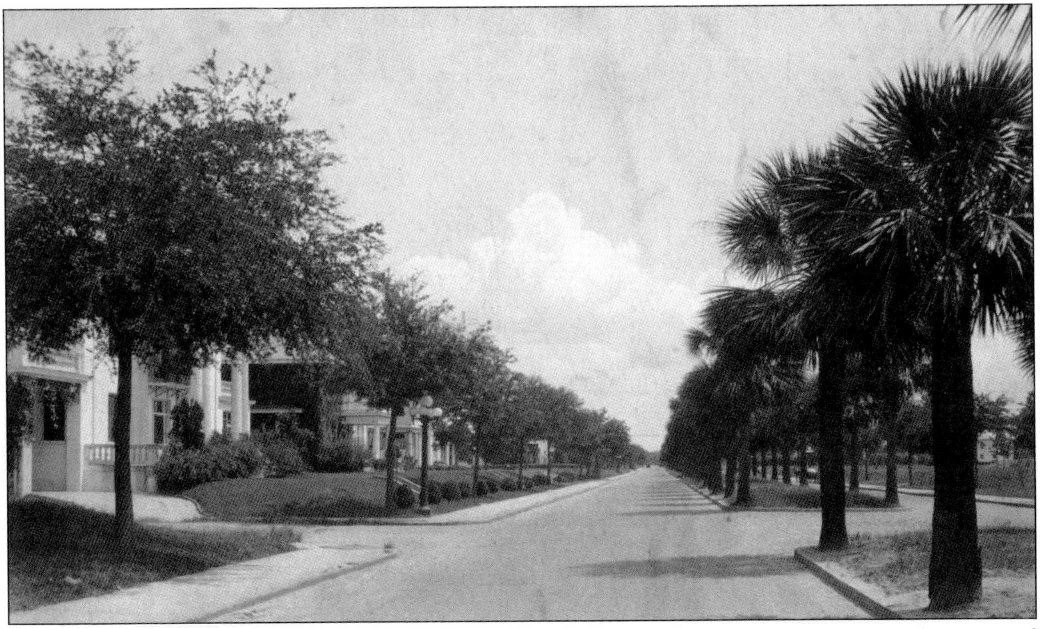

An early photo of Victory Drive at East Broad Street shows vintage street lamps and young trees.

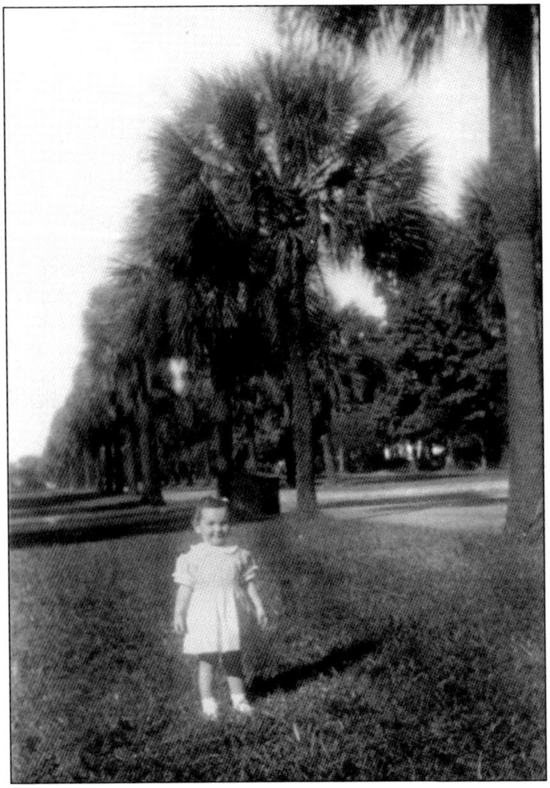

The palmetto-lined Atlantic mall has been the backdrop for numerous family photos, including this one of Dottie Eisenberg (Lynch).

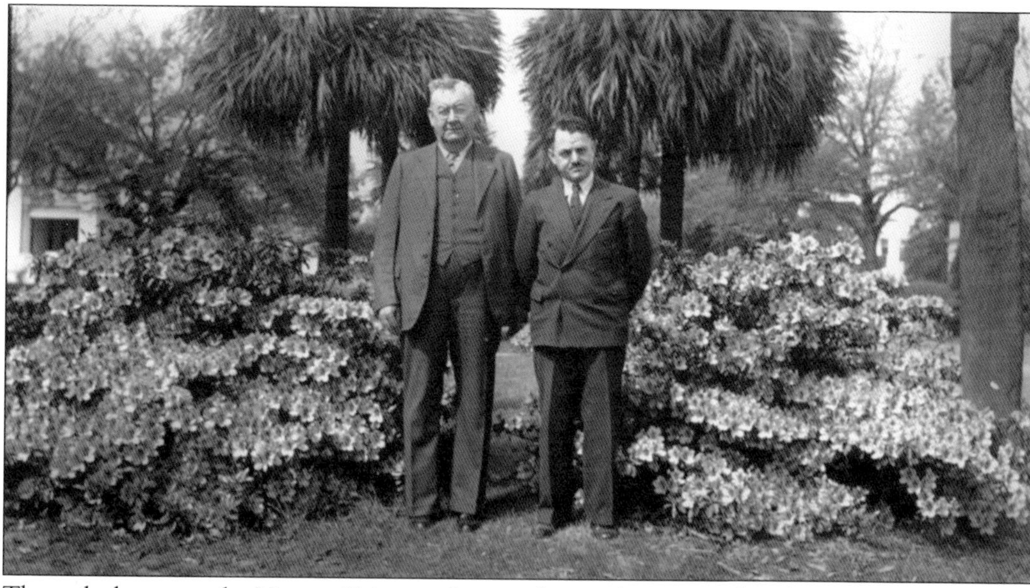

Through the years, the Victory Drive median, with its palmettos and azaleas, has been a popular spot for photographers and their subjects, like these two dapper gentlemen.

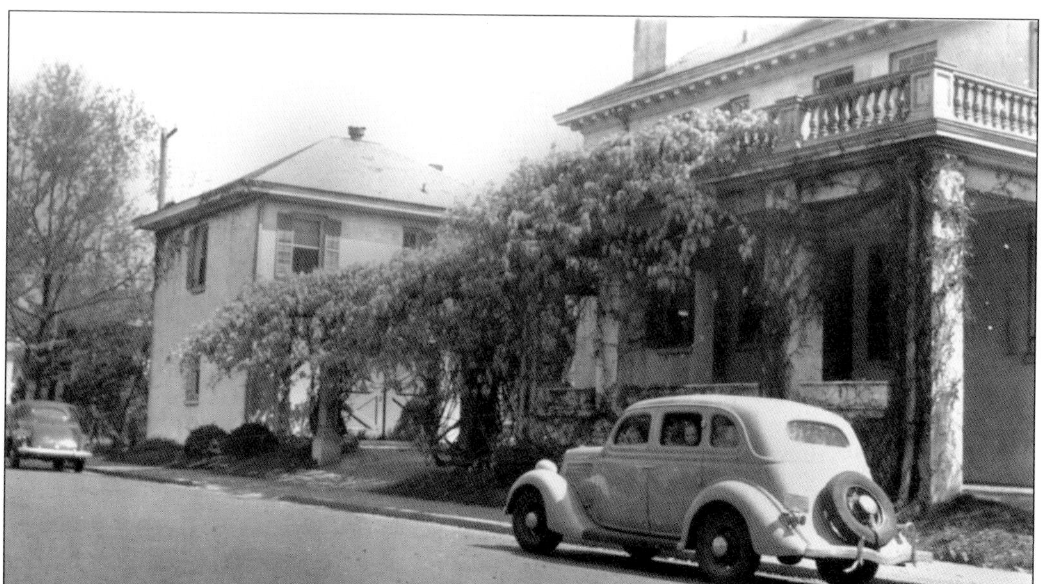

It wasn't too long ago that vehicles could park on streets like East Broad and Victory Drive. However, the person behind the camera may have been trying to show the wisteria that still blooms in the spring at 602 East Victory Drive near the carriage house and porte-cochere.

JOHN LAFFITEAU SUTLIVE
224 WASHINGTON AVENUE
SAVANNAH, GEORGIA 31405

The Reverend N. Robert Gill, Minister
First Christian Church,
711 East Victory Drive,
Savannah, Ga. 31405

Dear Mr. Gill,

Herewith is a print of the location of your church as it looked some 55 years ago. I had promised it to you some time ago, but retired persons do not do things as quickly as young active persons.

There is quite a local story behind the change of the names of the streets to Victory Drive as we know know it. Some contend that politics was involved but that was vigorously denied by the then Miss Eleanor Puder, whose father's house was across the street from where your church now is, and who suggested the change.

With all good wishes to you and yours in this greatest of the seasons,

Sincerely,

This letter written by John Sutlive, retired editor of the *Savannah Morning News*, offers insight into the reason why Estill Avenue was renamed Victory Drive.

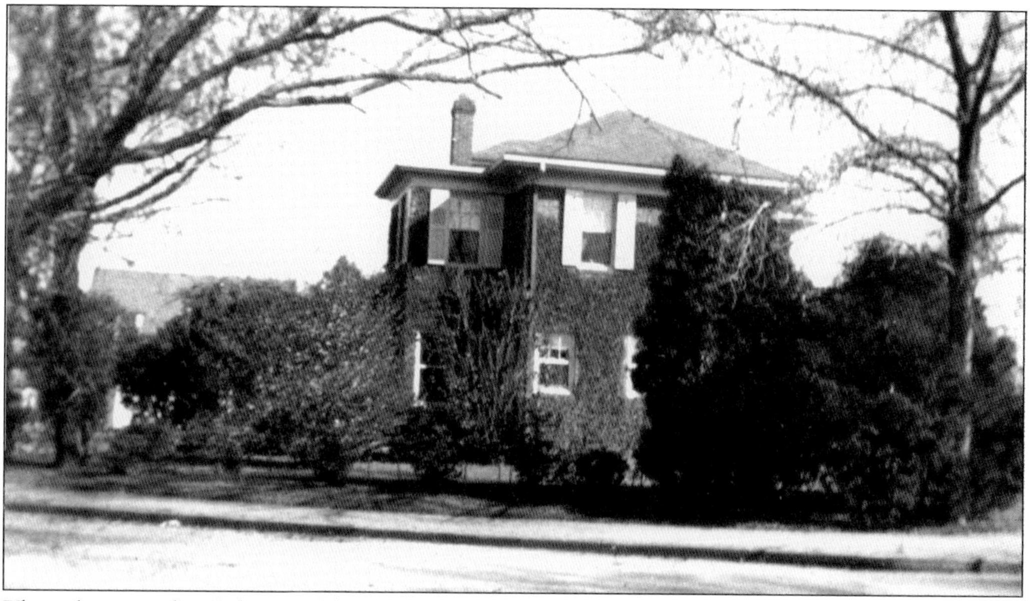

This photograph of the Strobhar home at 702 East 45th Street was taken in the 1940s by neighbor Sam Hornstein who wrote the following on the back: "A view of the Strobhar home taken from the Crescent. The lawn is unusually pretty and we could not resist the temptation to take this view not realizing the coloring of the flowers would not show in the picture." Hornstein was a city alderman.

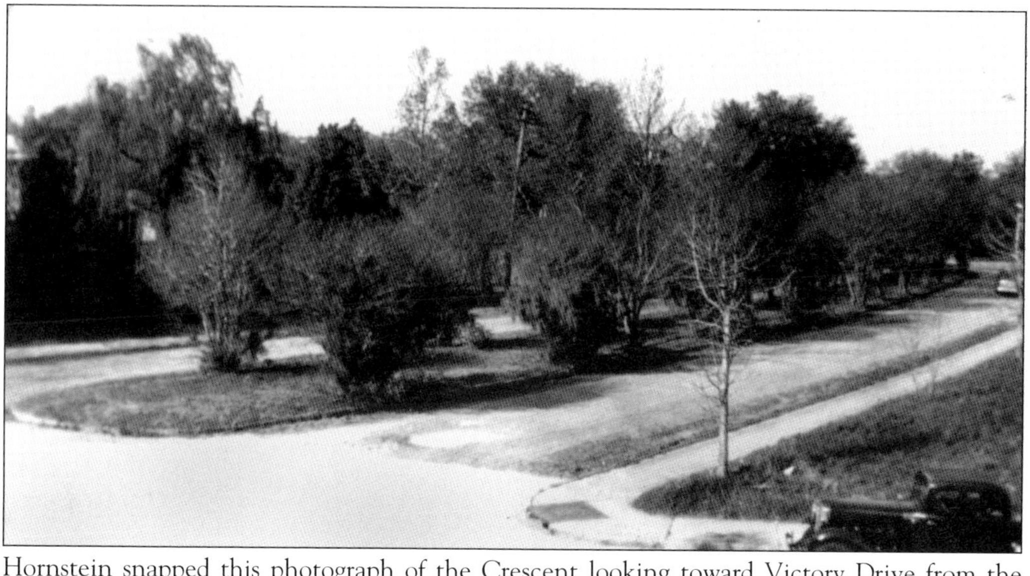

Hornstein snapped this photograph of the Crescent looking toward Victory Drive from the upstairs window of his house in the 700 block of East Forty-fourth Street.

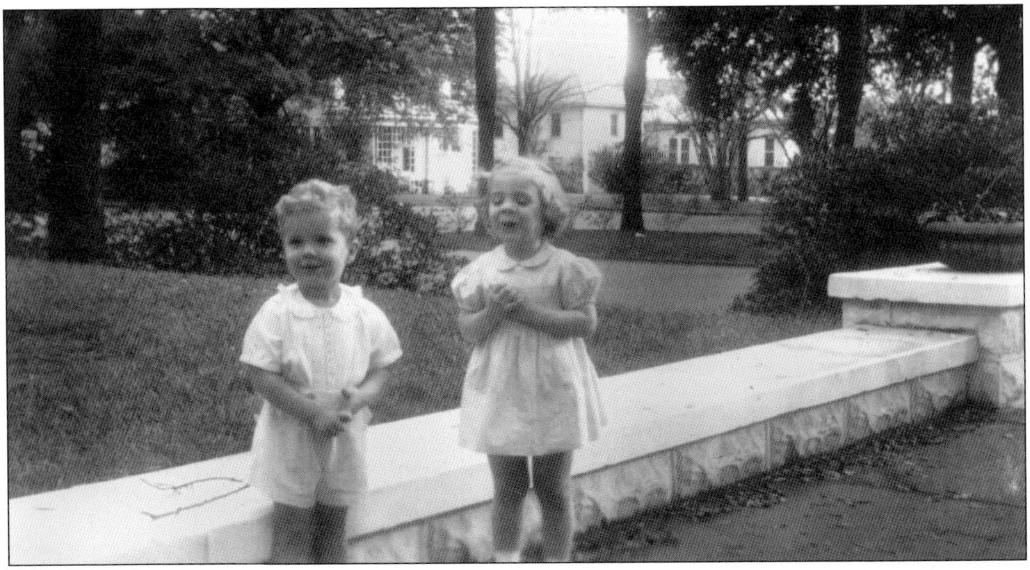

Johnny and Robbie Hoffman (Culver) play on the side porch of the Robertson home on Victory Drive in the early 1950s.

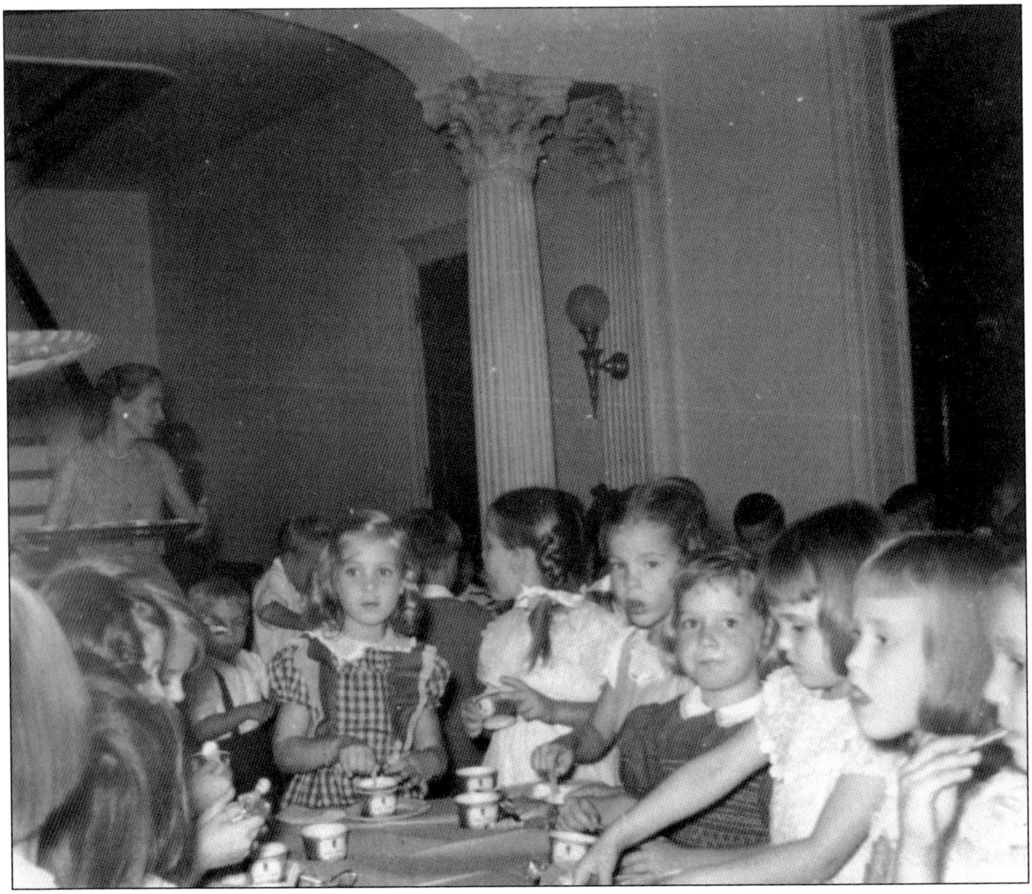

A birthday party at the Robertson home shows the ornate interior columns.

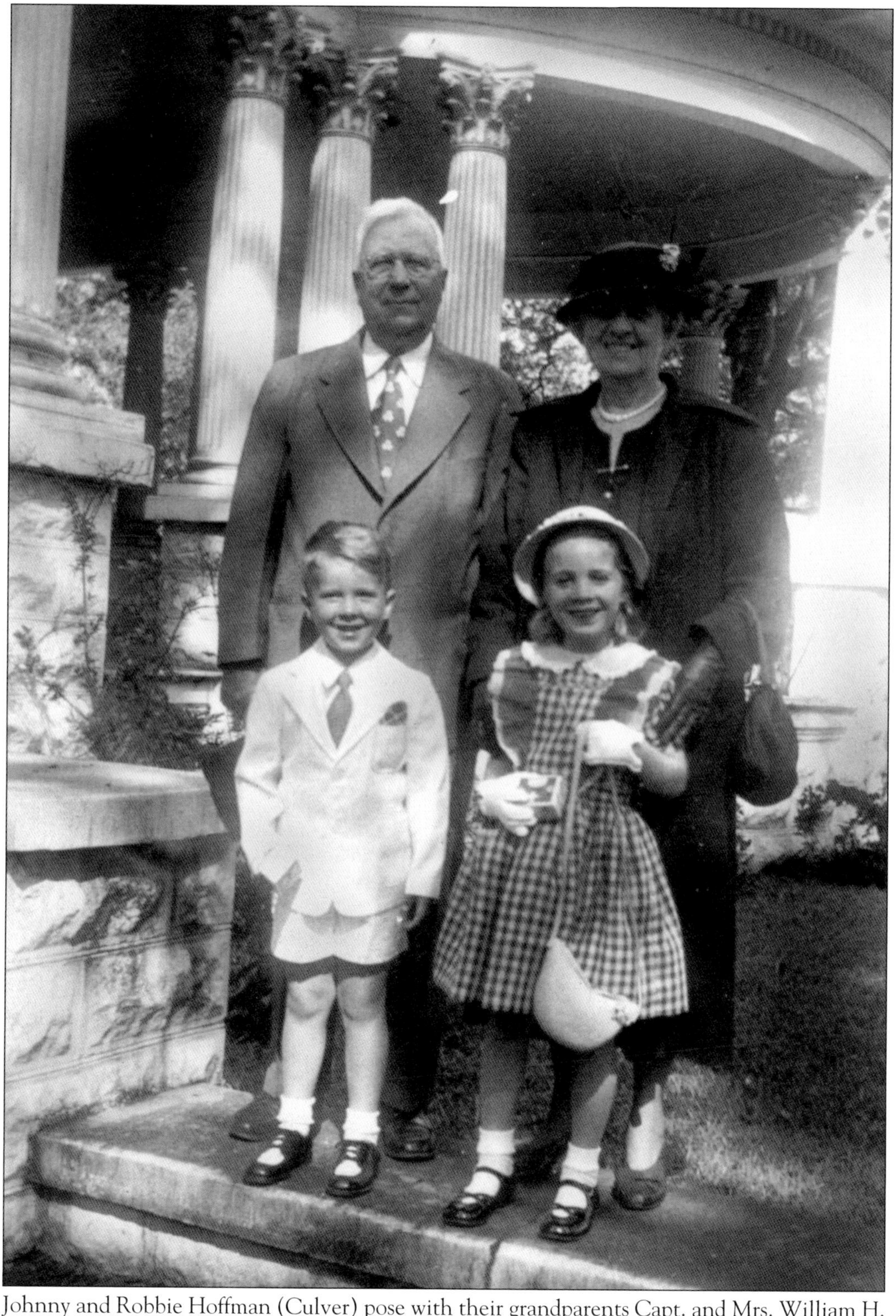

Johnny and Robbie Hoffman (Culver) pose with their grandparents Capt. and Mrs. William H. Robertson in front of their Victory Drive home.

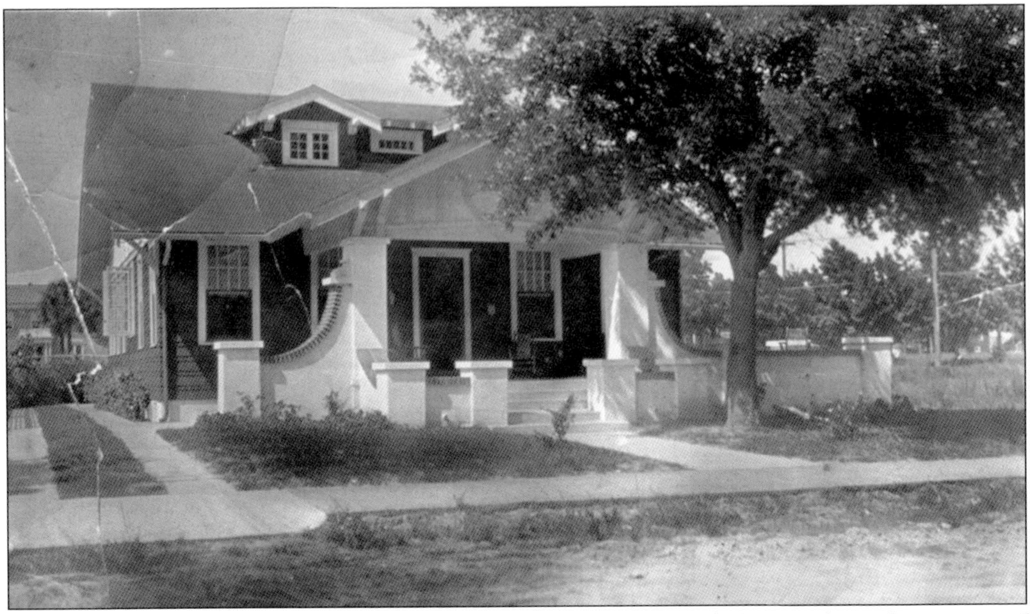

The simple lines of the Golson home, built in 1924 on East 44th Street, show the variety of architectural styles used in Chatham Crescent.

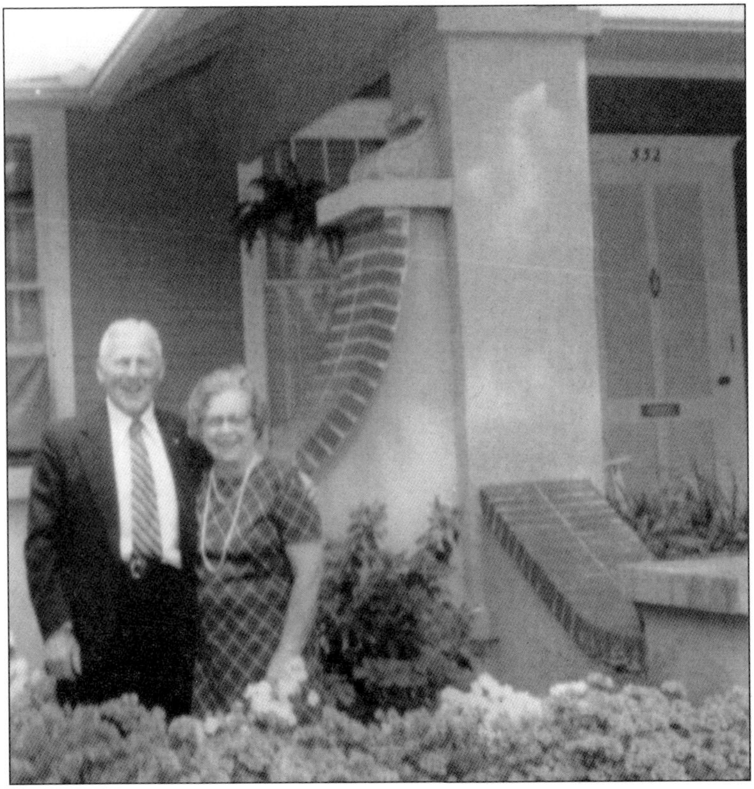

Mr. and Mrs. Jack Cubbedge lived at 532 East 44th Street for more than 30 years. During the 1950s Cubbedge was the publisher of the *Savannah Morning News*.

Three

Ardmore

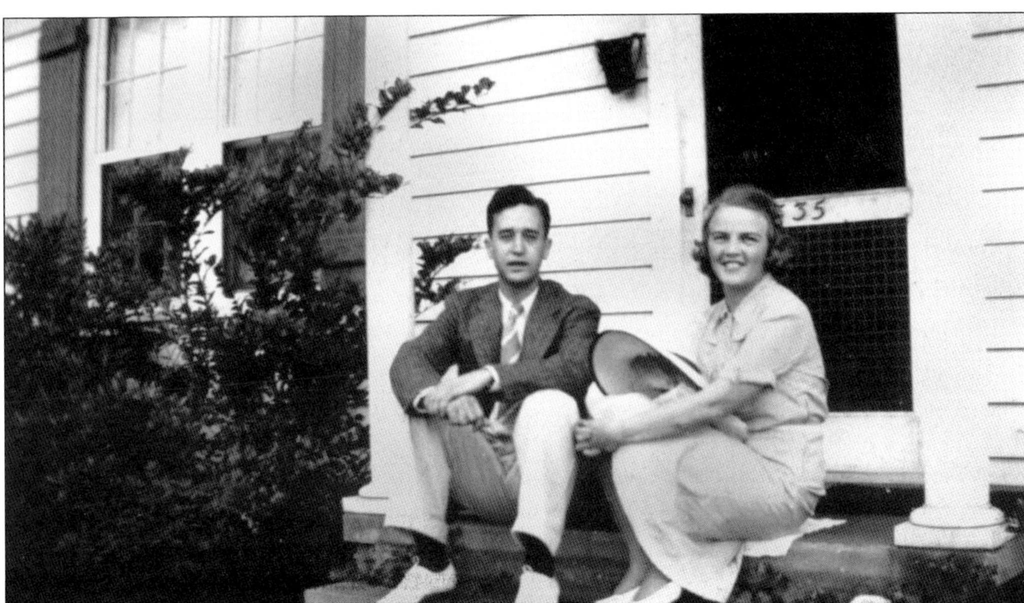

Mr. and Mrs. Edward A. Perkins relax on their front porch at 335 East 55th Street.

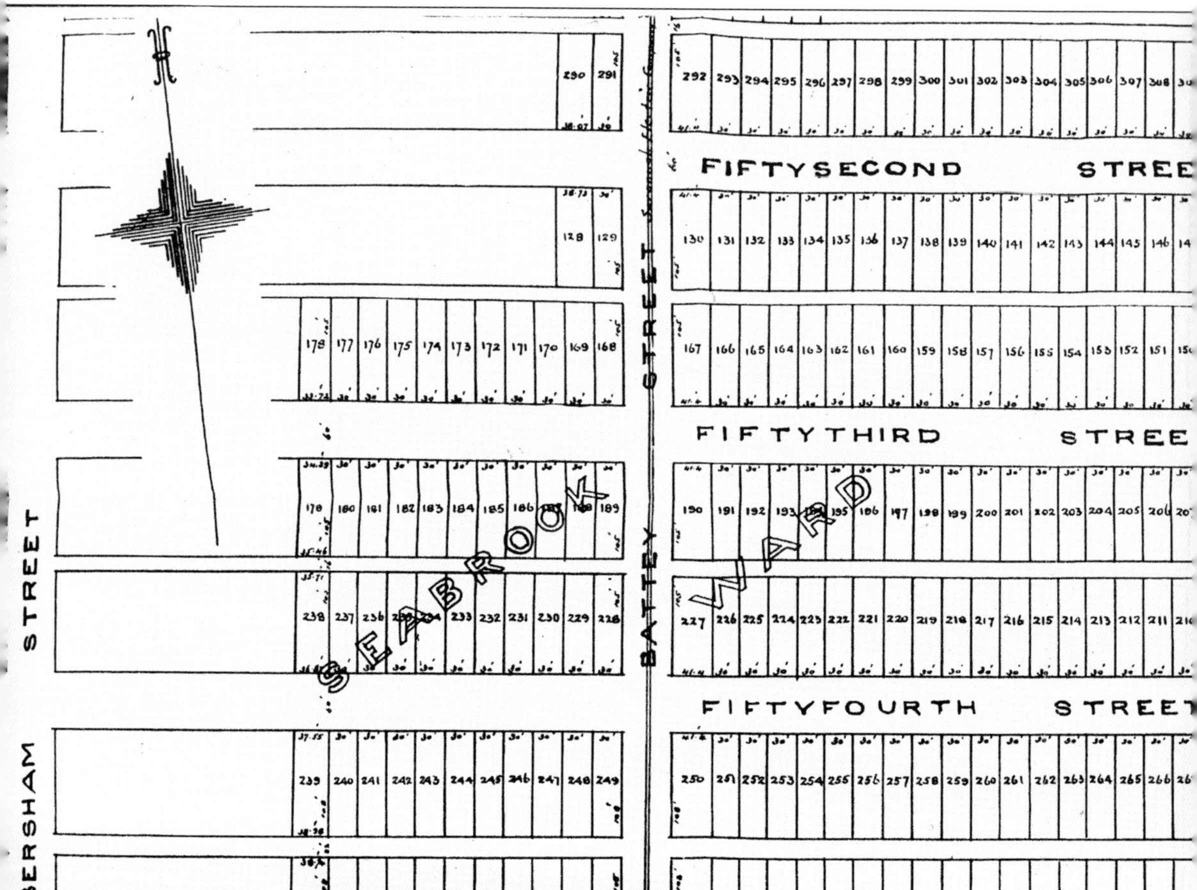
FIFTYSECOND STREET
FIFTYTHIRD STREET
FIFTYFOURTH STREET
FIFTYFIFTH STREET
HABERSHAM STREET
BATTEY STREET
SEABROOK
WARD
ARDMORE
SAVANNAH, GA.

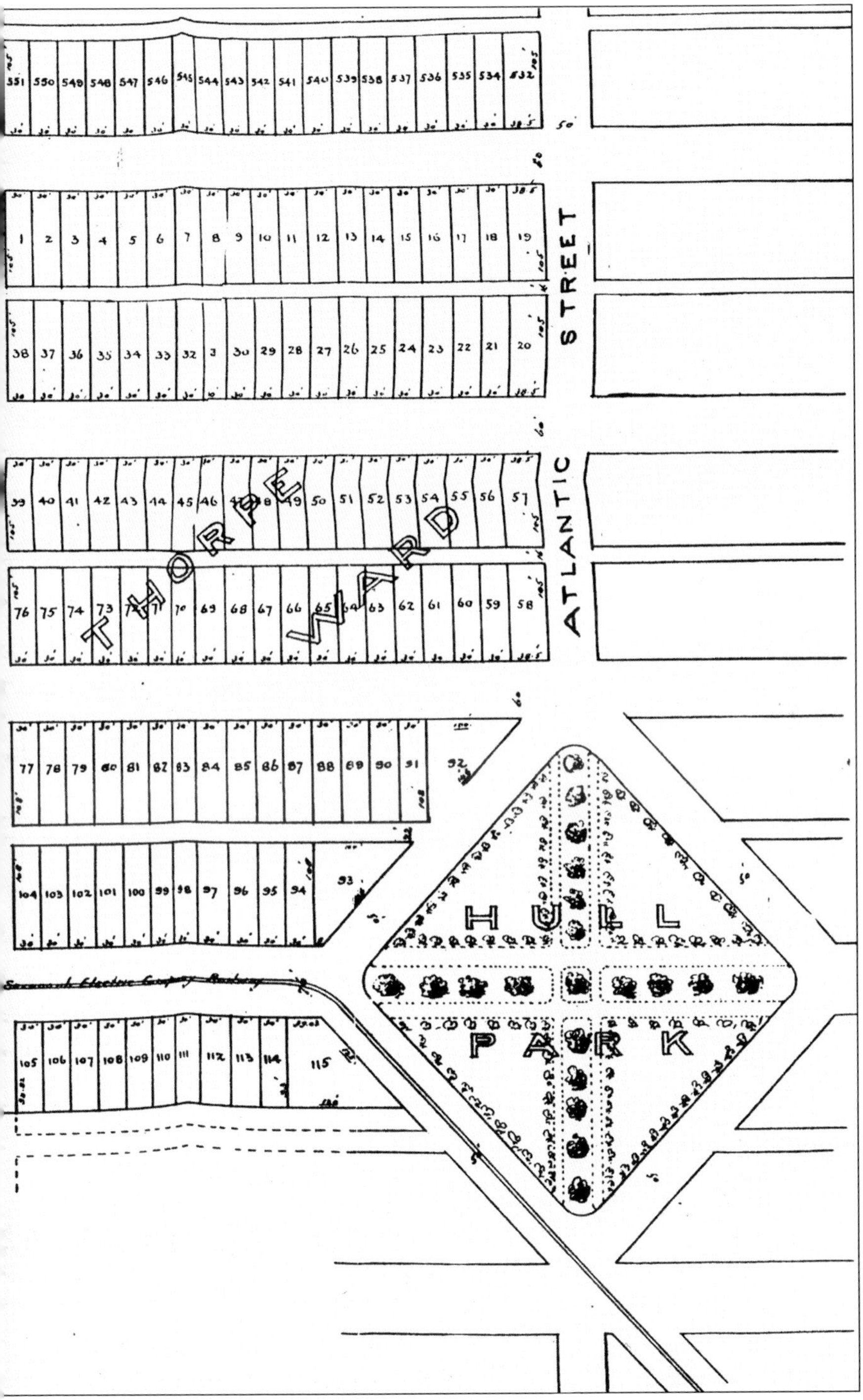

The Lattimores began developing Ardmore as a bungalow neighborhood in 1925. Originally, no house was to be more than two stories high, but that quickly changed and a variety of homes were built in the area.

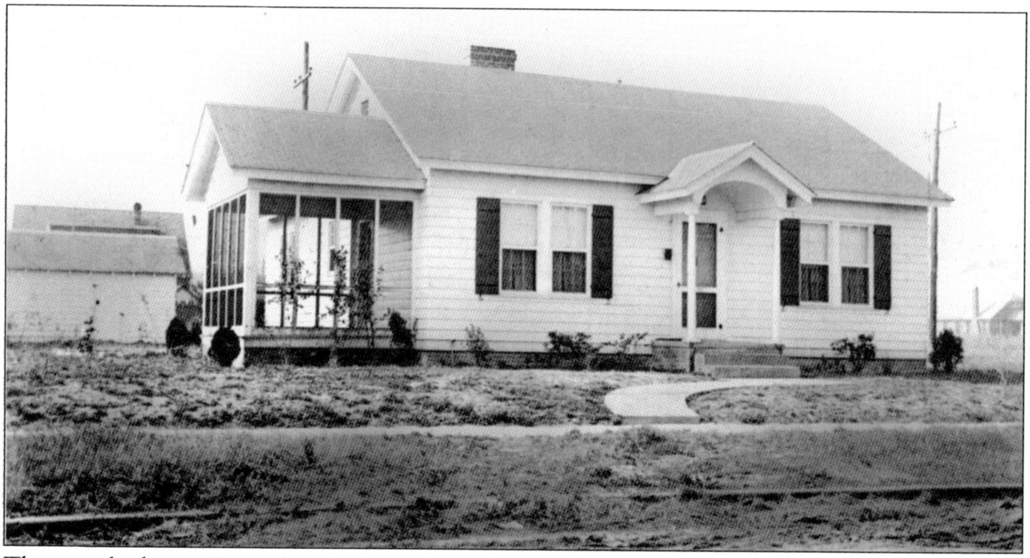

This two-bedroom Bungalow built in the early 1930s on East 55th Street is typical of many of the homes in Ardmore.

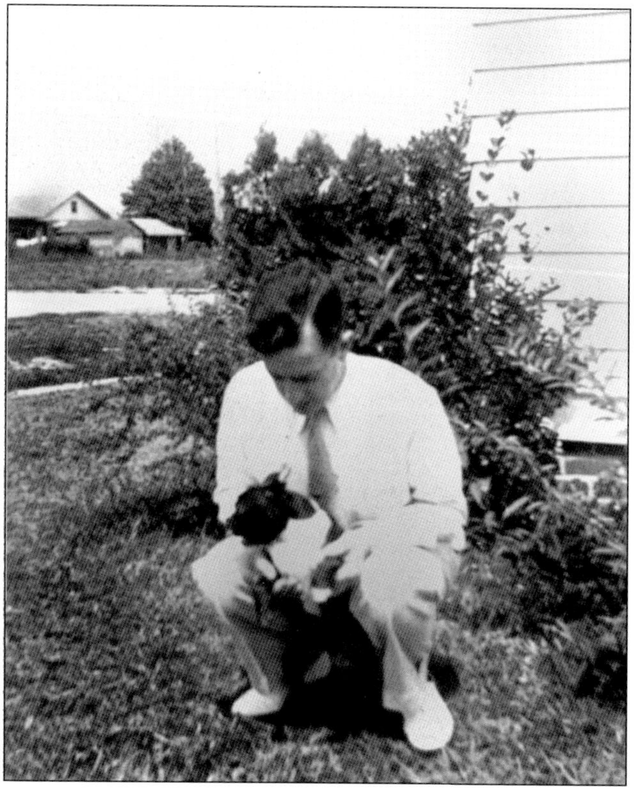

The background is similar to that seen in early photos of Ardsley park and Chatham Crescent—very few trees.

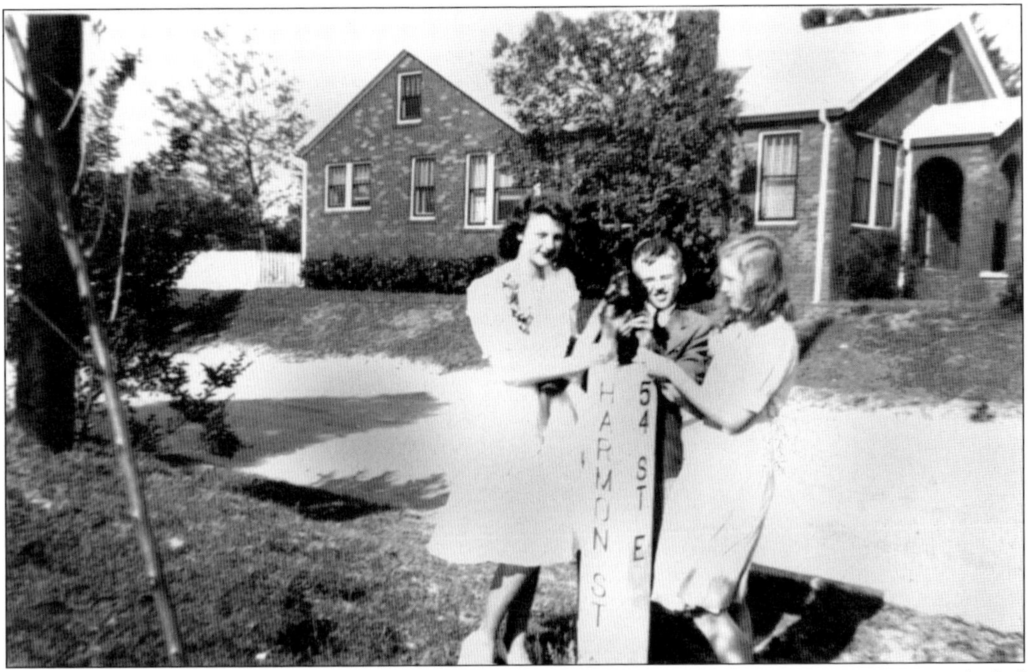

Although not officially Ardmore, the corner of East 54th and Harmon Streets is now included in the Ardsley Park Neighborhood Association.

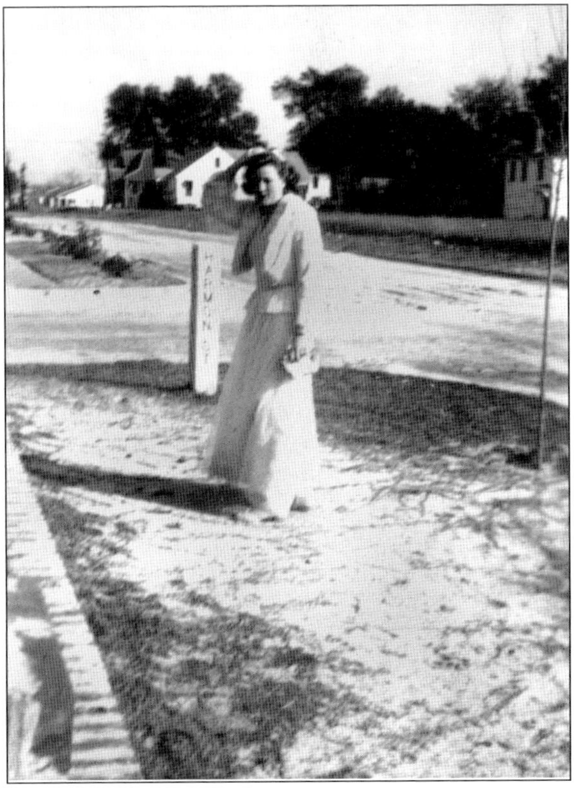

Before development, this area was part of a polo field.

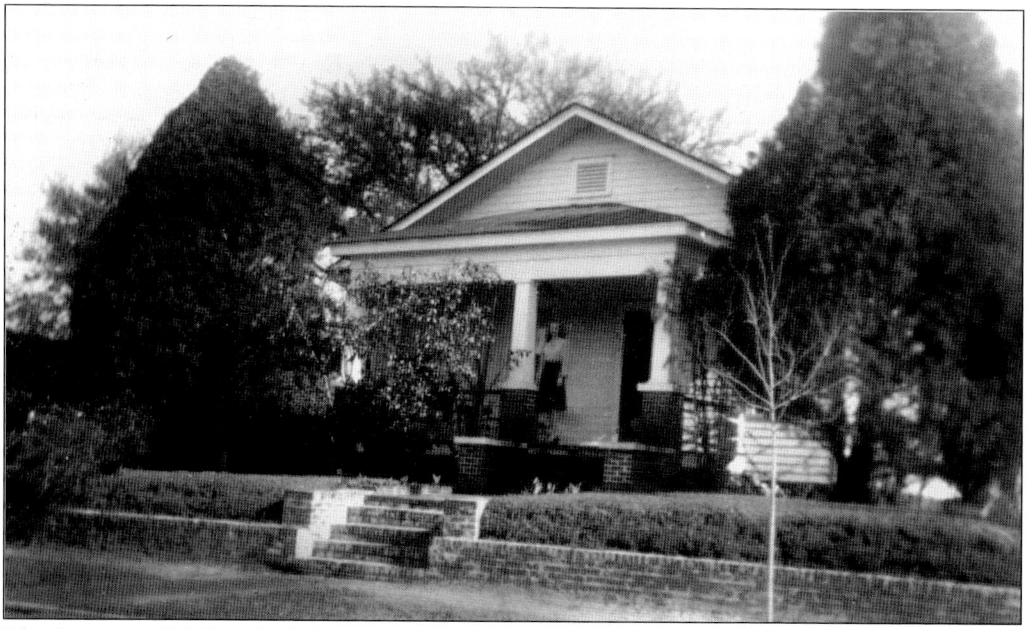

This house at 630 East 54th Street was thought to be the clubhouse for the polo fields.

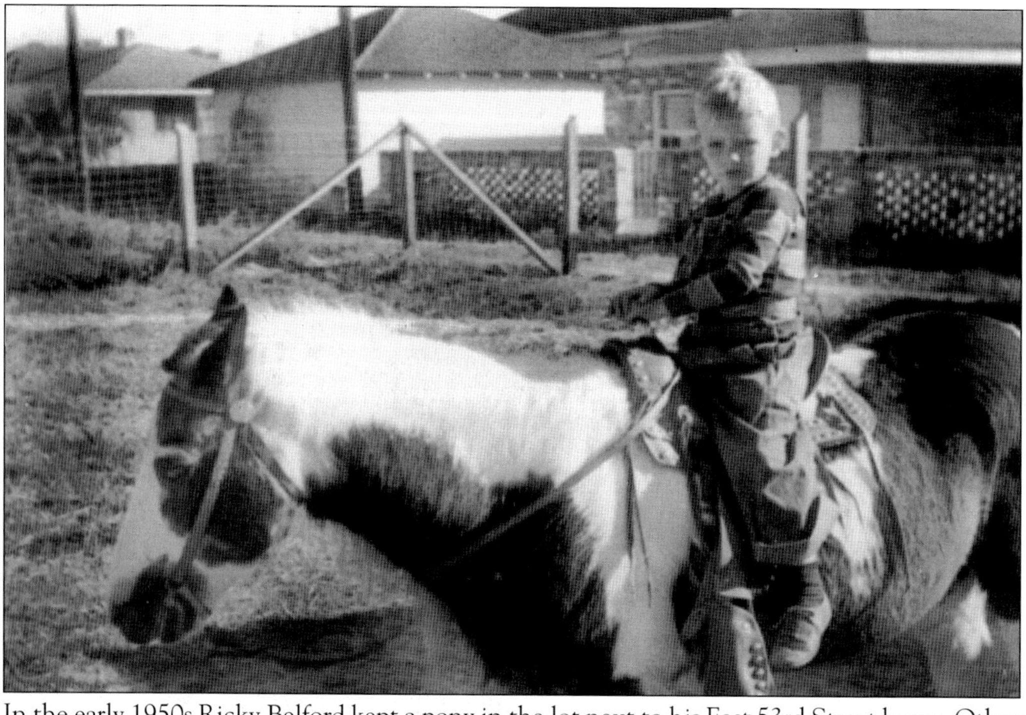

In the early 1950s Ricky Belford kept a pony in the lot next to his East 53rd Street home. Other Ardsley Park and Chatham Crescent youngsters had pet billy goats. A.J. Cohen's goat was named Ludowici.

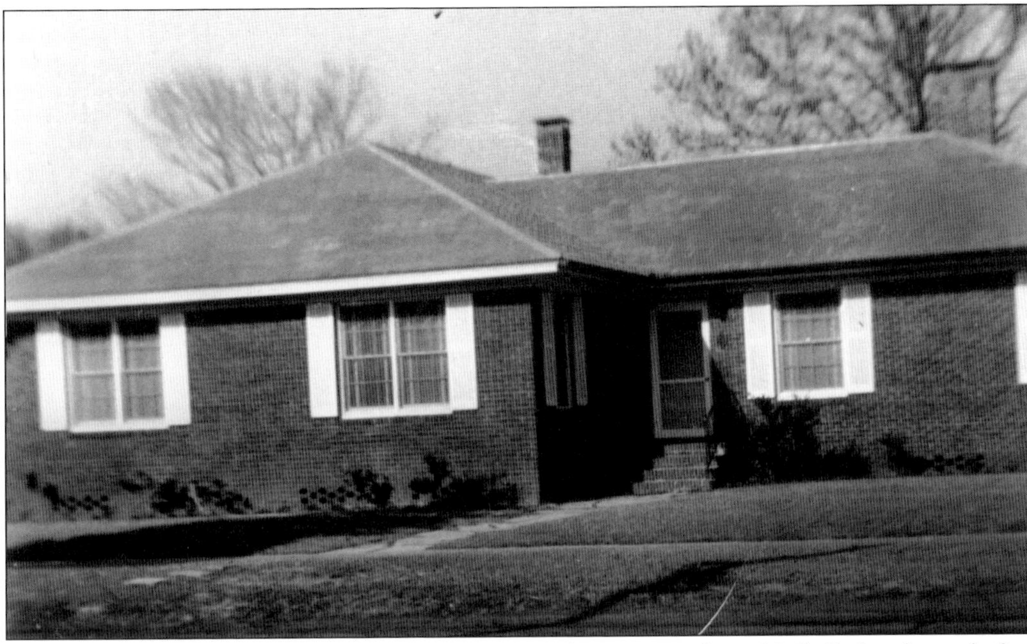

The Reed home was on East 55th Street, two doors away from Hull Park where, before refurbishment, children entertained themselves on the tall slide, swings, and merry-go-round. In the afternoon, the park lady would hand out basketballs and other equipment and turn on the spray pool.

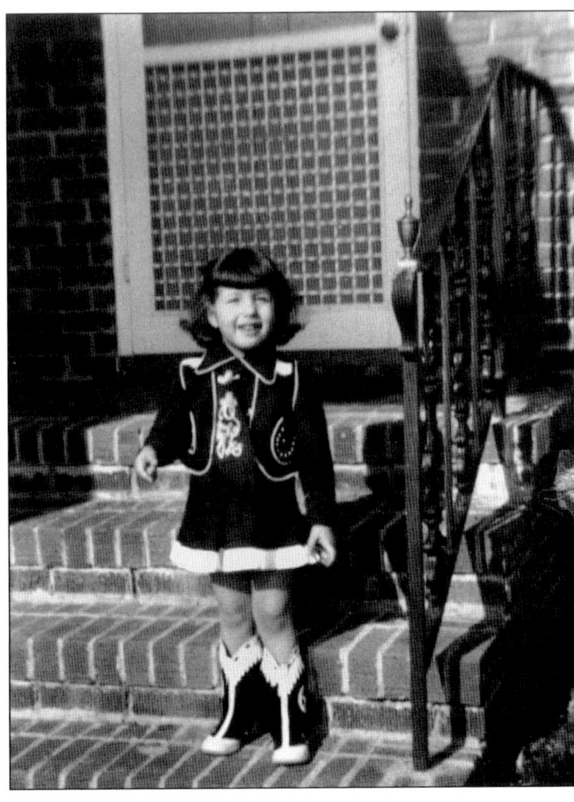

Linda Reed is decked out as a cowgirl for this photograph.

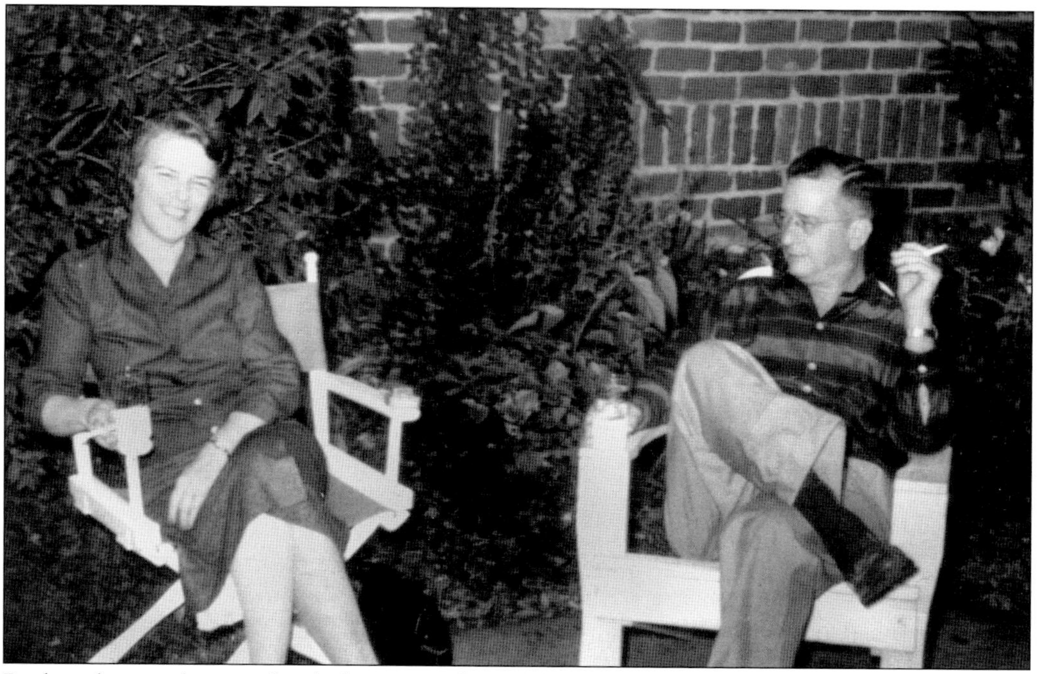

Backyards were havens for Ardmore residents like Edward Perkins and his wife, Lillie May. Perkins was the senior vice president of Savannah Bank and Trust Company when he retired after 50 years of employment. Mrs. Perkins was a longtime teacher at Waters Avenue (later renamed Romana Riley) School.

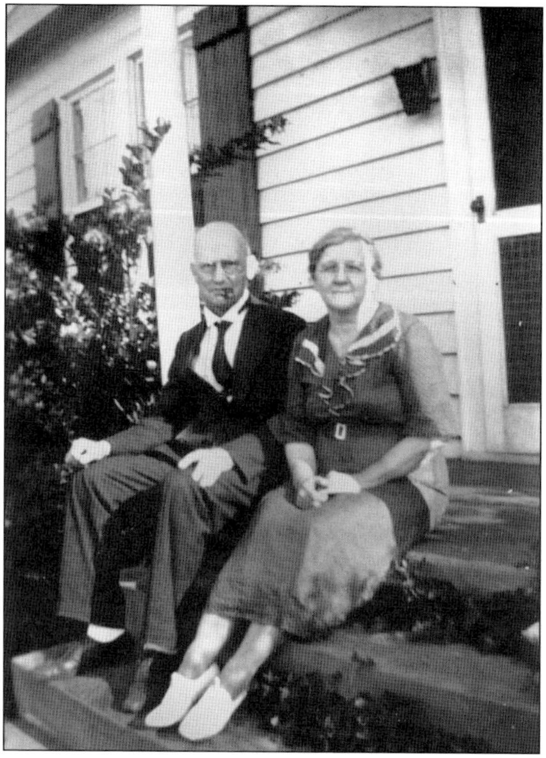

Mrs. Perkins's parents, Mr. and Mrs. George Cargill, posed for this photograph in the late 1930s or early 1940s on the front stoop of the Perkins home. Cargill was an attorney and an assistant to Judge Peter Meldrim.

Four

Families and Friends

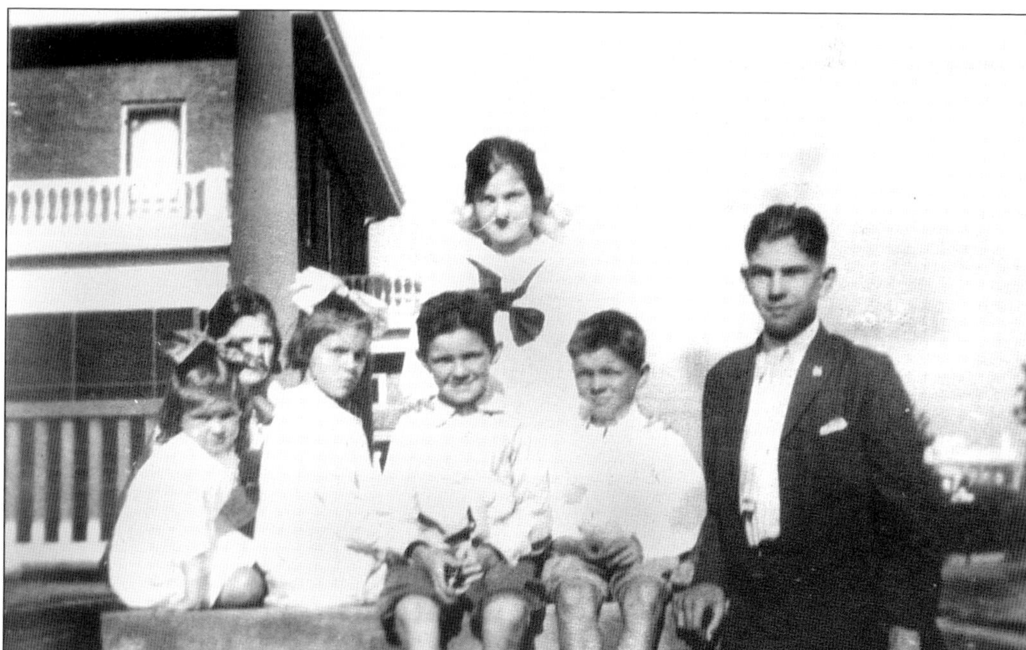

In 1916 the Thompson family and a neighbor gathered in front of their home at 111 East 49th Street. From left to right are Helen Thompson (Brooks); Meta Thompson (McDonough); Kathryn Thompson (Walsh);Virginia Arden; and Coakley, Marion, and Robert Thompson. The Emmerson/Livingston home can be seen in the distance to the right of Robert Thompson.

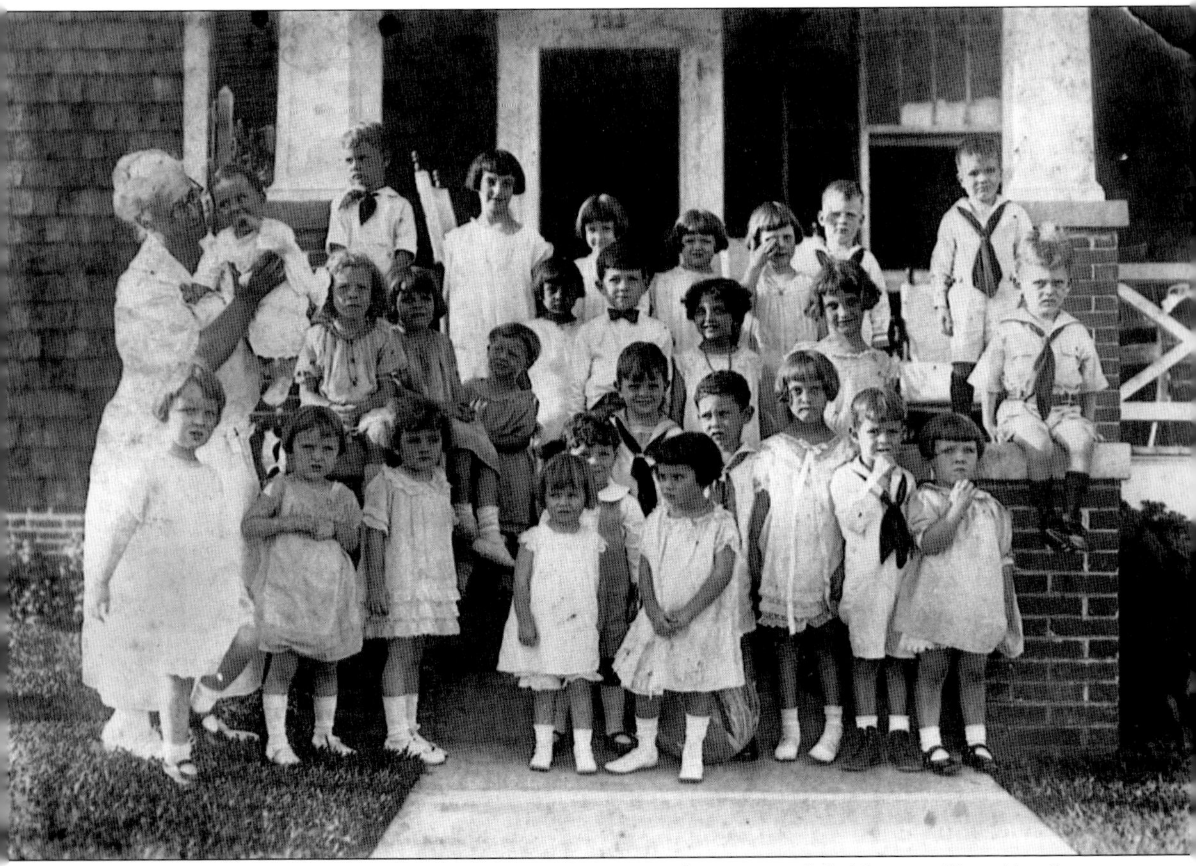

Eugenia Myers Minis (holding Frances Minis) poses with a group of children on East 41st Street. Florance Minis is fifth from the left on the front row.

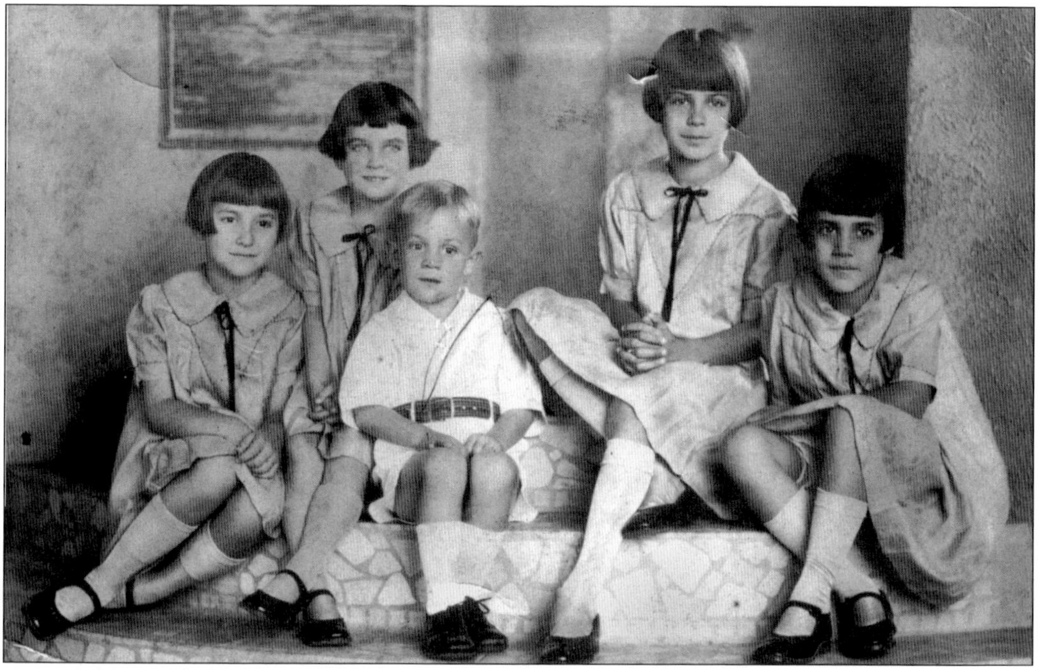

Five of the six children of Mary C. Smith and Harry Melville Dodd were (from left to right) Pat, Connie, Harry Jr. (Icky), Joan, and Muriel. In the 1930s Harry Dodd was the manager of the Lucas Theater. Joan Dodd was killed in an automobile accident in the late 1930s while attending Armstrong Junior College.

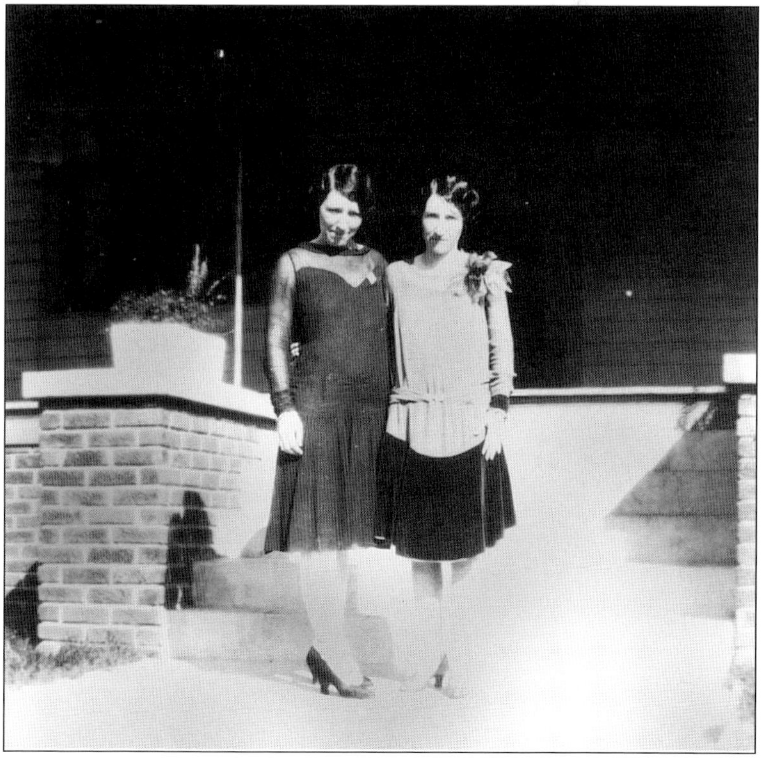

Etta Bart and her sister Chris Lester are all dressed up in front of 316 East 51st Street.

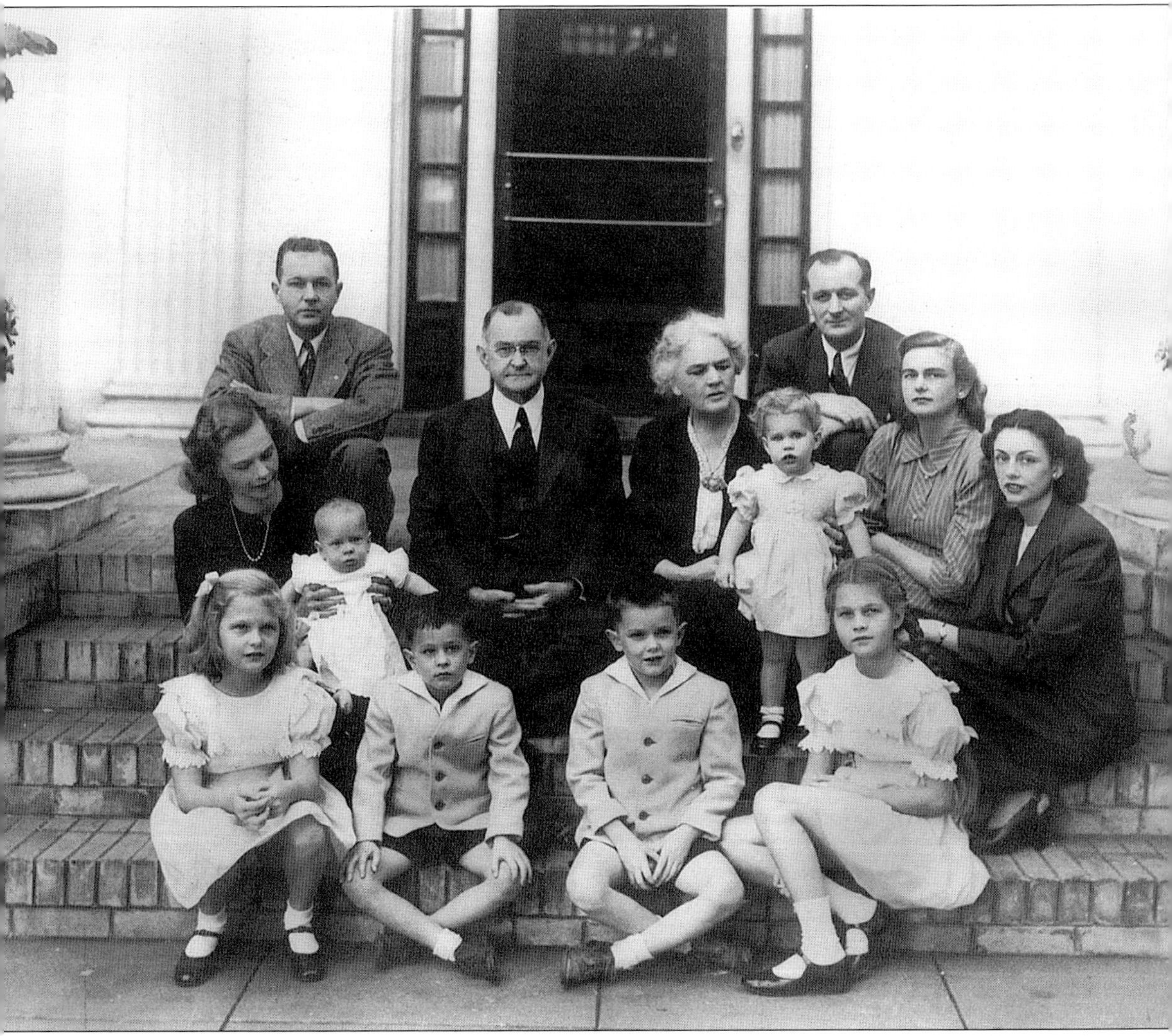

The Oliver family lived at 602 East Victory Drive for more than 50 years and had this family portrait taken in 1946. Pictured, from left to right, are (front row) Julia Oliver (Conrade), Dana Oliver, Mac Oliver, and Louise Oliver (Maner); (middle row) Louise Myers Oliver with baby Joe, Joseph M. Oliver, Julia Oliver, Krista Clausen, Caroline Oliver Clausen Strang (in striped suit), and Corrine Stevens Oliver (Johnson); (back row) Frank M. Oliver and Pete Clausen.

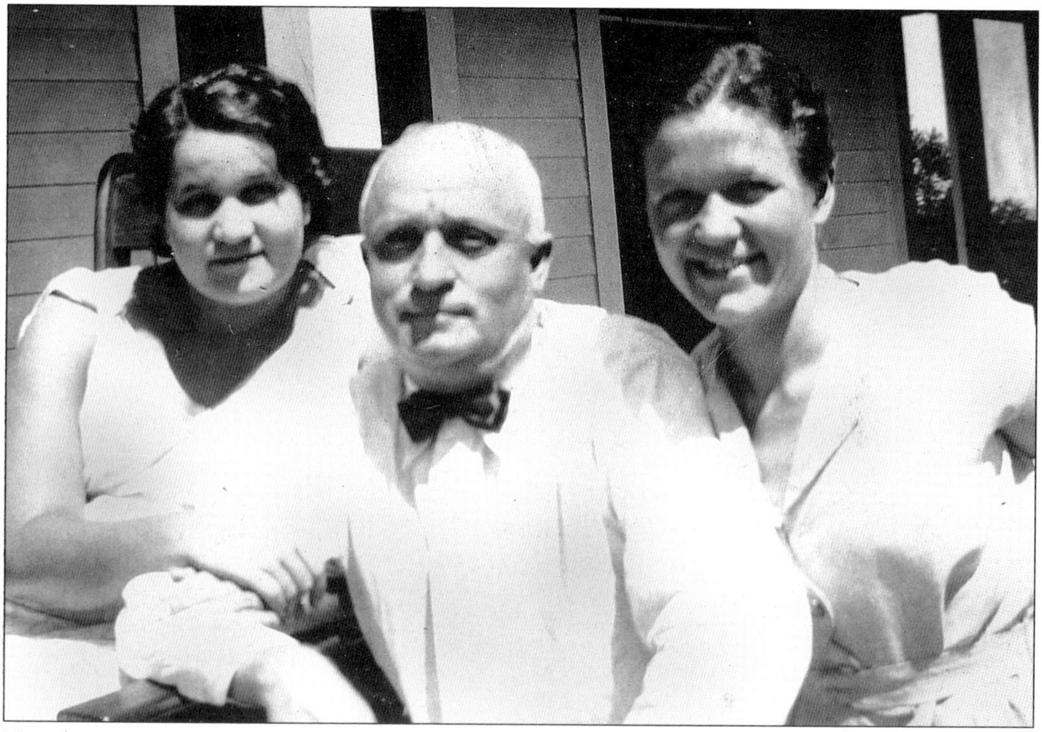

Naval stores executive David T. Furse is flanked by daughters Elise Furse and Anne Furse (Sipple).

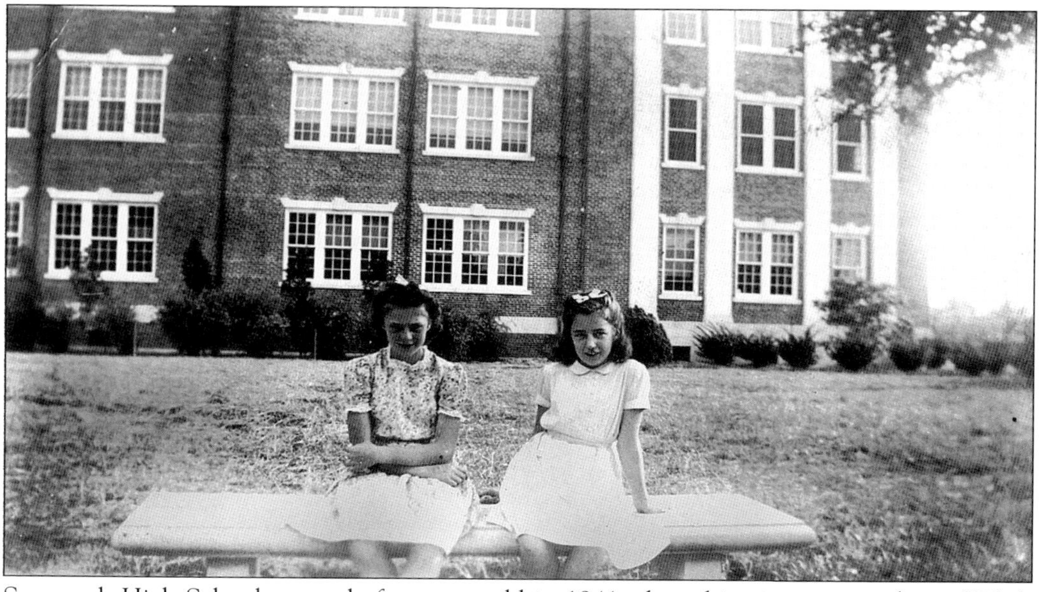

Savannah High School was only four years old in 1941 when this picture was taken of Edith Rehm and Marge Hasselton.

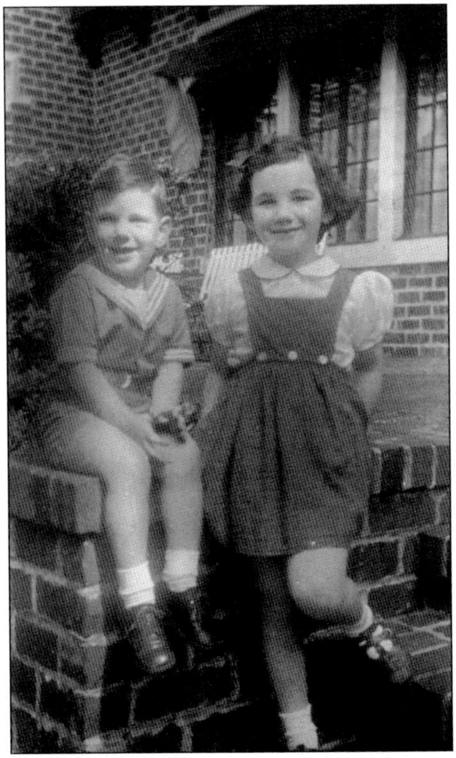

Everett Eisenberg and Dottie Eisenberg (Lynch) pose in front of their East 46th Street home, which they shared with their parents and grandparents.

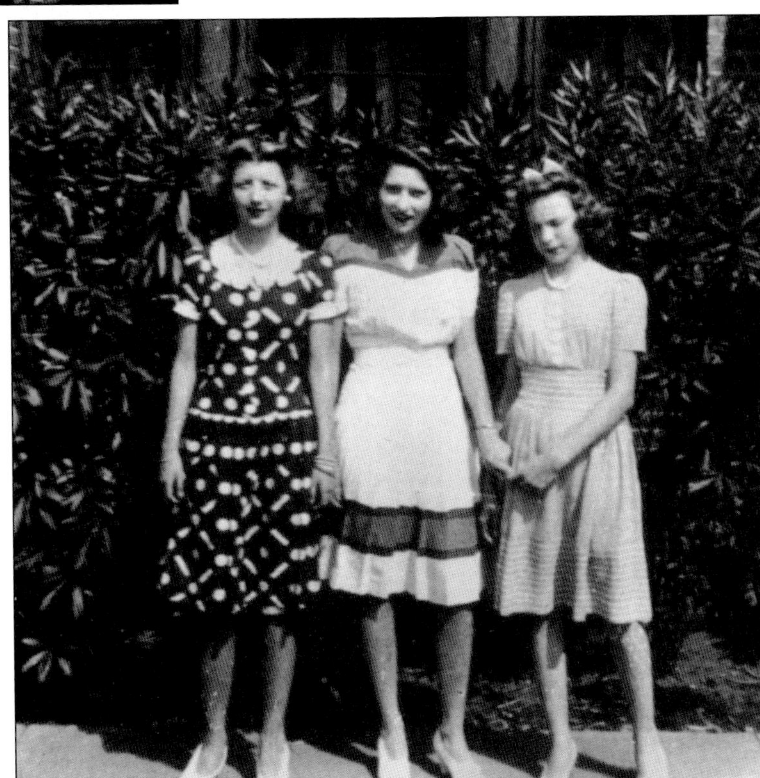

In 1942 (from left to right) sisters and good friend Claire Tharin (Robertson), Mary Ann Suddath (McDowell), and Lucille Suddath (Bates) stood beside the Suddath home on Washington Avenue.

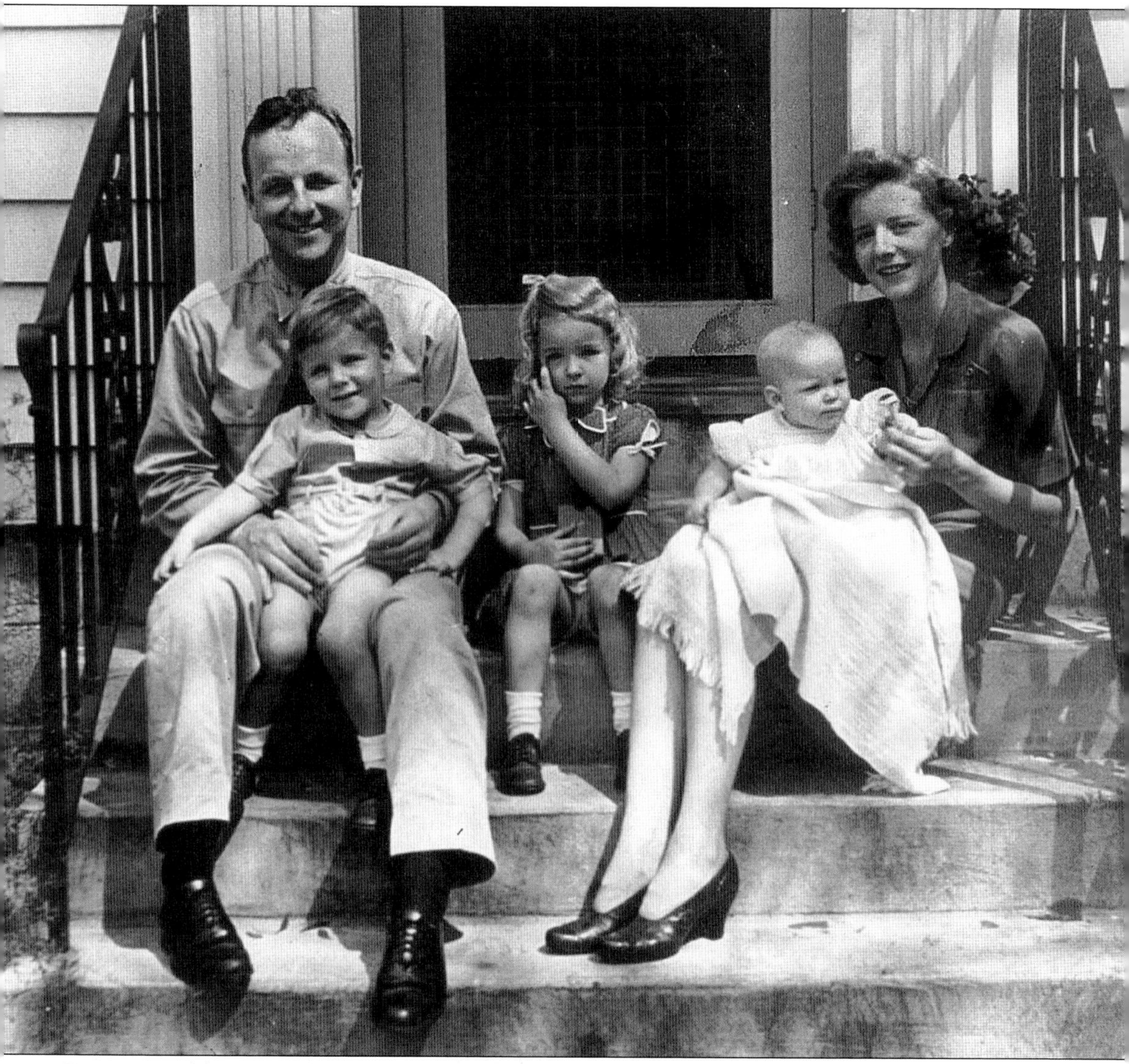

During World War II the Wylly family sat on the front porch of their home at 34 East 53rd Street. From left to right are John Wylly Sr. holding Johnny, Polly Wylly (Cooper), and Polly Chisholm Wylly (Brooks) holding baby Sue.

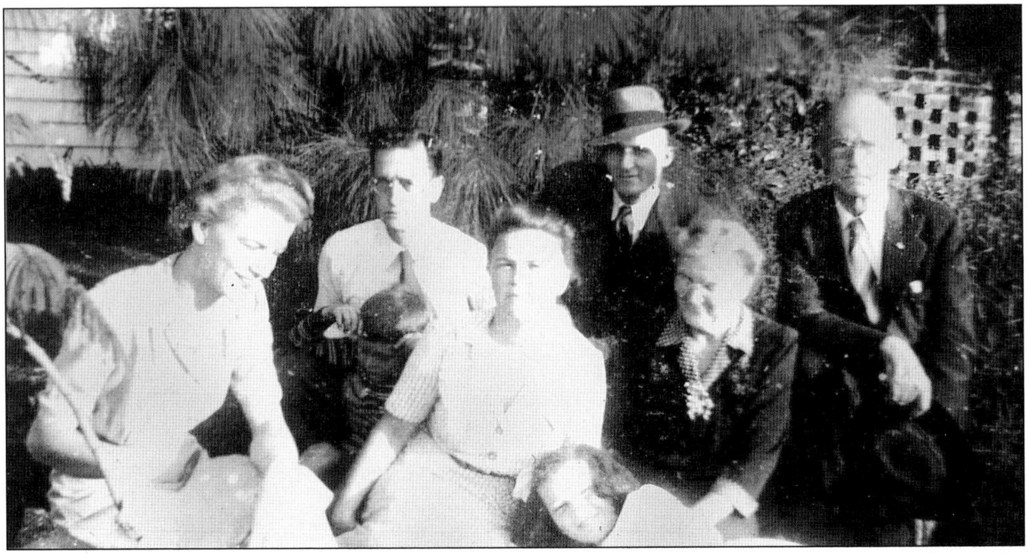

Members of the Cargill family got together for this picture in the late 1930s or early 1940s. From left to right are (front row) Pauline Cargill (Powers), Lillie May Cargill Perkins, Mary Cargill (Waddell), and Mattie Cargill; (back row) Edward Perkins with Jimmie Cargill, John Cargill, and George S. Cargill.

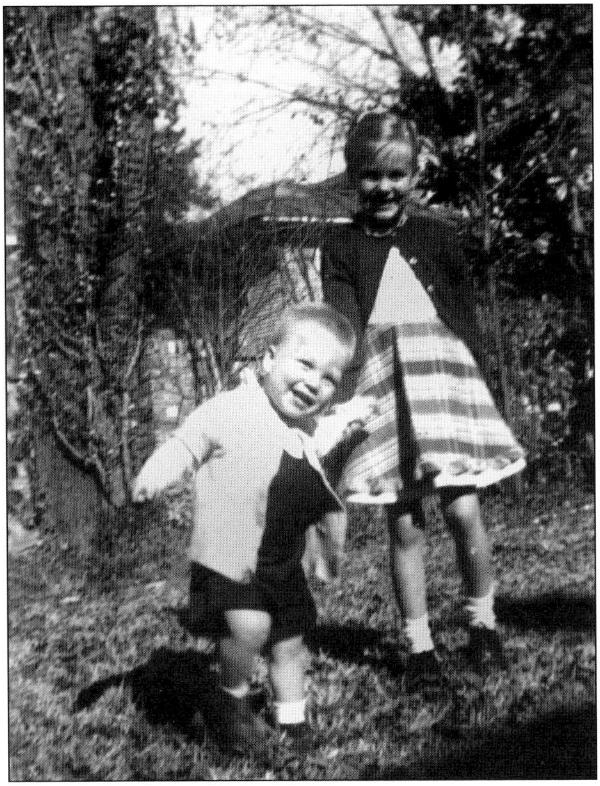

Billy and Marian McIntosh play in the backyard of their Washington Avenue home.

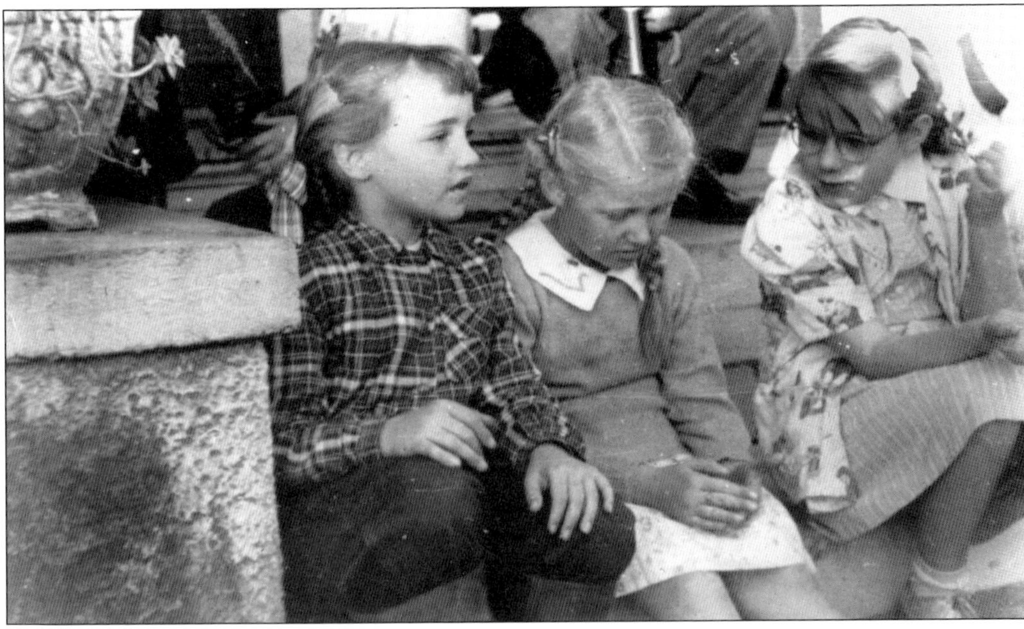

The Pacifici girls relax on the steps of a bungalow in the 700 block of East 48th Street.

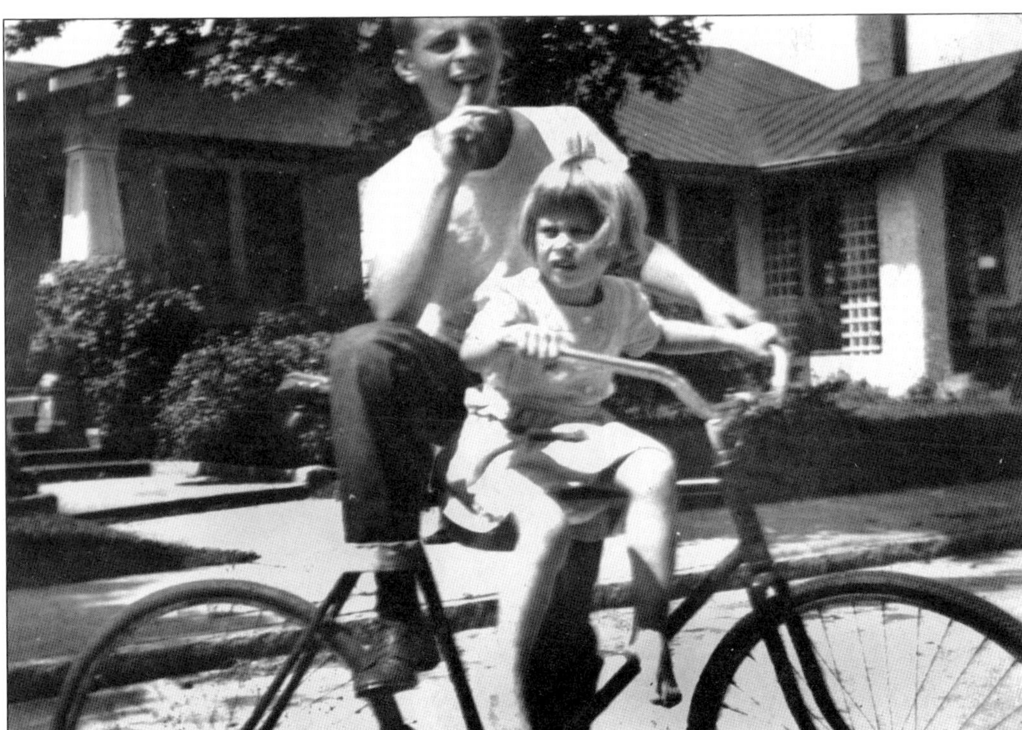

Wally Butler looks as if he can't decide whether of not to give Cookie Pacifici a tow on his bicycle.

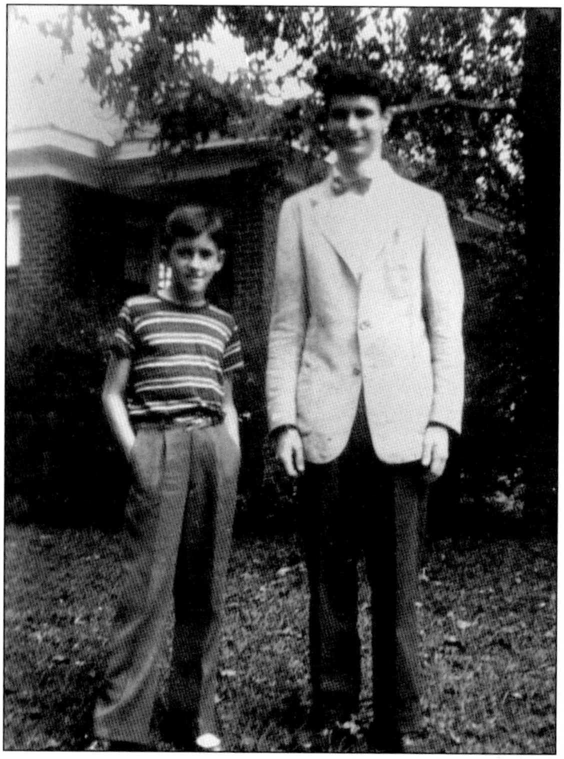

Stanley Martin and Ken Palmer look long and lean in this 1947 photo taken in the 700 block of East 48th Street.

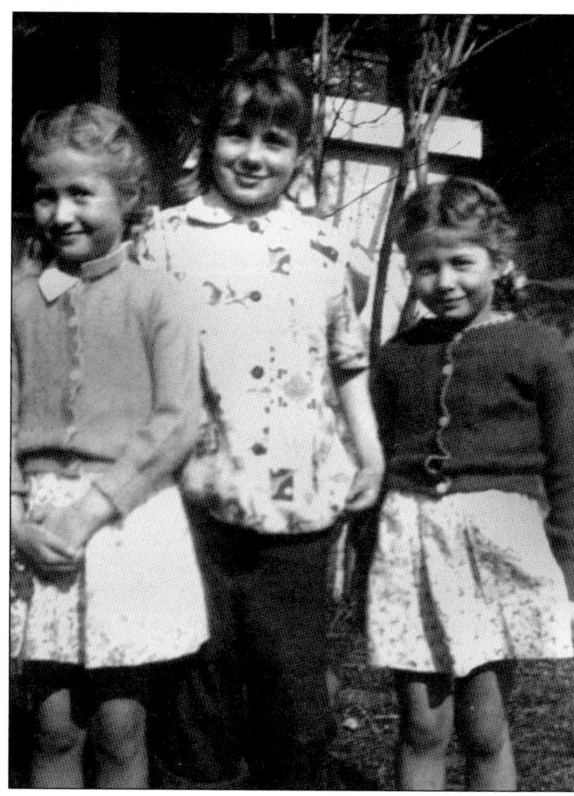

Karen Davis is flanked by two of the Pacifici sisters in this1947 photograph.

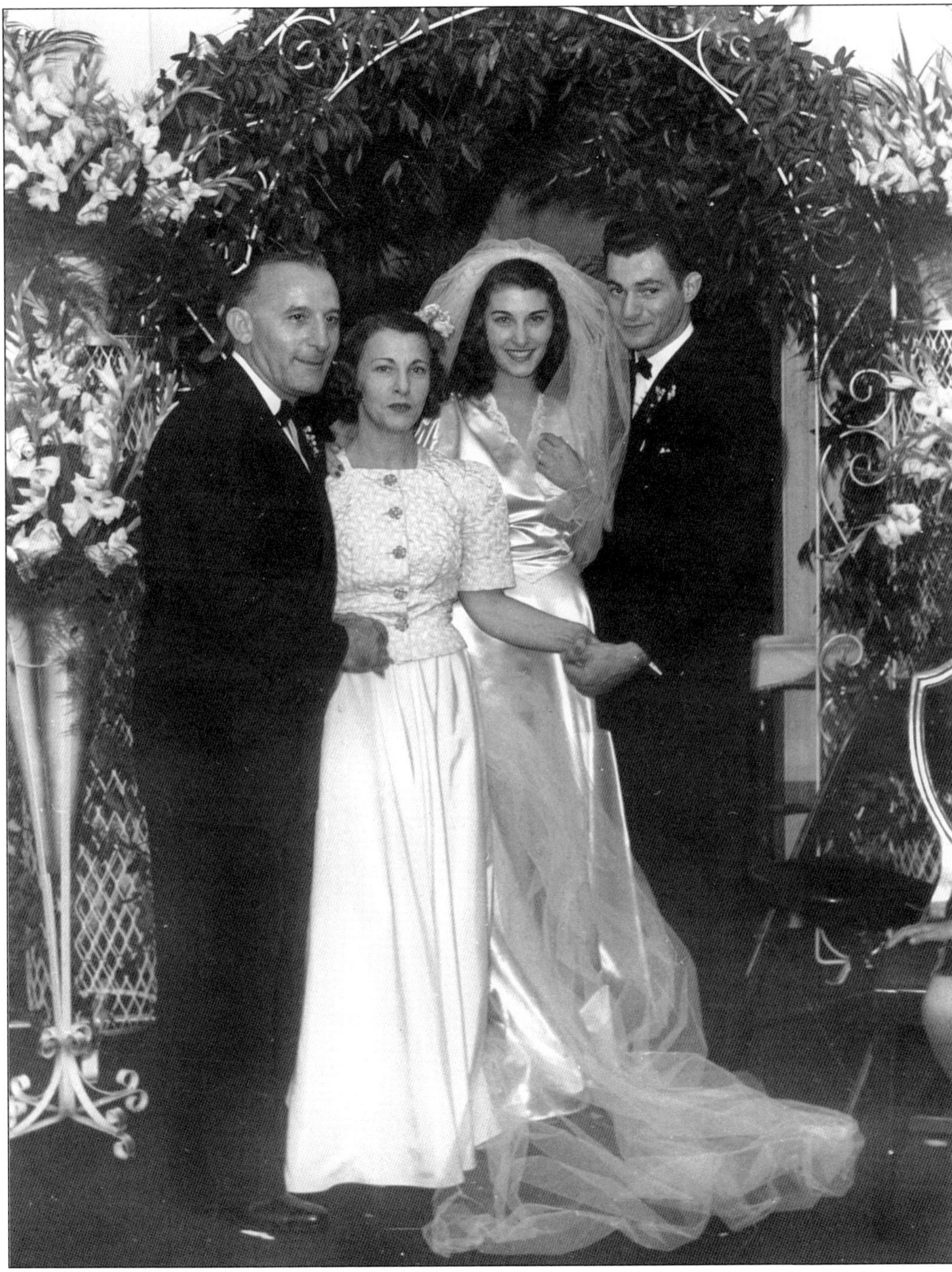

The wedding of Frances Hornstein and Joe Goldberg, with her parents, Mr. and Mrs. Sam Hornstein looking on, took place at the Hornstein's East 44th Street home. The Jewish nuptials included the traditional chupa, or arch, seen in the photograph.

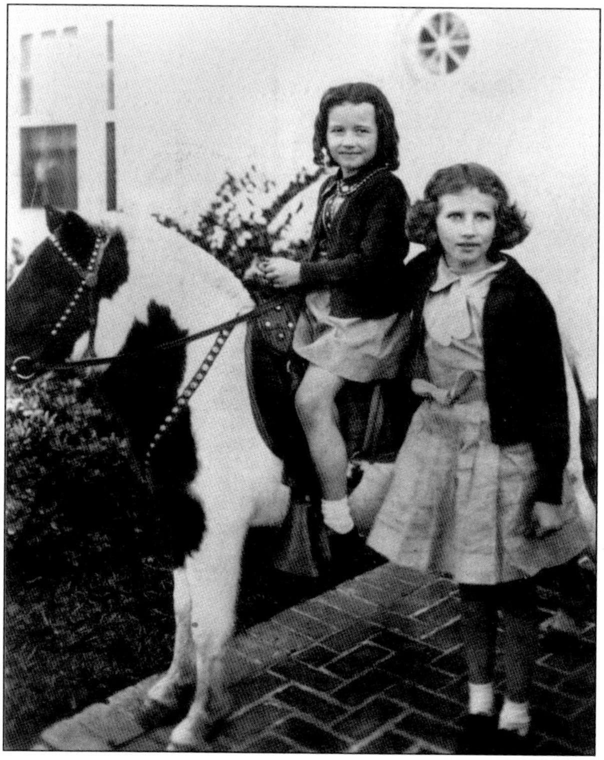

During the 1940s, photographers, with ponies in tow, often went door to door in the neighborhoods. Dinky Crutcher (Foster) takes her turn while sister Katherine Crutcher (Chisholm) stands by.

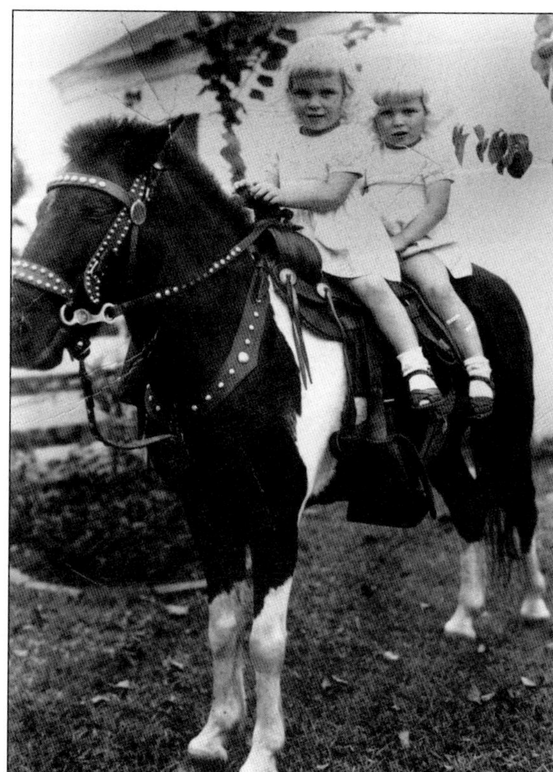

The Powers twins, Jean Powers (Sparks) and Jane Powers (Sparks) managed to fit on one pony.

Frances Goldberg tries to keep sons Steve and Lanny in line on the lawn of their 44th Street home.

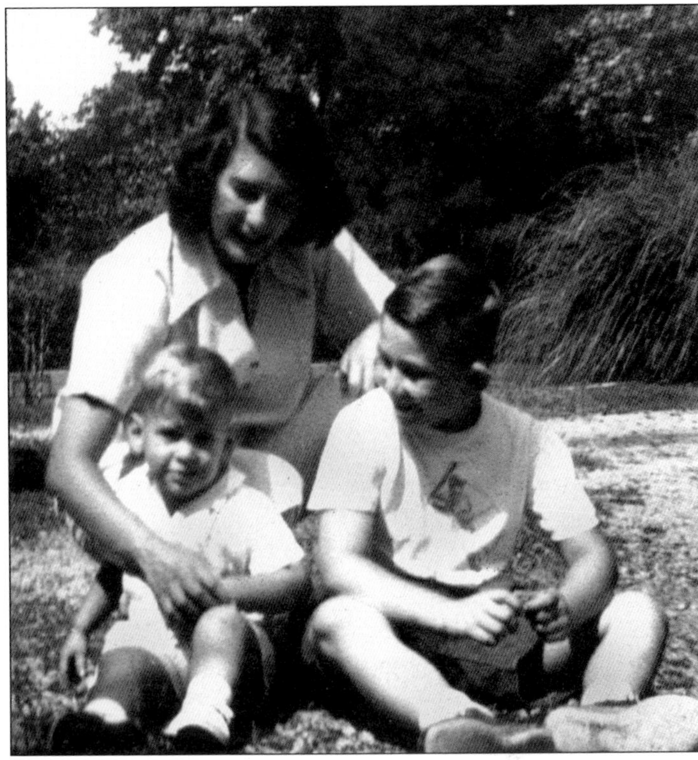

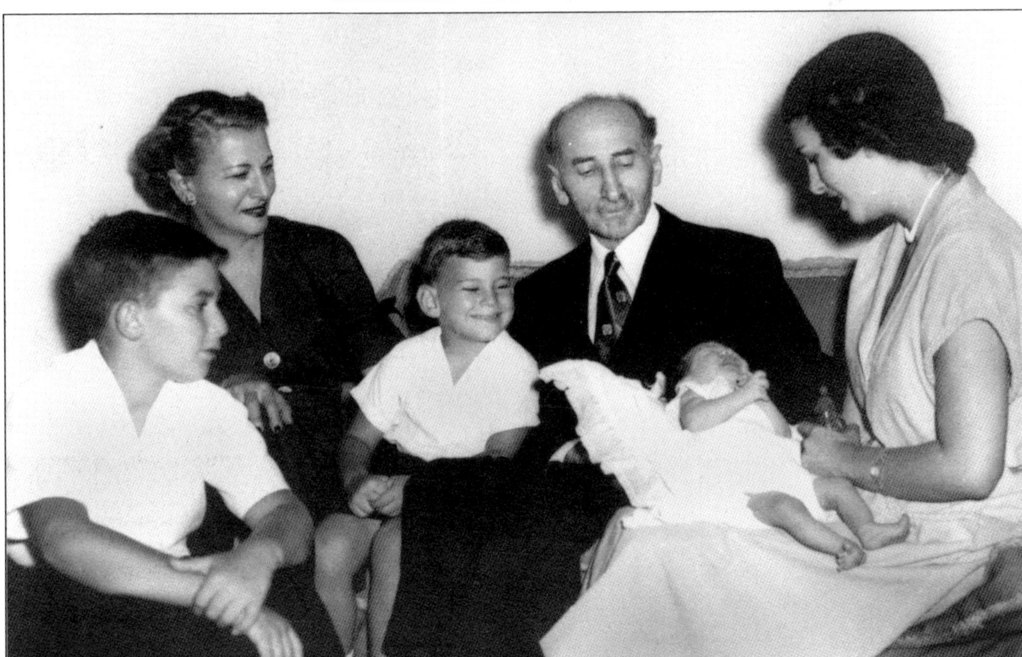

The 1951 birth of Sissy Goldberg (Hoffman) was a great celebration for the Goldberg, Hornstein, and Blumenthal families. From left to right are brother Lanny Goldberg, grandmother Dorothy Blumenthal Hornstein, brother Steve Goldberg, great grandfather Rabbi Charles Blumenthal, and mother Frances Hornstein Goldberg holding Sissy.

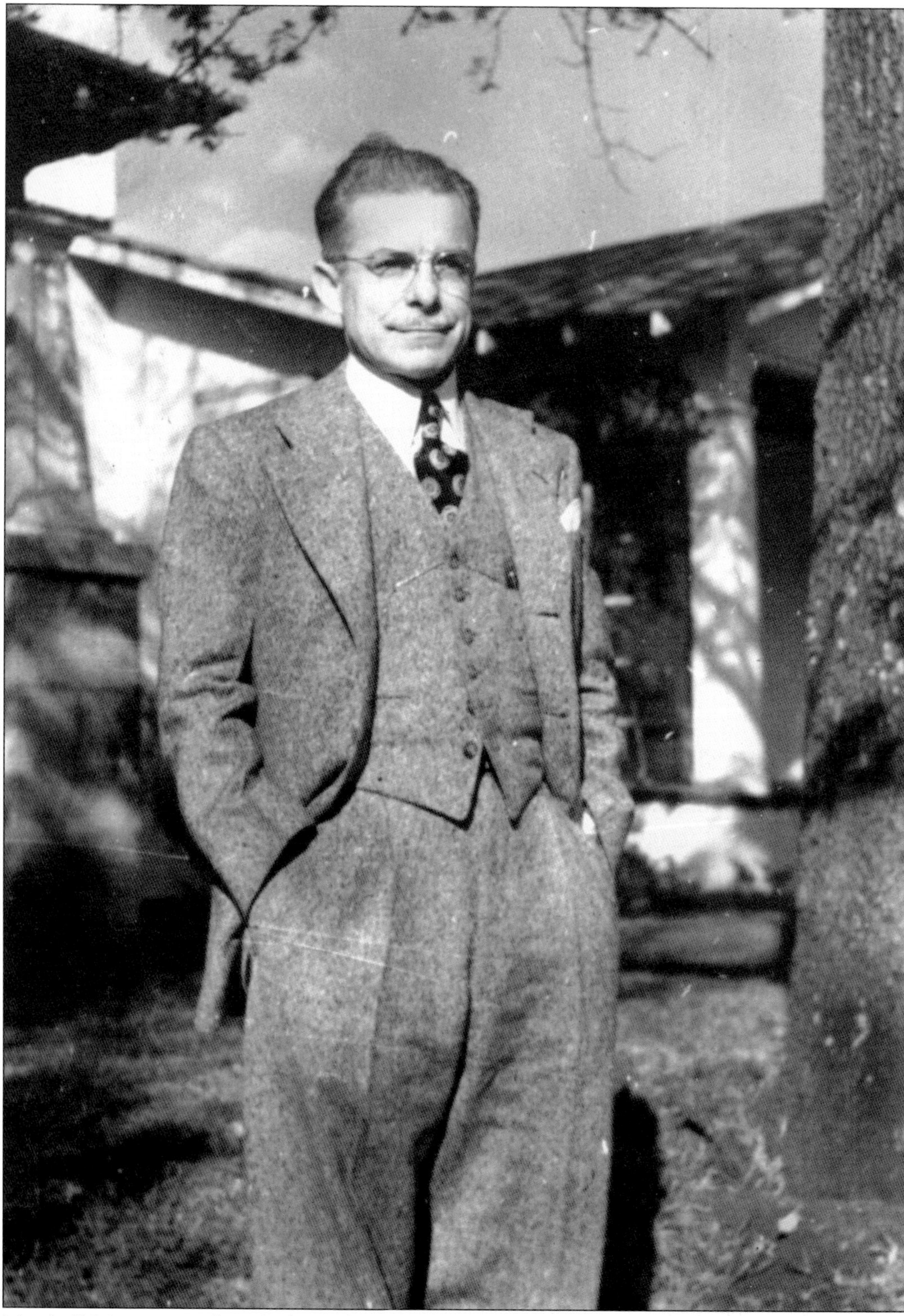

Marshall Morgan purchased a bungalow on East 48th street for his family in 1923. The Morgan family owned the home until 1998.

After a 1940 storm Agnes Hill and Jo Kelly stood in the 200 block of East 45th Street, which was unpaved, to check out tree damage.

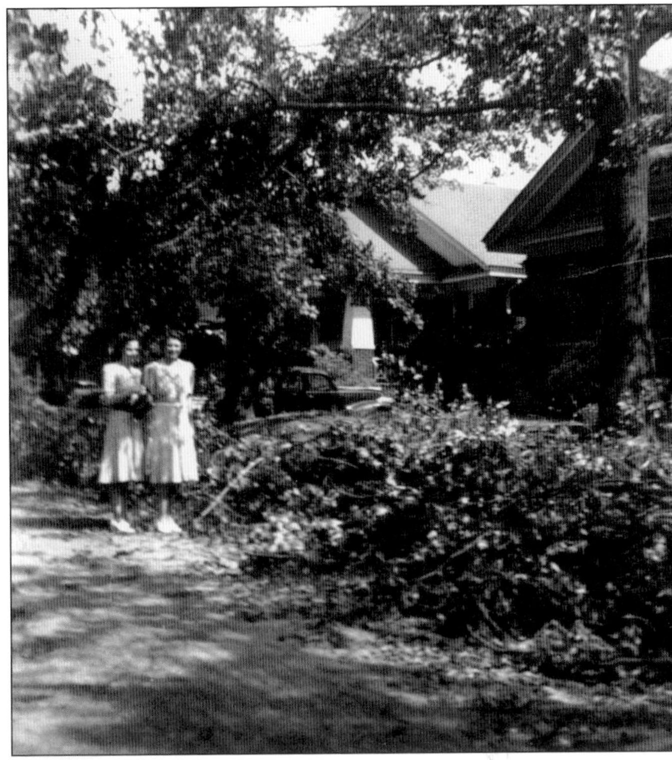

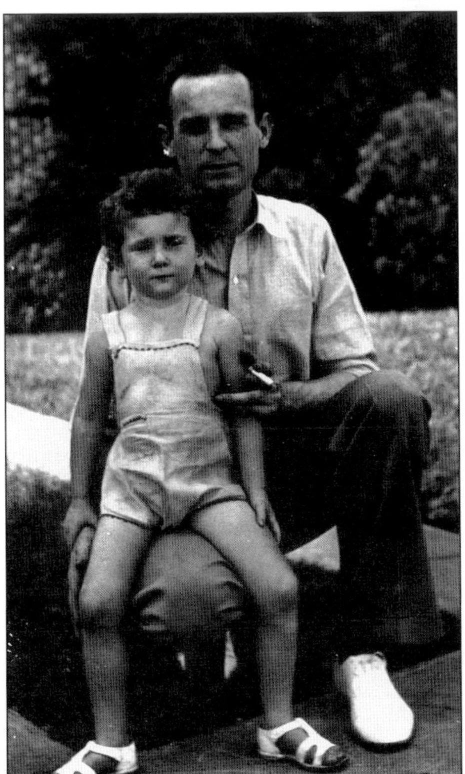

Dr. Lester Neville poses with his daughter Beth Neville (Whelan).

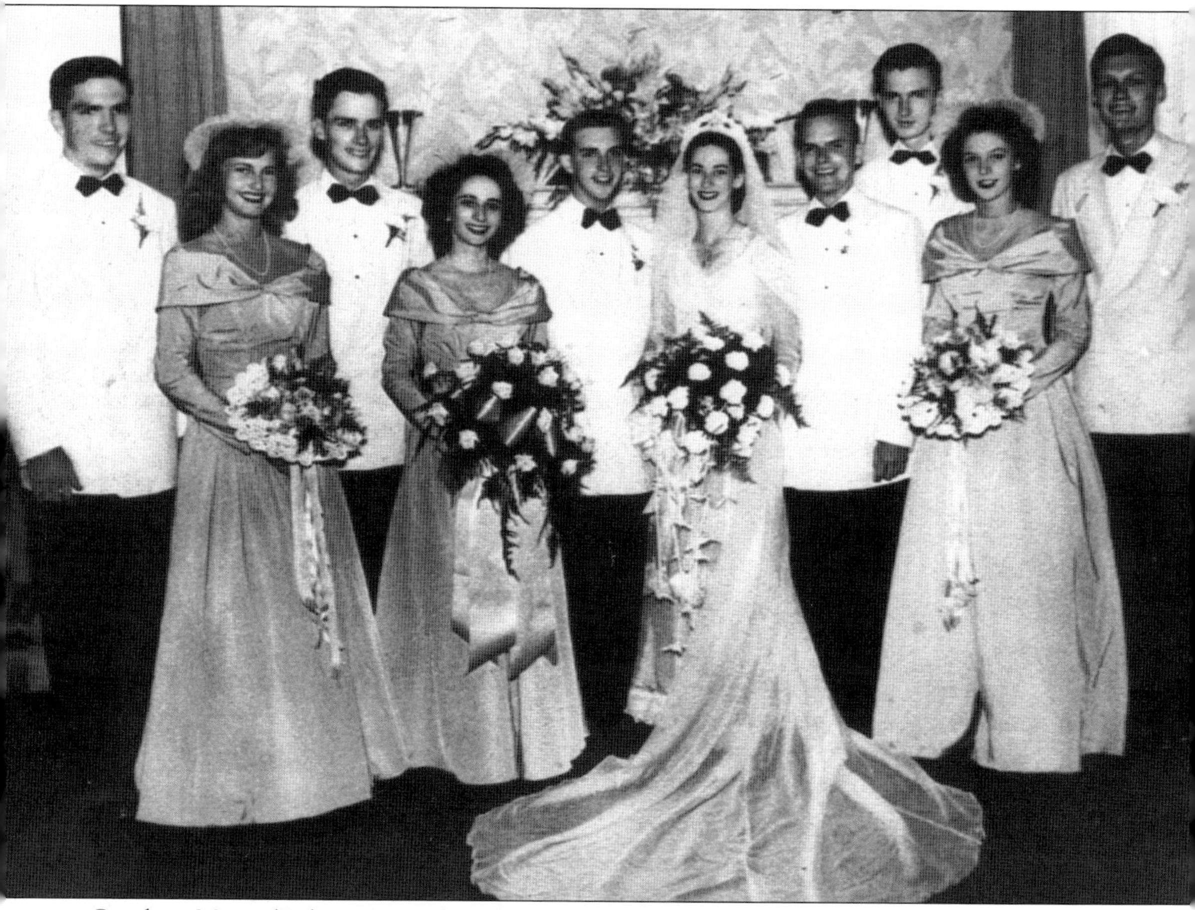

Caroline Minis (Rehm, Cowart) and Raymond Rehm were married at St. John's Episcopal Church in 1947. The reception was held at the East 51st Street home of the bride's parents, Mr. and Mrs. Isaac Minis. The wedding party included Edward Neal of Columbus, Eva Sessoms, Jimmie Tootle, Frances Minis (Earle), Raymond and Caroline, Austin Hinely, Lee McClure, Edith Rehm, and Ross Holland.

George and Etta Bart sit on the steps of their home at 316 East 51st Street.

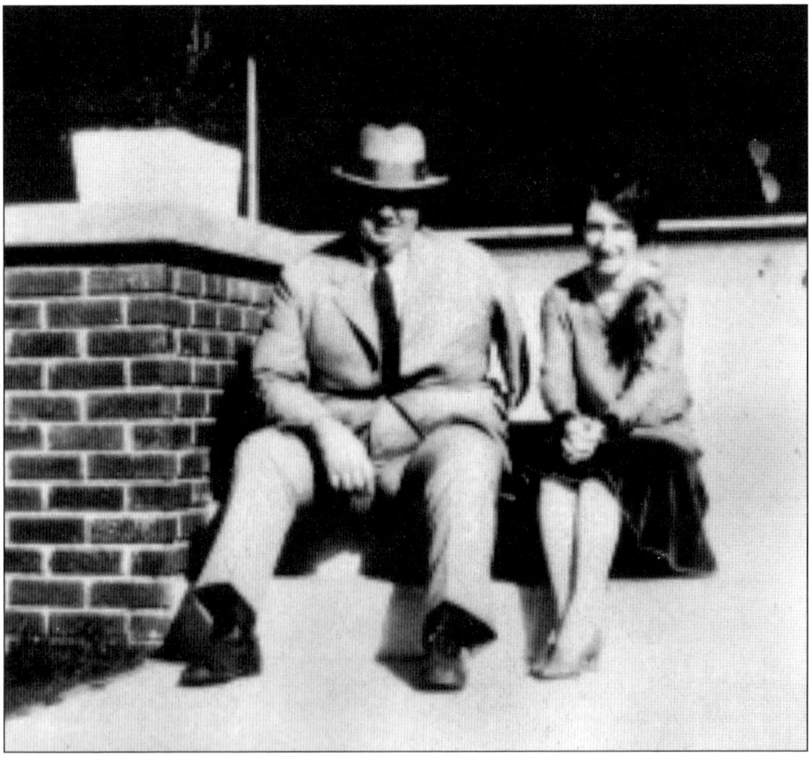

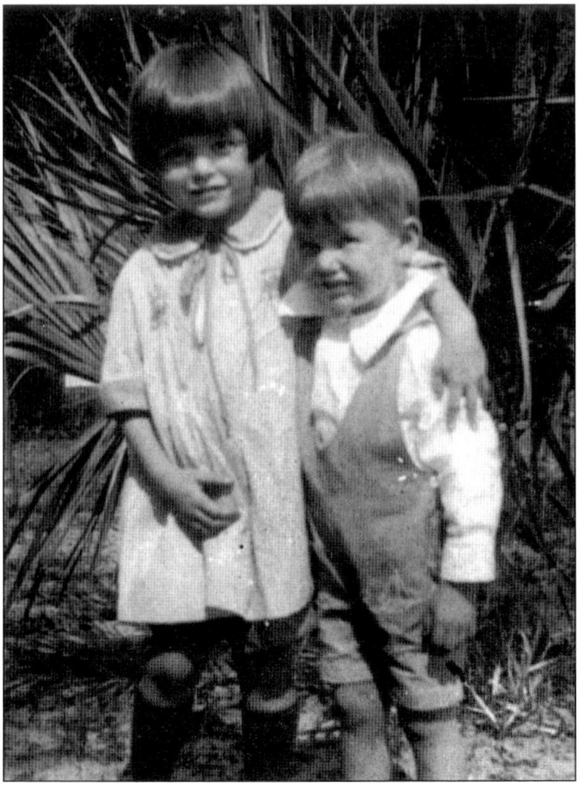

Marjory and George Heyward look sweet for the camera.

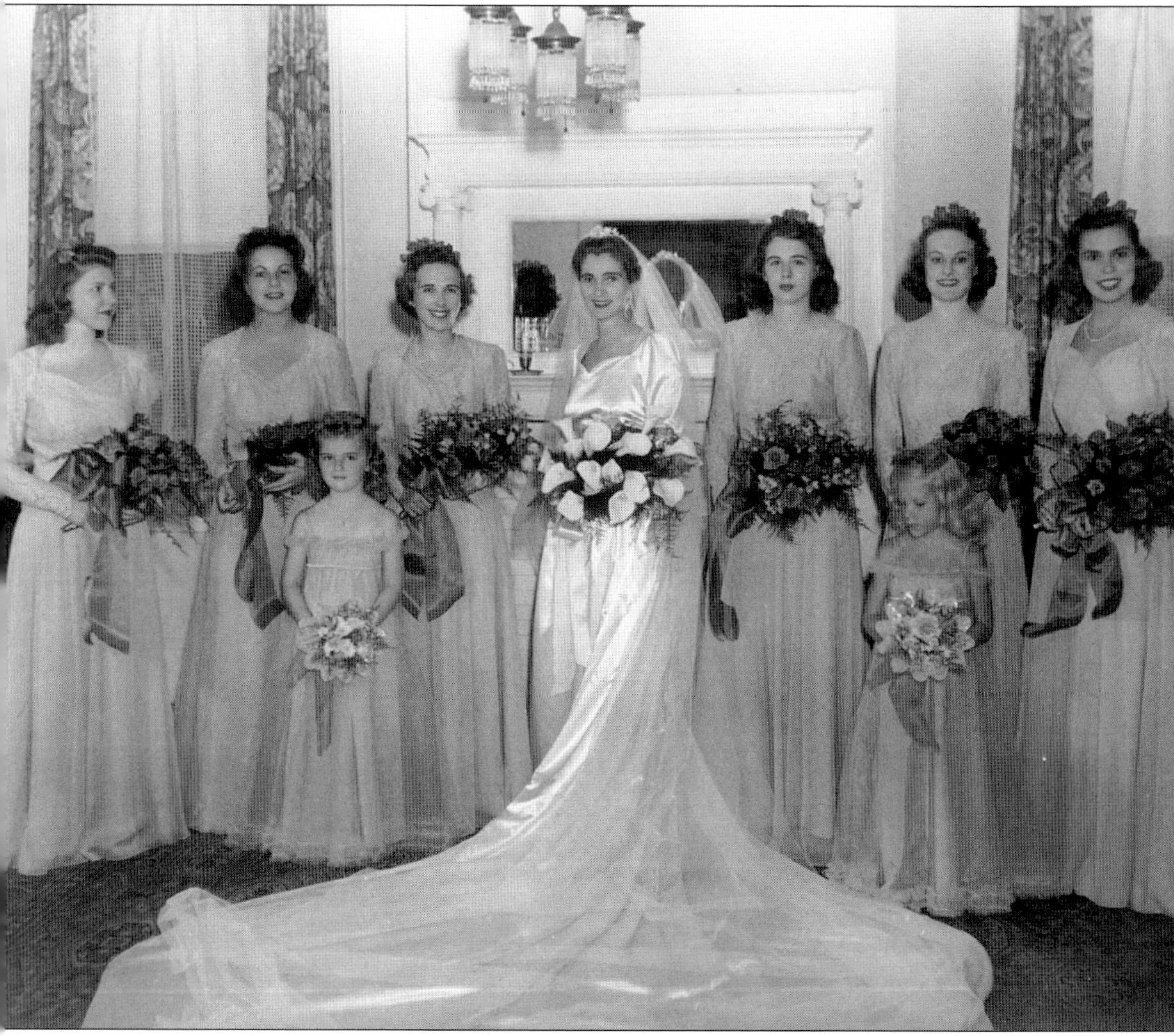

Electa Robertson married Howard Hoffman in the mid-1940s. Here she is with her bridesmaids and flower girls in the Robertson family home at 920 East Victory Drive.

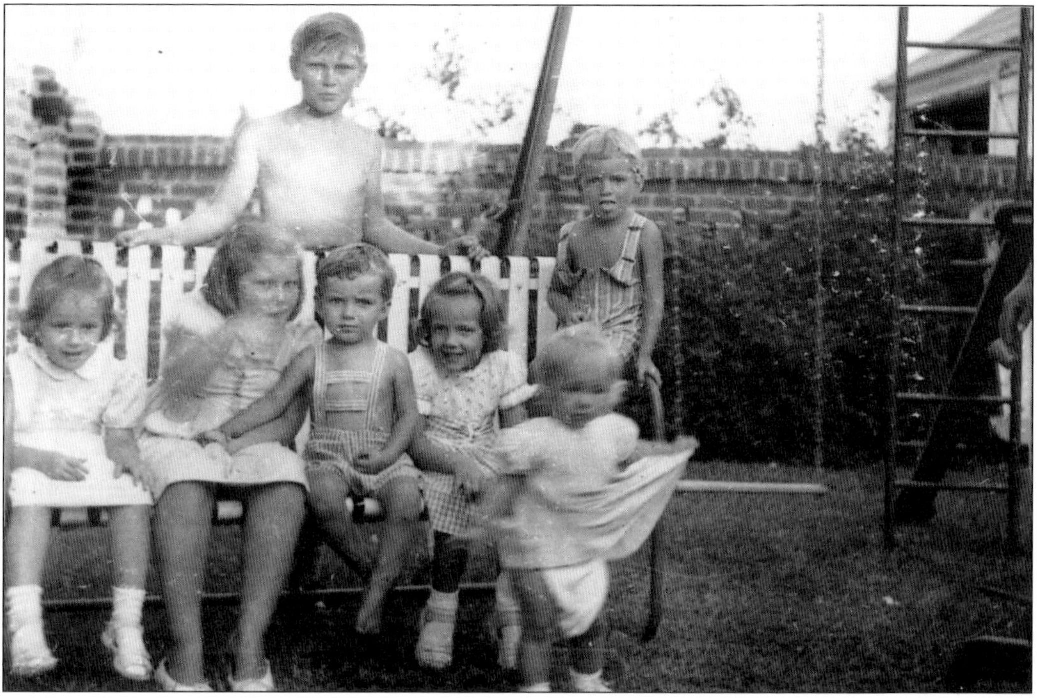

Backyards were full of fun in the late 1940s and early 1950s. Enjoying a ride on a glider are (from left to right) Mary Olsen, Barbie Little, Lee Belford, Lois Olsen, Ricky Belford, Ann Olsen (baby), and Pat Little (standing).

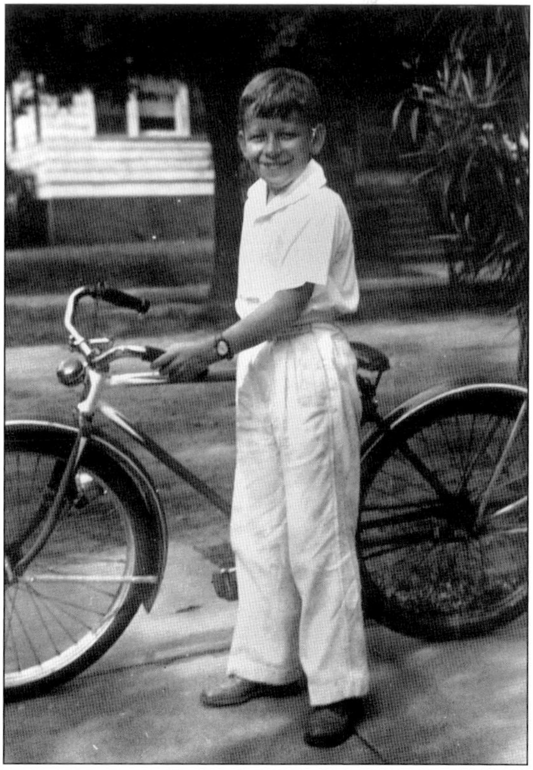

Like many neighborhood children in the 1930s, Harvey Morgan could hop on his bicycle and ride to his grandmother's home.

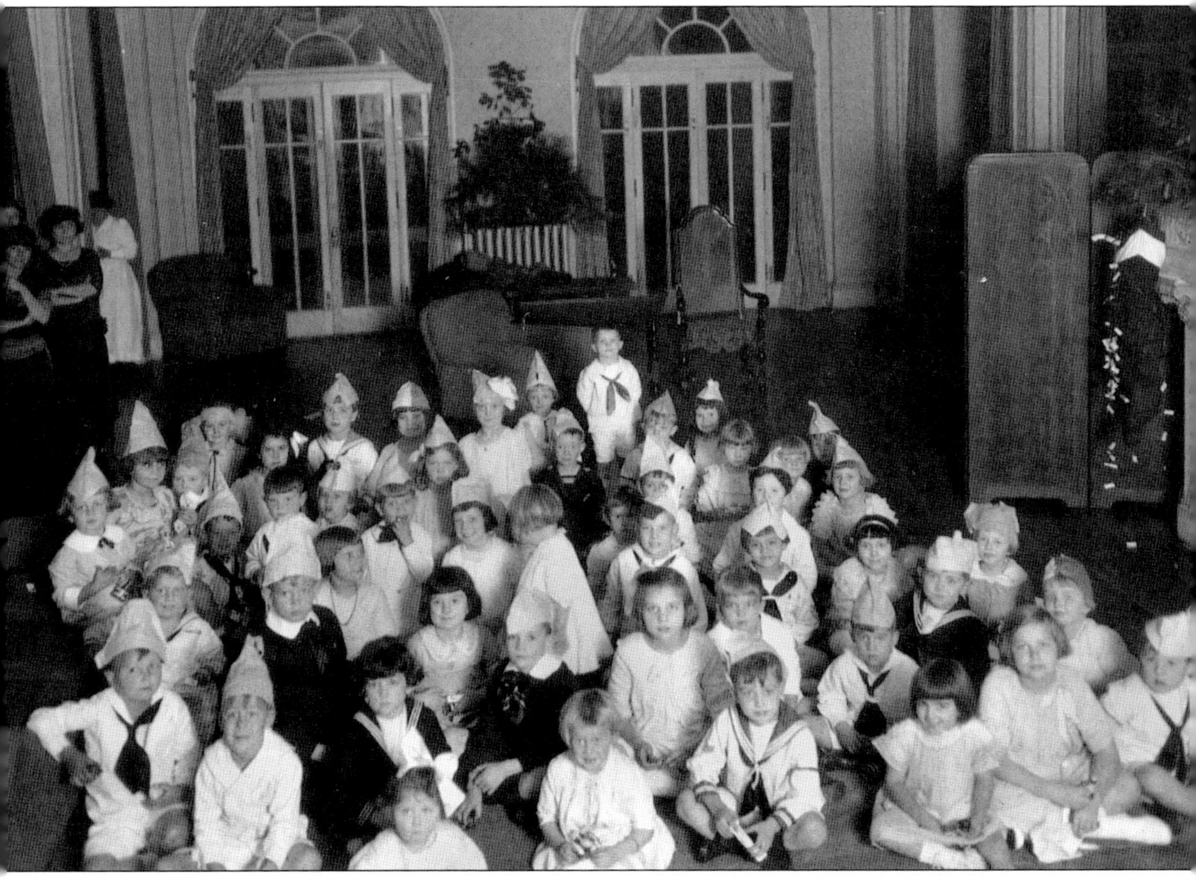

Birthday parties sometimes involved leaving the neighborhood for a larger location, such as the old Savannah Golf Club. The occasion for this celebration was Bobby Groves's seventh birthday.

Five

Churches

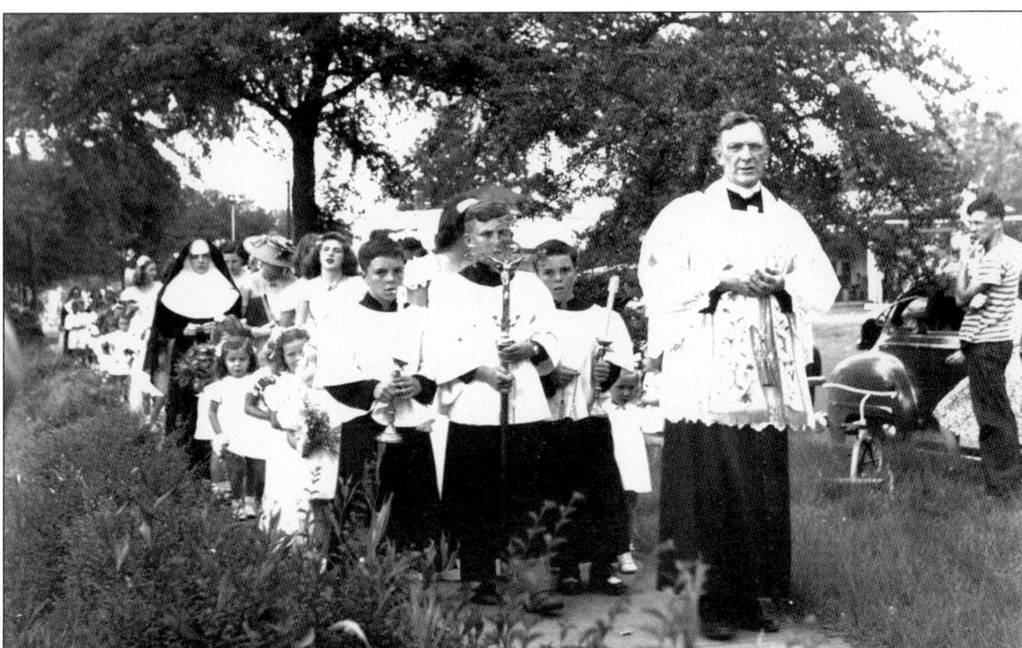

The Reverend Daniel J. McCarthy leads a procession to the original Blessed Sacrament Catholic Church at the corner of Waters Avenue and East 44th Street.

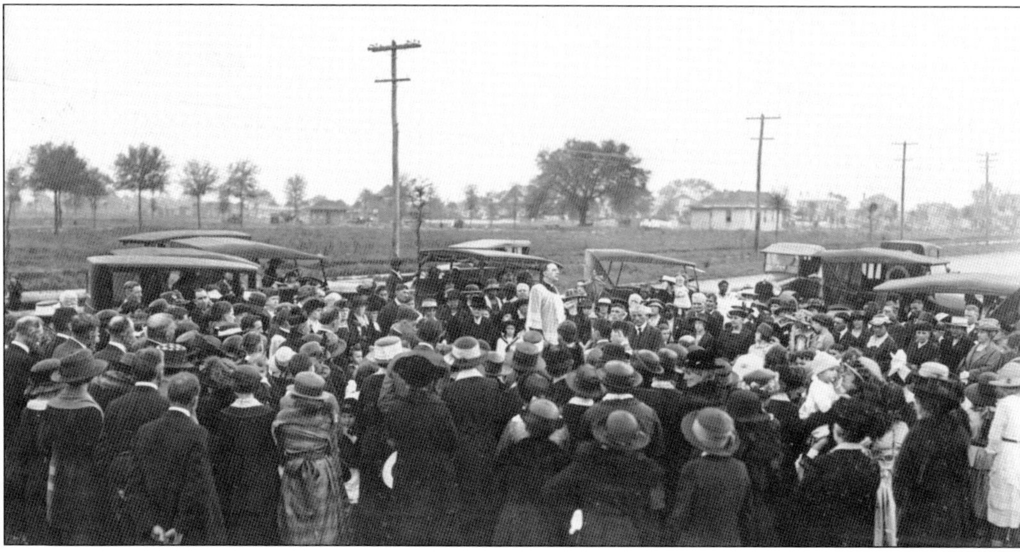

Groundbreaking for the original Blessed Sacrament Catholic Church was held in 1920.

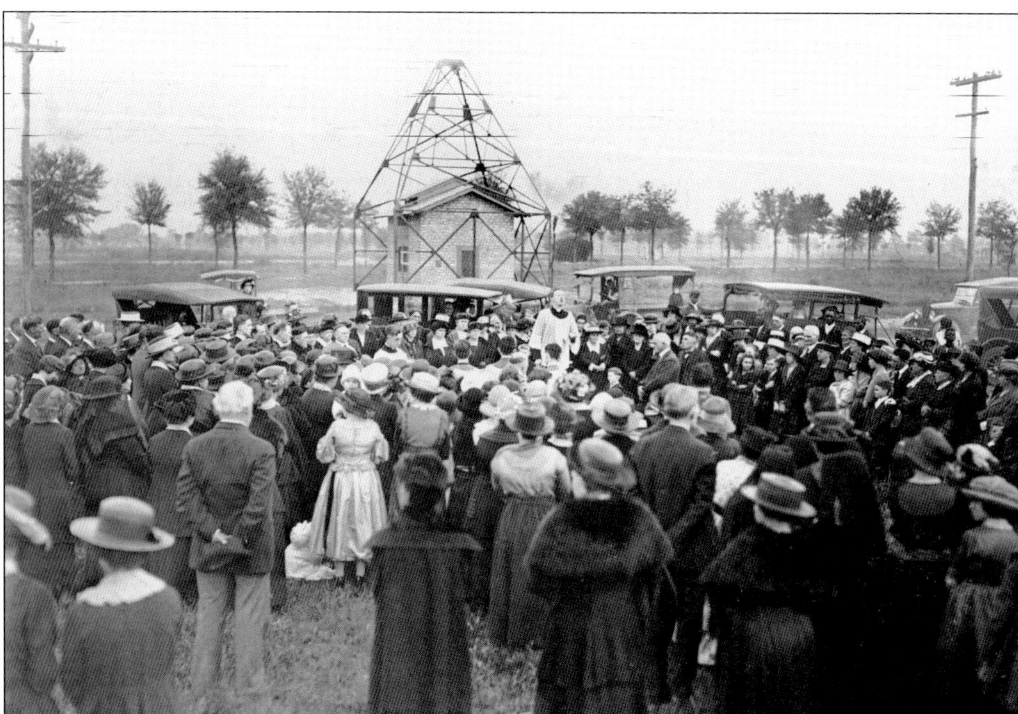

Catholic Bishop Benjamin J. Keiley formally dedicated the original Blessed Sacrament church building on July 10, 1921.

The Blessed Sacrament parish grew to such a point that a new church and school were necessary. In July 1941 the little wooden church was placed on rollers and moved to the adjoining lot on 44th Street. Later, the building was converted to an auditorium and finally demolished to make room for a school addition.

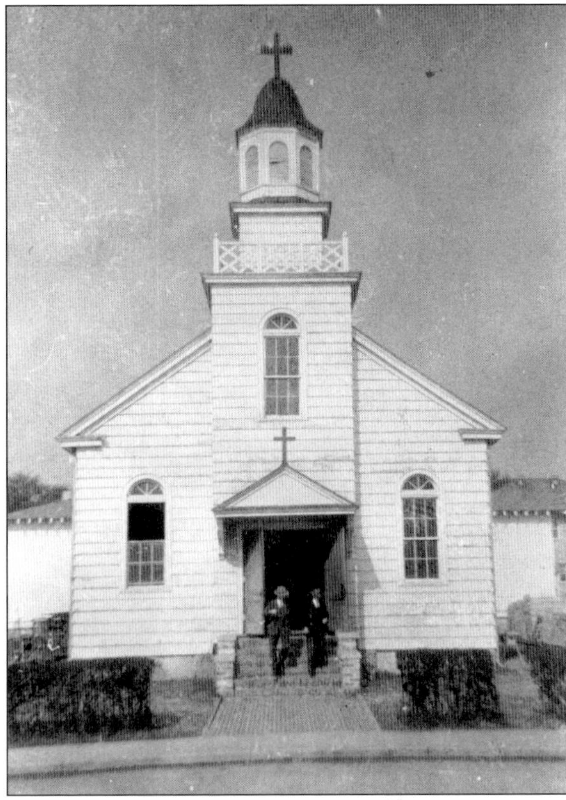

Bishop Gerald P. O'Hara is shown in 1942 laying the cornerstone for a new combination church and school building. When St. Patrick's Church was damaged in the storm of 1940, it was dismantled and bricks were used in the construction of Blessed Sacrament. (Courtesy of Catholic Diocese Archives.)

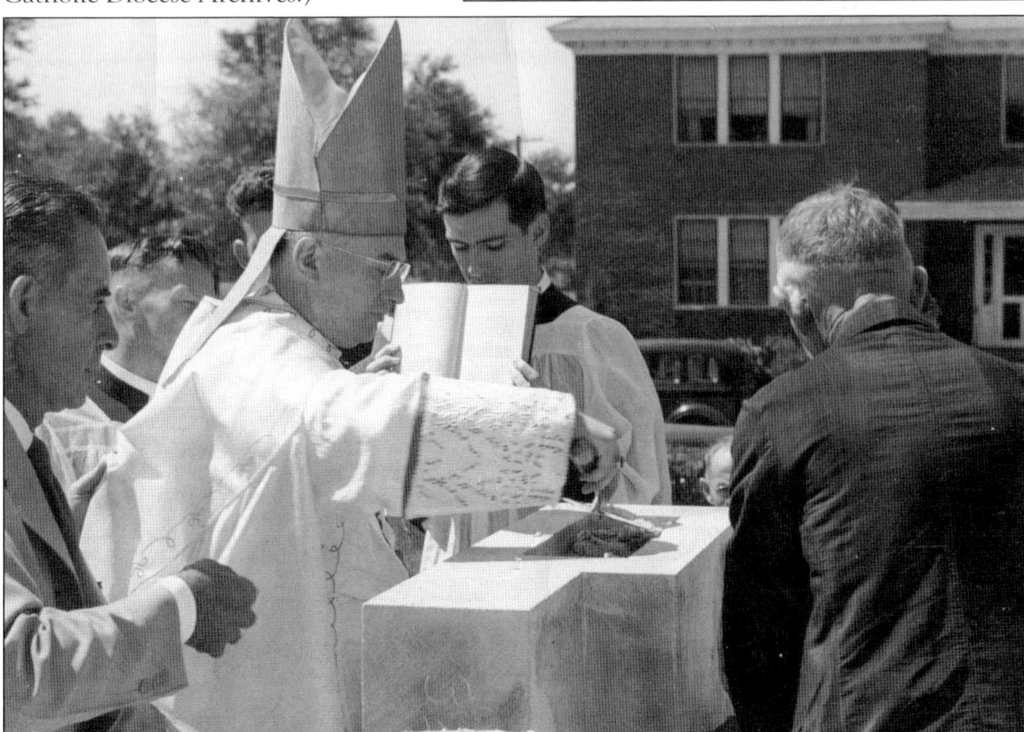

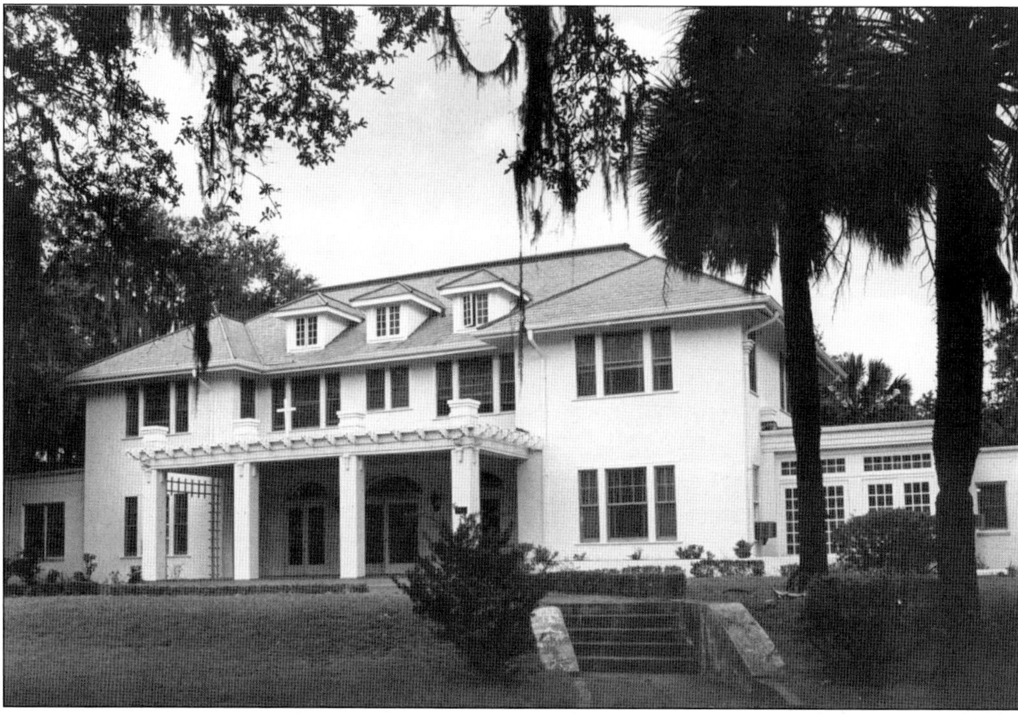

The Stovall house on Estill Avenue (Victory Drive) was built in 1920 and was purchased in 1952 by the Catholic Diocese for use as a convent for the Sisters of Mercy teaching at Blessed Sacrament School. (Courtesy of Catholic Diocese Archives.)

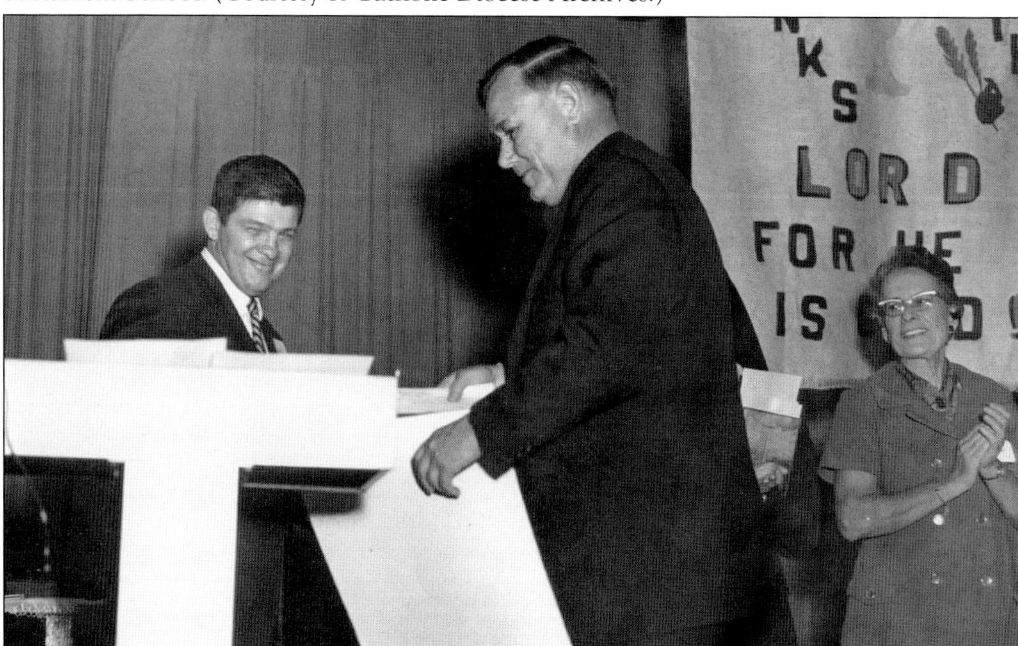

In 1969 longtime church member Tom Coleman, now director of the Georgia Department of Transportation, and Bishop Gerard Frey led the Thanksgiving service to celebrate the debt-free status of the Blessed Sacrament parish. (Courtesy of Catholic Diocese Archives.)

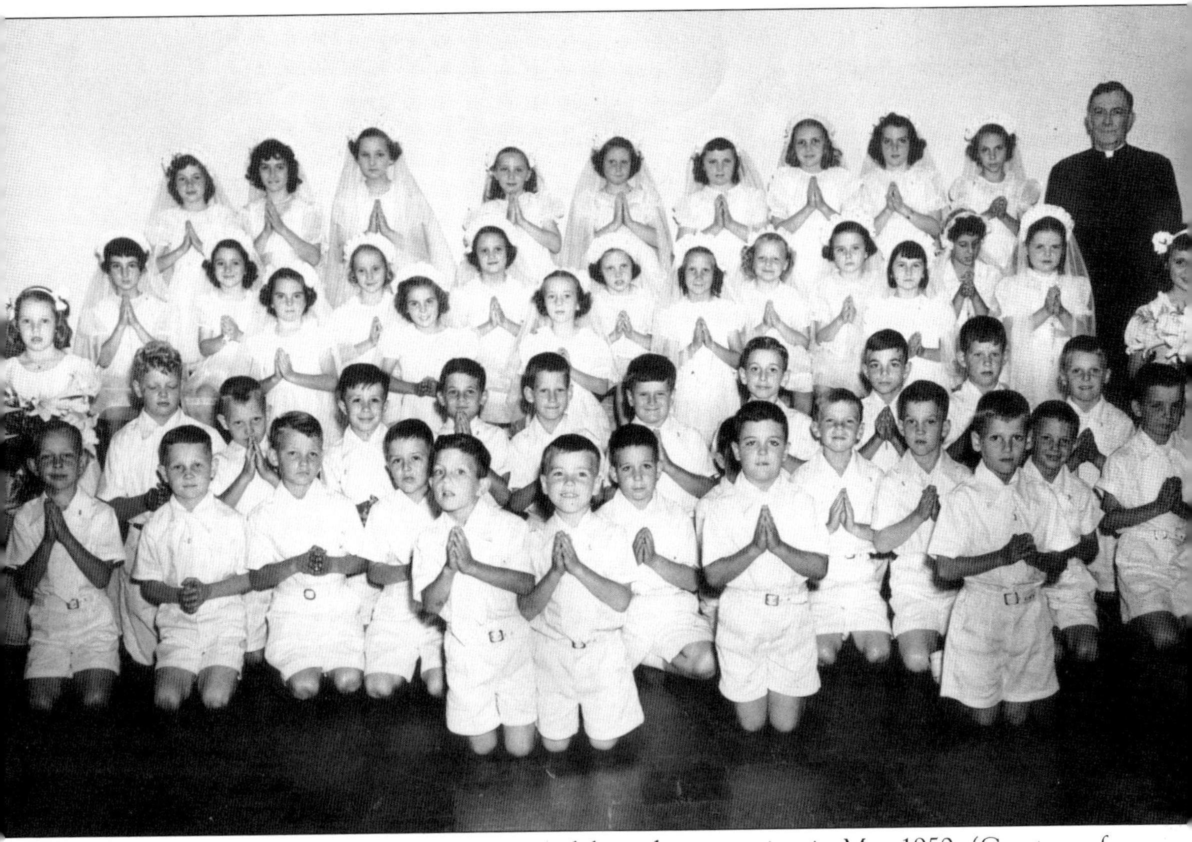

A group of Blessed Sacrament youngsters celebrated communion in May 1950. (Courtesy of Catholic Diocese Archives.)

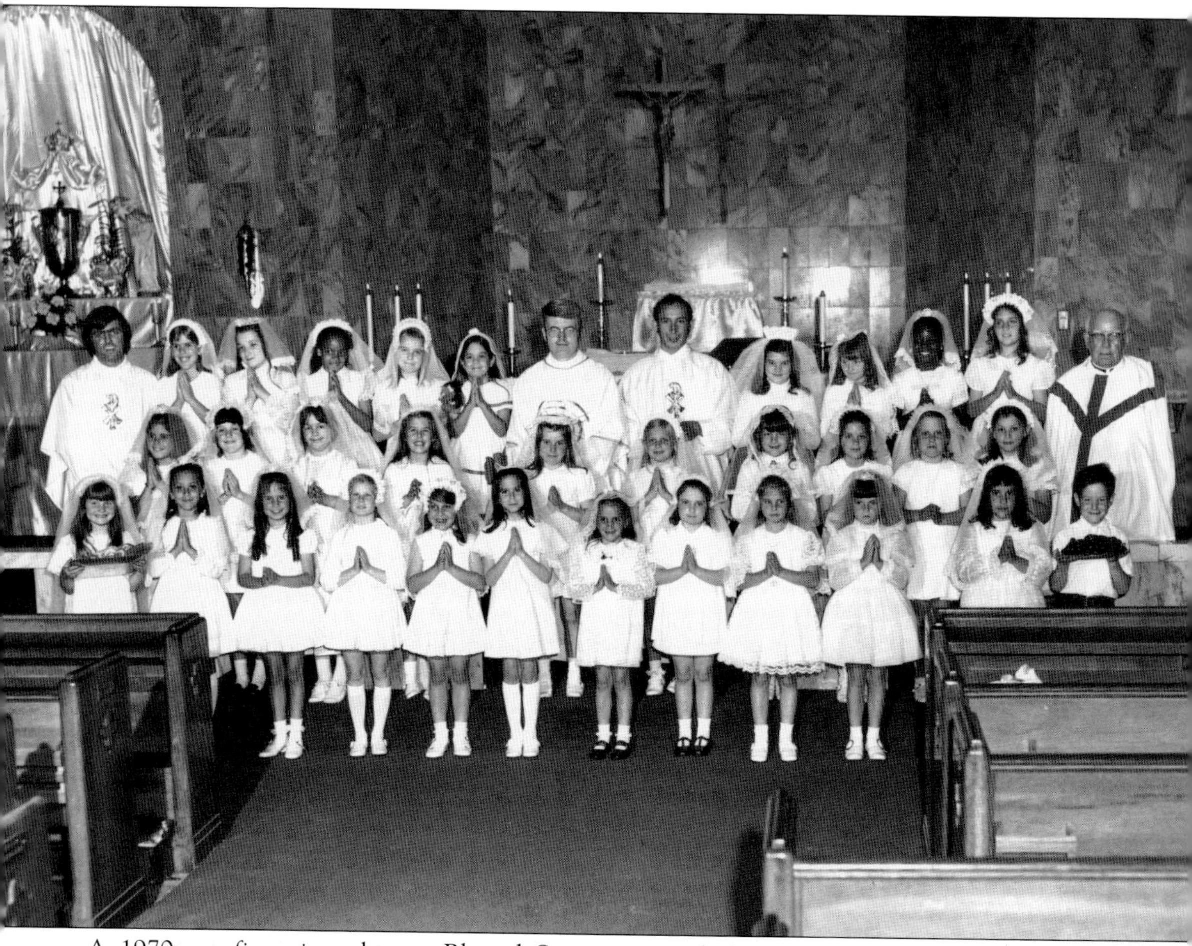

A 1970s confirmation class at Blessed Sacrament includes then-Rev. Kevin Boland, who was appointed bishop of the Catholic Diocese of Savannah in 1995. Bishop Boland is in the middle of the top row (with glasses). (Courtesy of Catholic Diocese Archives.)

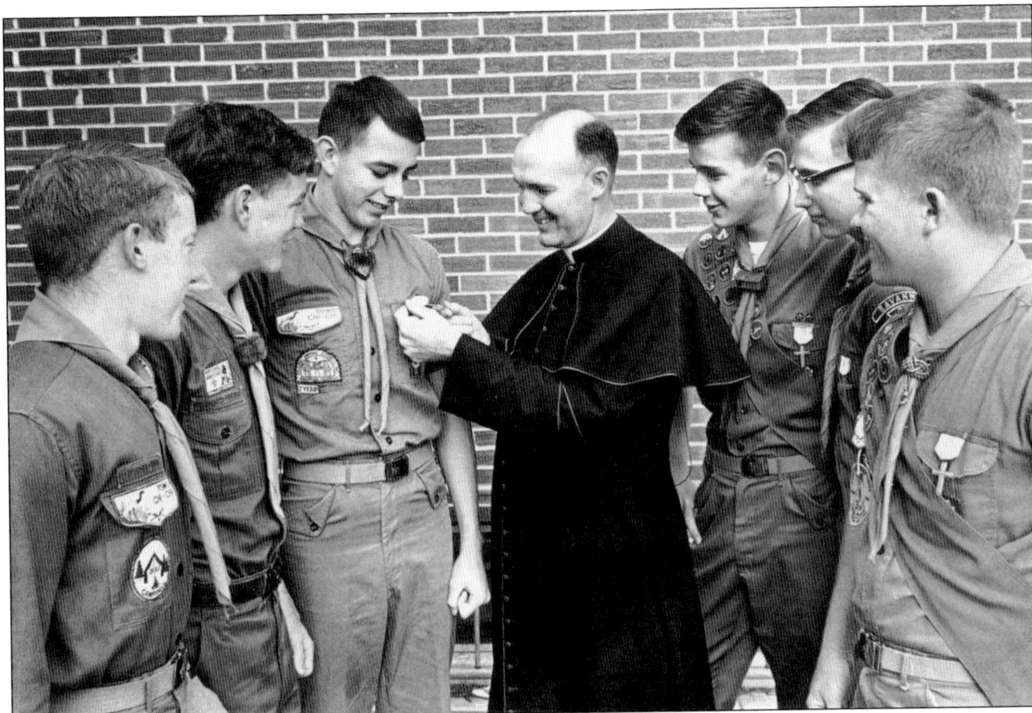

Monsignor Andrew J. McDonald honors Boy Scouts from a troop sponsored by Blessed Sacrament. From left to right are Pat Harper, George Barry, Michael Dillon, Robert Innes, Scotty Paul, and Michael Hennessy. (Courtesy of Catholic Diocese Archives.)

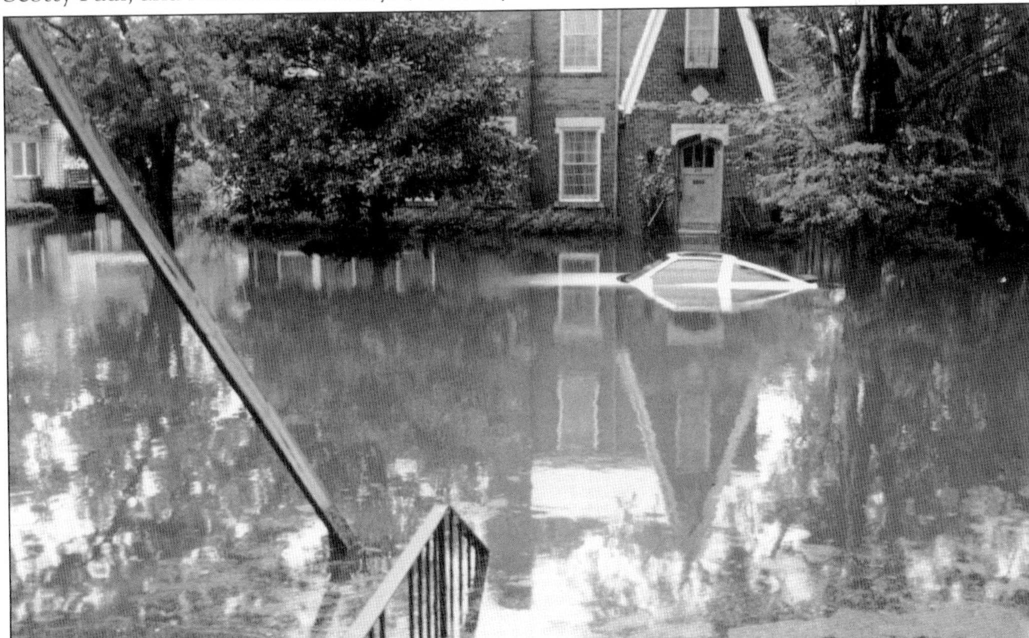

Unfortunately, through the years, all three neighborhoods have been plagued by flooding problems. This photograph of the 700 block of East 44th Street was taken from Blessed Sacrament after a torrential downpour.

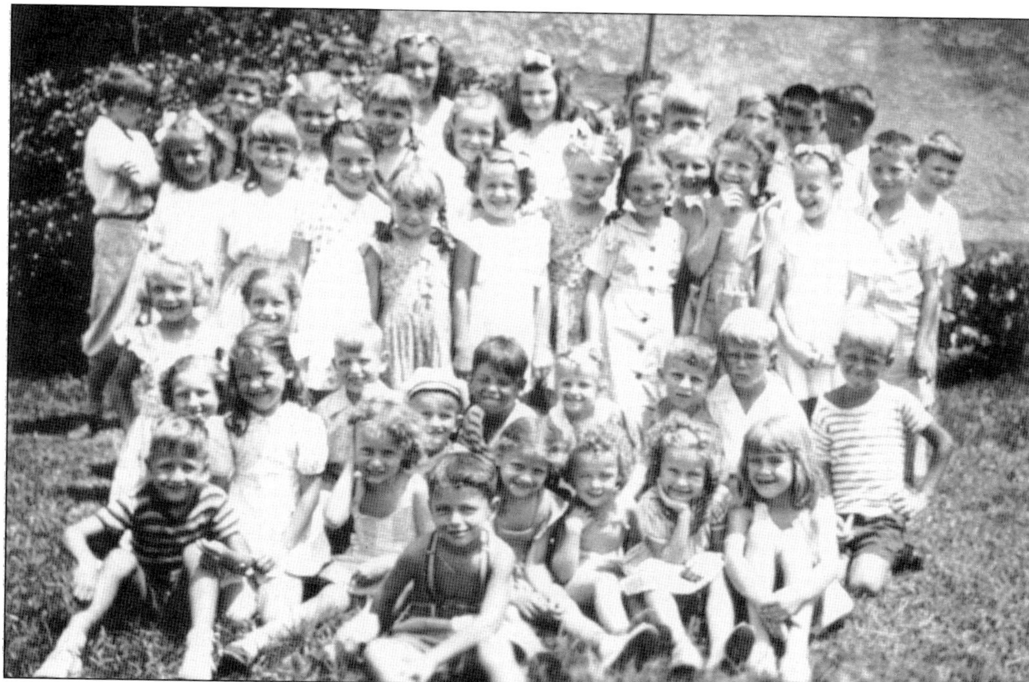

A 1944 Vacation Bible School group at First Presbyterian Church on Washington Avenue attracted quite a crowd in 1944.

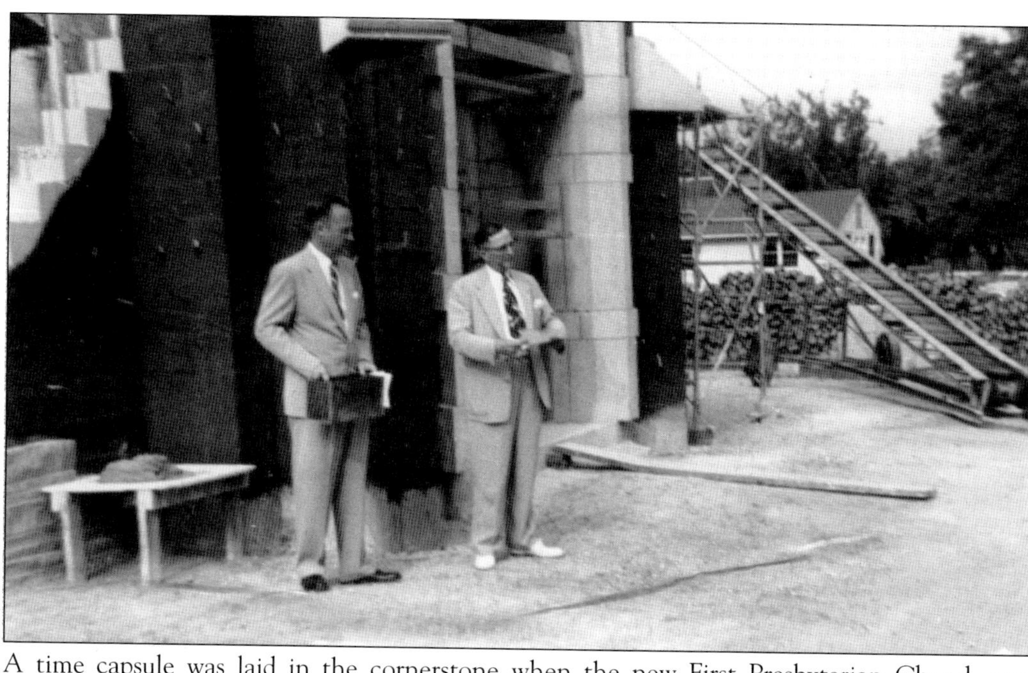

A time capsule was laid in the cornerstone when the new First Presbyterian Church was dedicated on June 10, 1956. The former sanctuary had been constructed on the site in 1927. The Reverend J. Walton Stewart holds the box while Ralph Metzger reads a list of the articles placed inside.

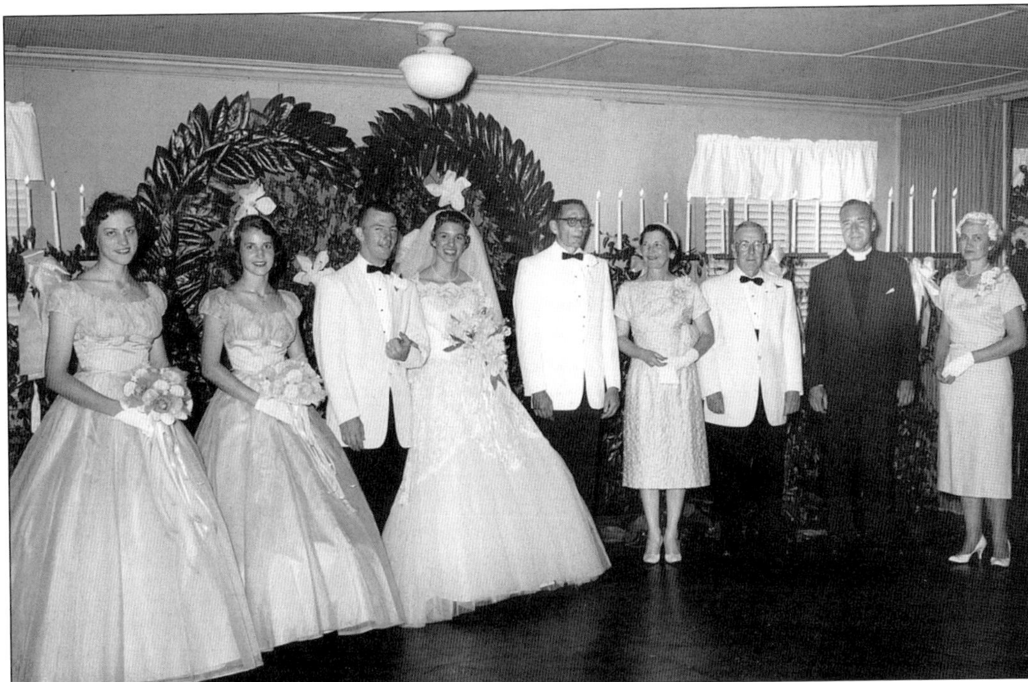

In 1959 the women of First Presbyterian Church gave a reception for the Reverend James Walton Stewart's daughter Margaret Stewart when she married Claude Ashton McMillion.

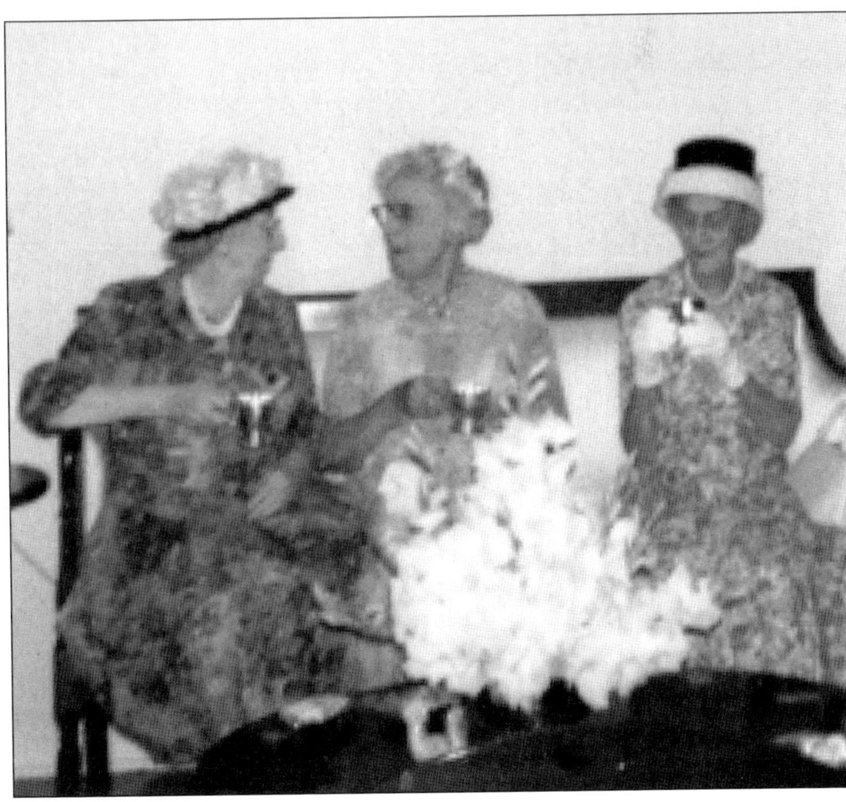

In 1963 Miss Lucile Charlton, Mrs. Bertha Hodge, and Miss Nellie Coney enjoy refreshments at a church gathering.

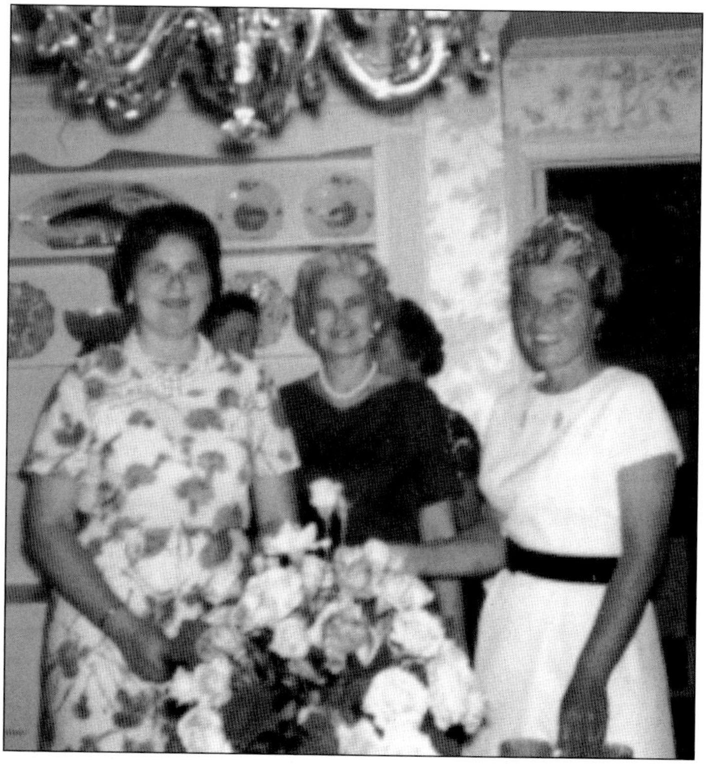

Three members of the Women of the Church at First Presbyterian—Mrs. Rufus Herring, Mrs. Walton Stewart, and Mrs. Norman McGee—are pictured in 1963 at a reception.

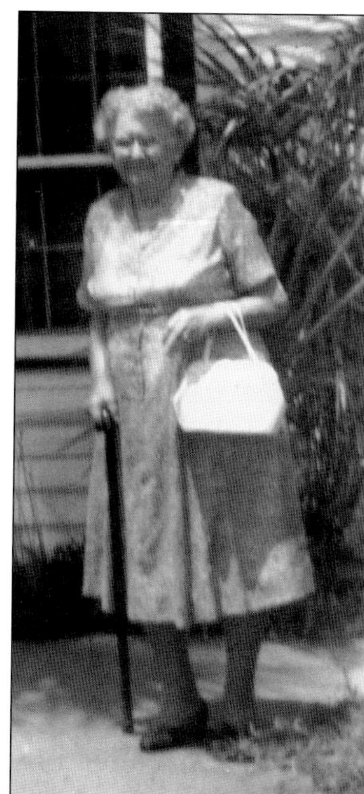

In 1960 Mrs. J. Lee Johnson was the oldest active member of the Women of the Church at First Presbyterian.

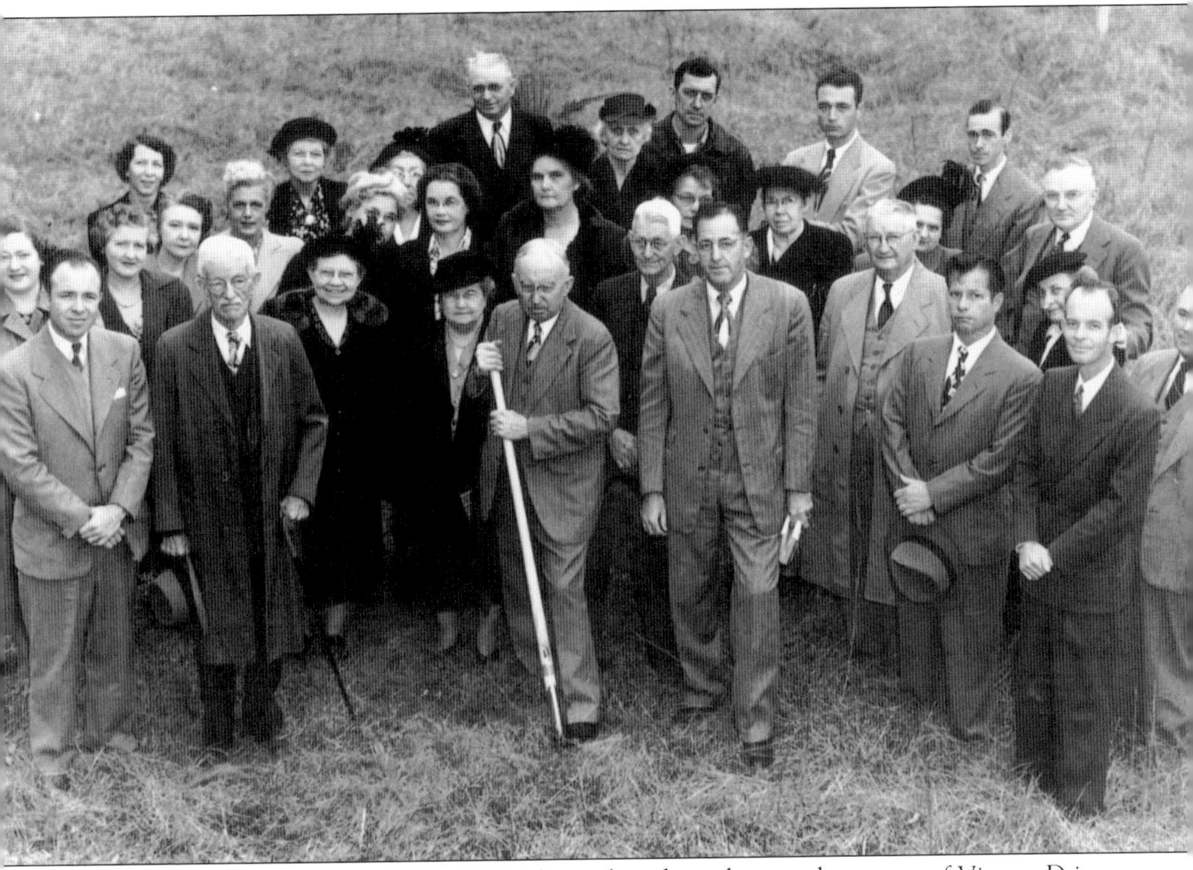

On March 28, 1944 First Christian Church purchased two lots on the corner of Victory Drive and Atlantic Avenue. Additional lots were added later. Groundbreaking for a youth center named Artley Hall was held on January 5, 1949. Pictured, from left to right, are (front row) Dennis Crosby; Capt. Tom Daniels; O. Highsmith (chairman of the board); Rev. Harry J. Berry, Billy Clark, and Stanley Clark; (second row) Mrs. Frank O. Hixon, Mrs. Harry E. Himes, Mrs. Ferdinand E. Davis, Mrs. W.L. Salter, F.E. Davis, E.D. Biggs, Mrs. Clarence F. Griffin, and Asa Buntyn; (third row) Mrs. J.N. Crosby, Mrs. Theo Medernach, Mrs. E.D. Biggs, Mrs. F.J. LaRoche, Mrs. W.H. Reed Sr., Mrs. R.L. Kersh, Mrs. ? Crosby, Mrs. Asa Buntyn, and C.F. Griffin; (fourth row) Mrs. J.R. Beach, Mrs. J.Q. Hodges, Mrs. ? Wall, Mrs. J.A. Getty, and W. Kershaw Getty Sr.

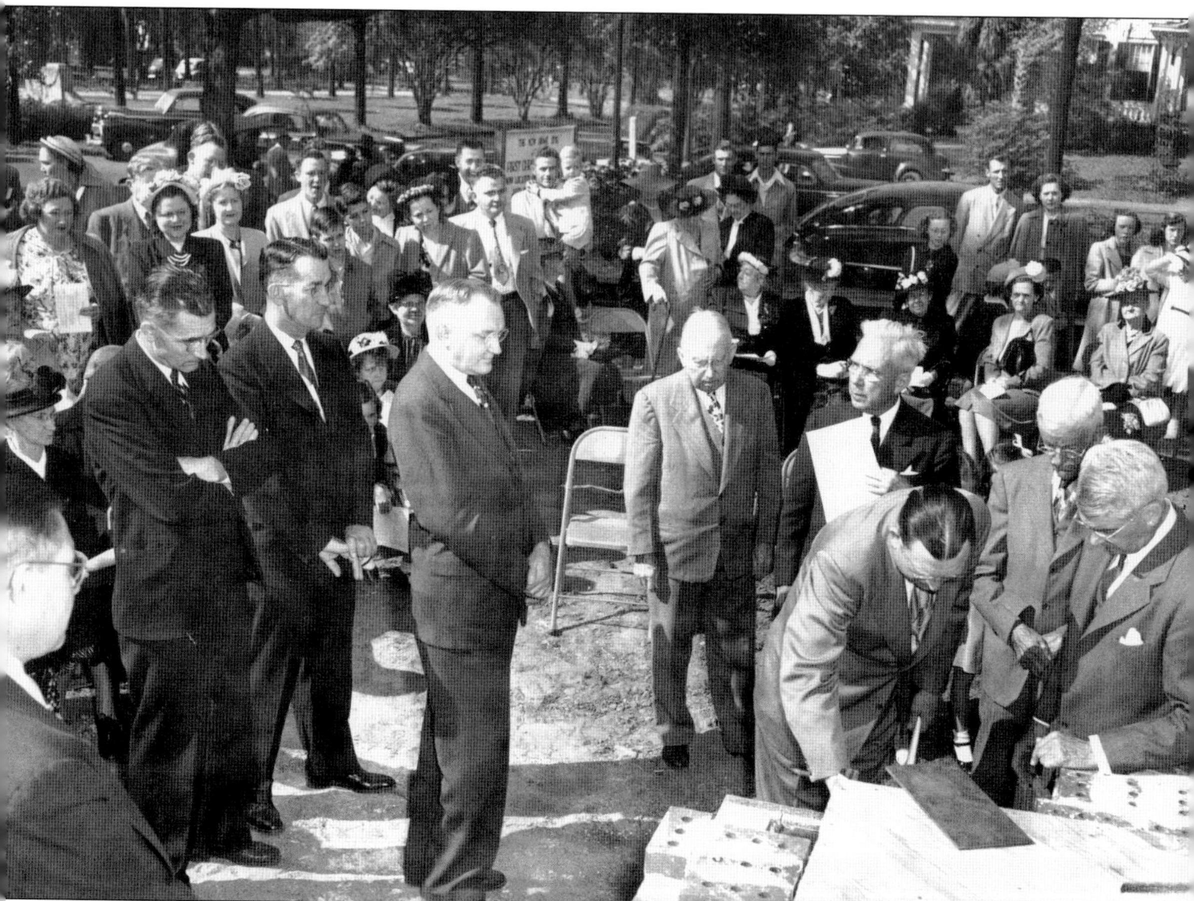

On April 16, 1950 church officials laid the cornerstone for a new sanctuary at First Christian Church, which was founded in 1819 and previously located downtown. From left to right are James R. Beach, ? Feagin, C.F. Griffin, O. Highsmith Sr., A.D. Strobhar, Capt. Tom Daniels, Will Artley, and Harry Peterson fixing the stone.

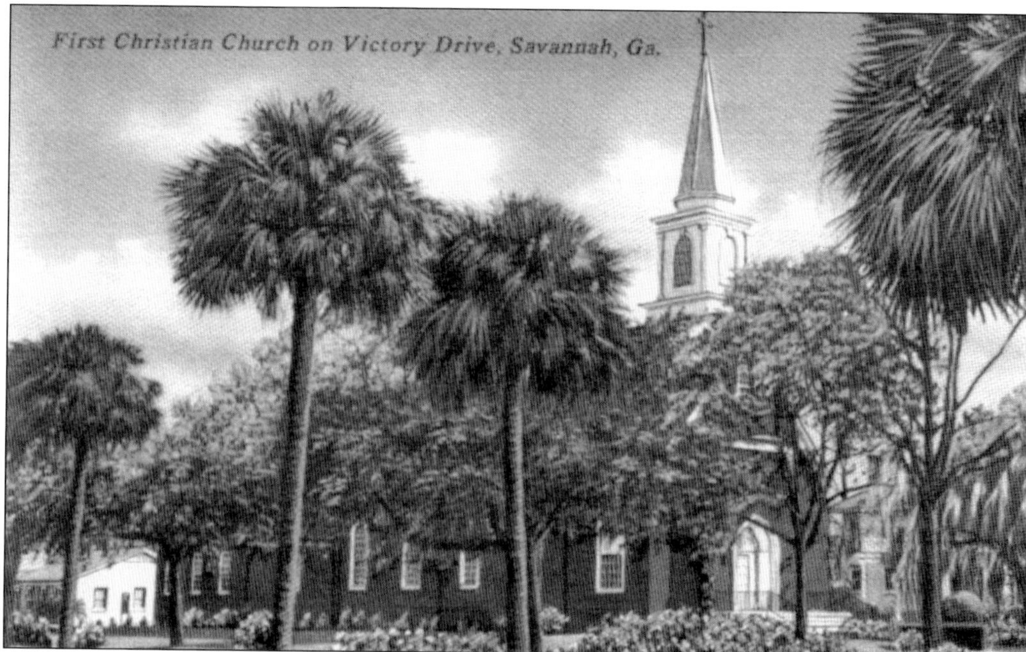

This vintage postcard shows First Christian Church, a standout on scenic Victory Drive.

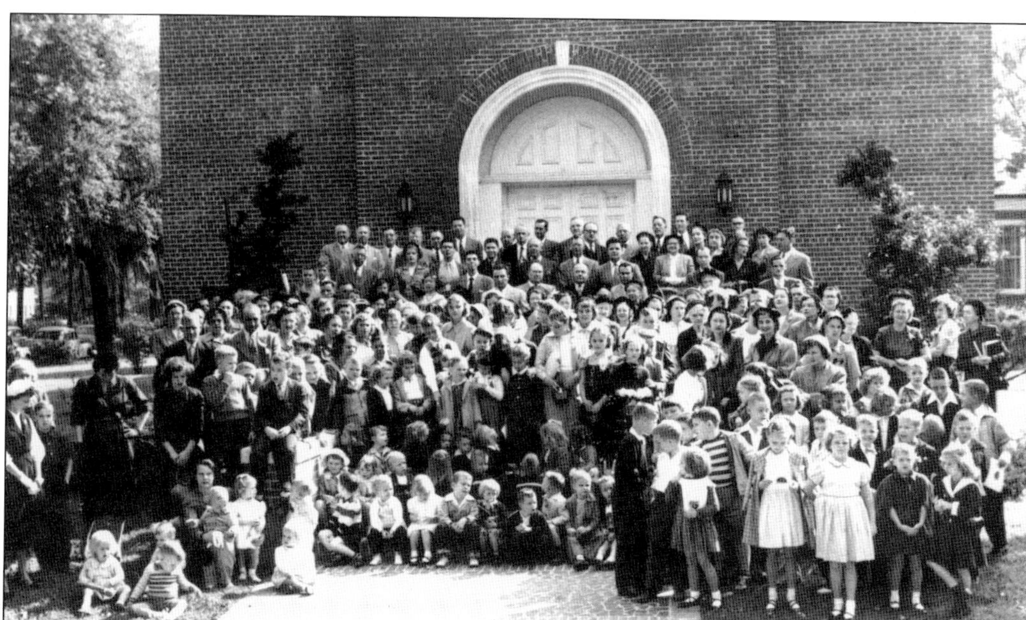
A crowd gathered in front of First Christian Church after the January 28, 1951 dedication service. The First Christian kindergarten has been a mainstay in the Chatham Crescent neighborhood since the early 1950s.

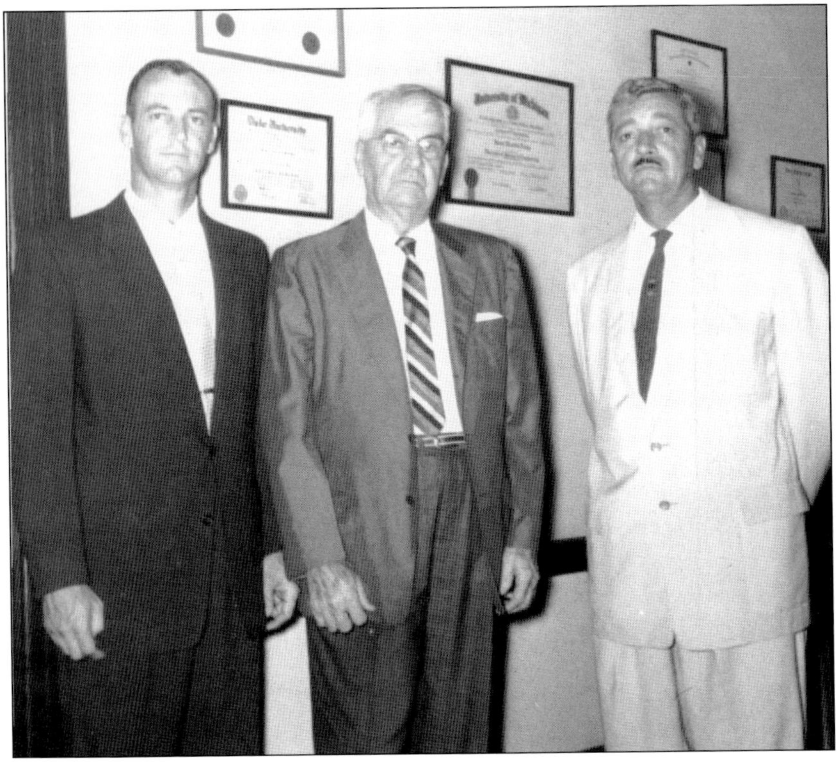

The Artley family played a key role in First Christian Church as well as in the development of Ardsley Park and Chatham Crescent. The Artley Company, founded by A.A. Artley, was one of the principal contracting firms in both neighborhoods. From left to right are Jim Artley, Will H. Artley Sr., and Will Artley Jr.

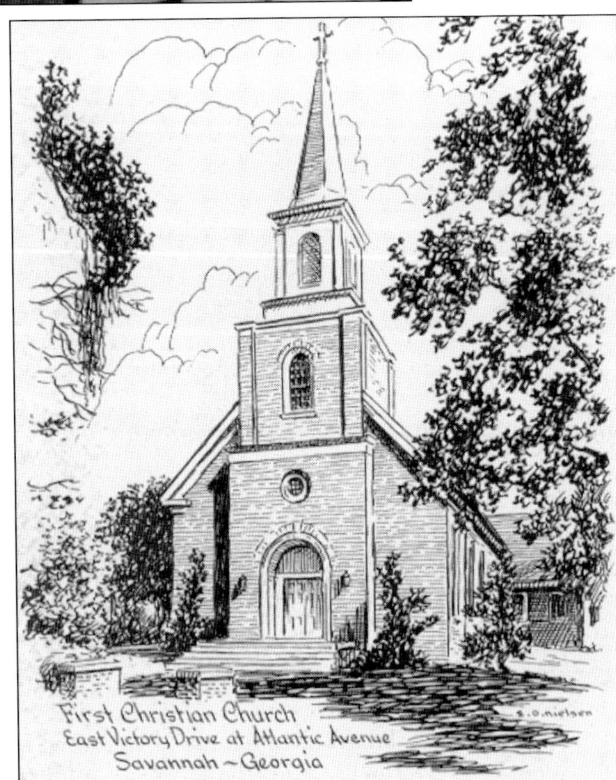

Here is a sketch of the church as it looks today.

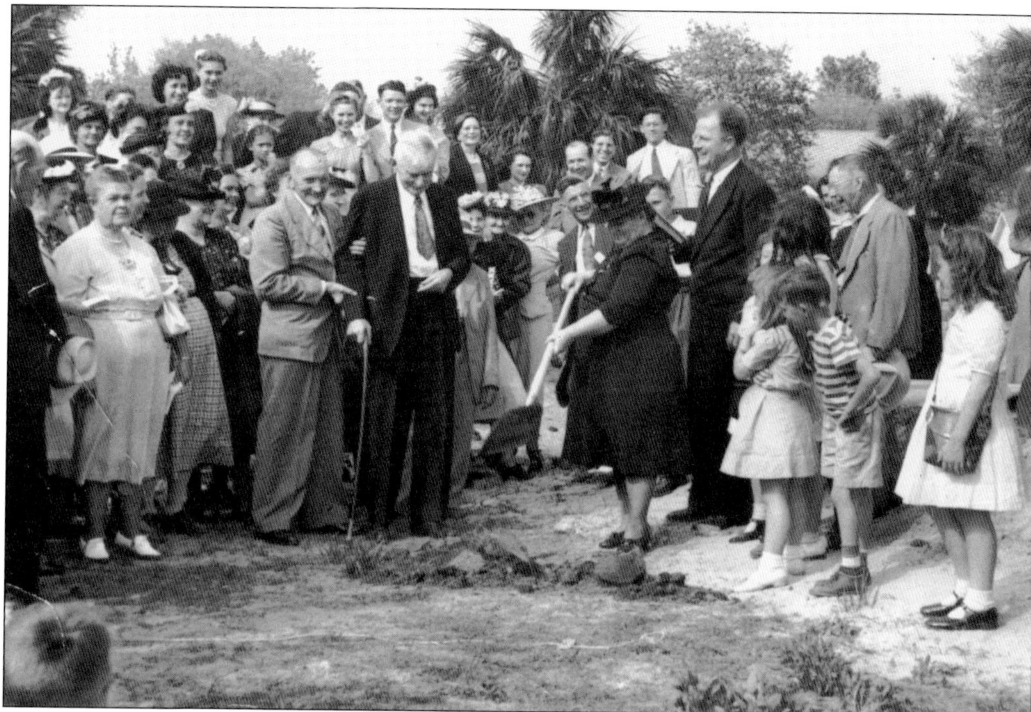

Groundbreaking for Robert McIntire United Methodist Church at East 54th and Bull Streets was held in 1947. Lillie Priester, with the shovel, does the honors

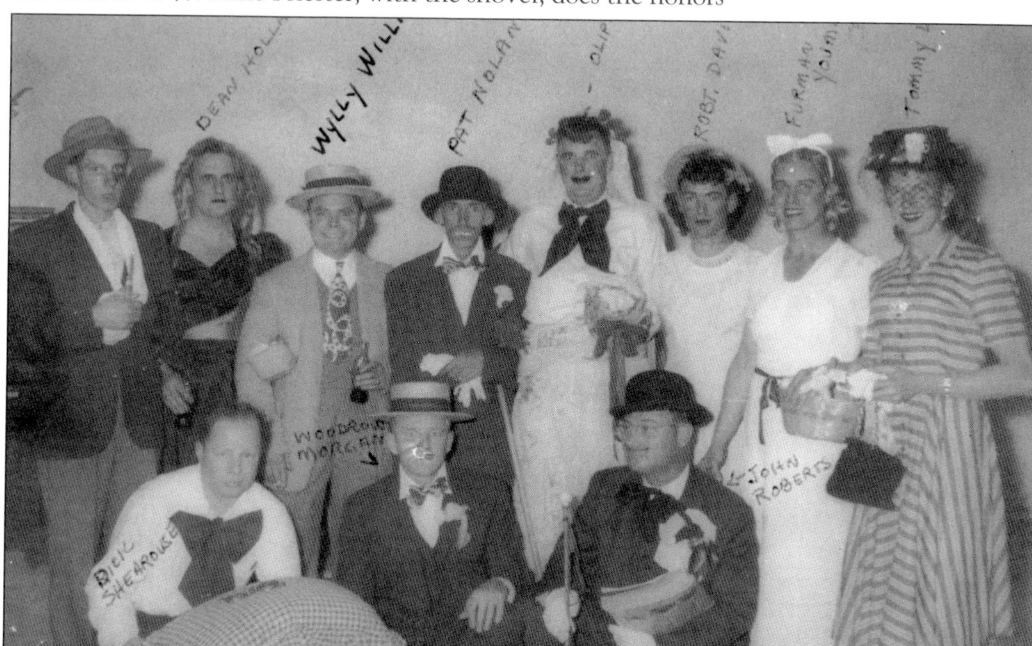

Church activities aren't always serious and solemn as indicated by this womanless wedding at McIntire Methodist. From left to right are (front row) Dick Shearouse, Woodrow Morgan, and John Roberts; (back row) Dean Holland, Wylly Williams, Pat Nolan, ? Oliphant, Rob Davis, Furman Youmans, and Tommy Long.

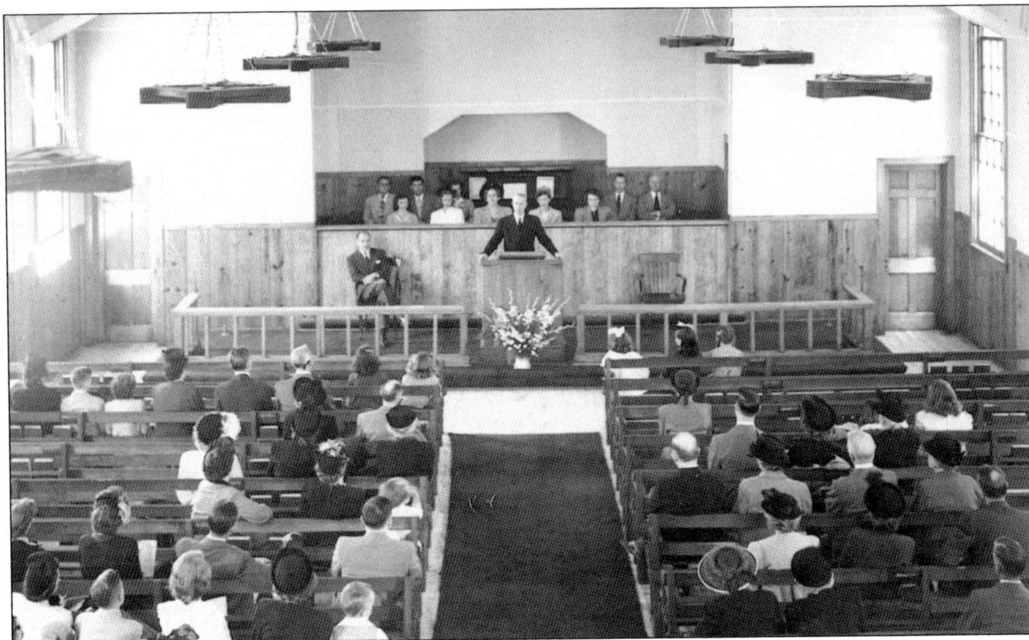

The first service at Whitefield United Methodist Church was held on October 10, 1948. The church building formerly was a chapel at Hunter Field and was purchased from the government when the base closed after World War II. The chapel was moved from Hunter along DeRenne Avenue to the corner of East Fifty-fifth Street and Waters Avenue, which was quite a production.

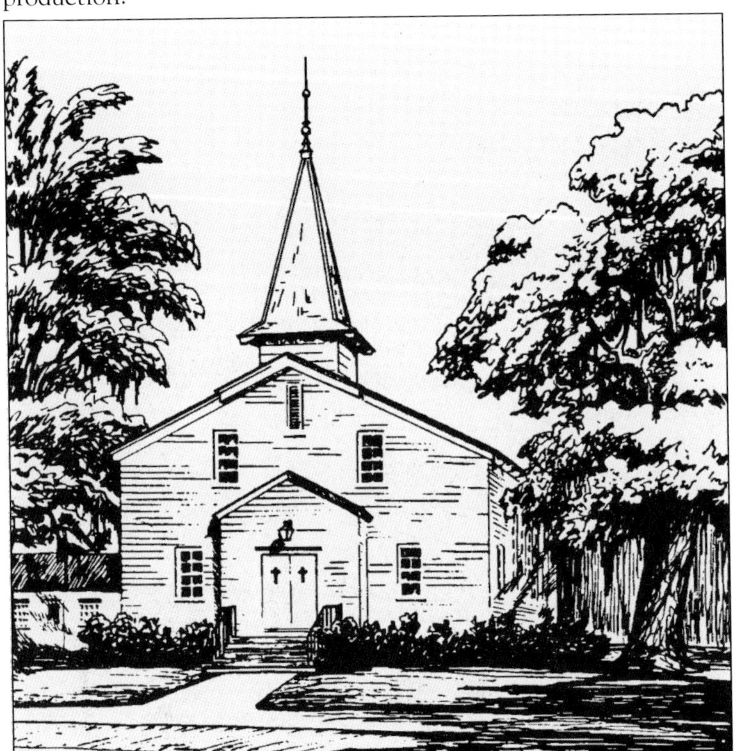

The late Leonora Quarterman worked out of a studio in Chatham Crescent and sketched this rendition of Whitefield Methodist.

A 1942 fire destroyed the original Ardsley Park Baptist Church at East 55th and Bull Streets. The church had its beginnings in January 1905 when 27 worshippers met in the West 54th Street home of Mr. and Mrs. R.W. Griffith. Three months later it became the Green Street (now 55th) Mission. In 1908 it was constituted as a missionary church of First Baptist and renamed Fourth Baptist Church. The name was changed to Ardsley Park Baptist in 1927.

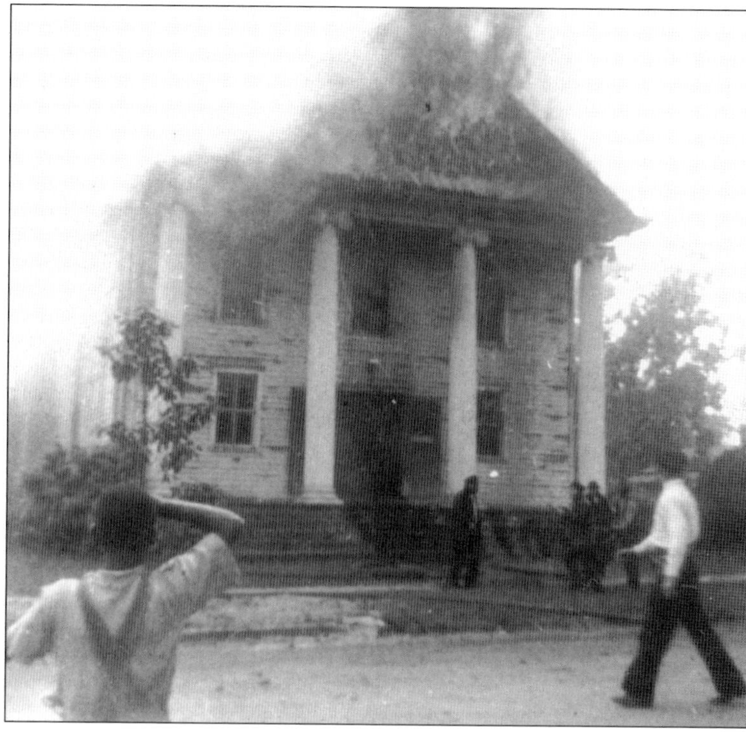

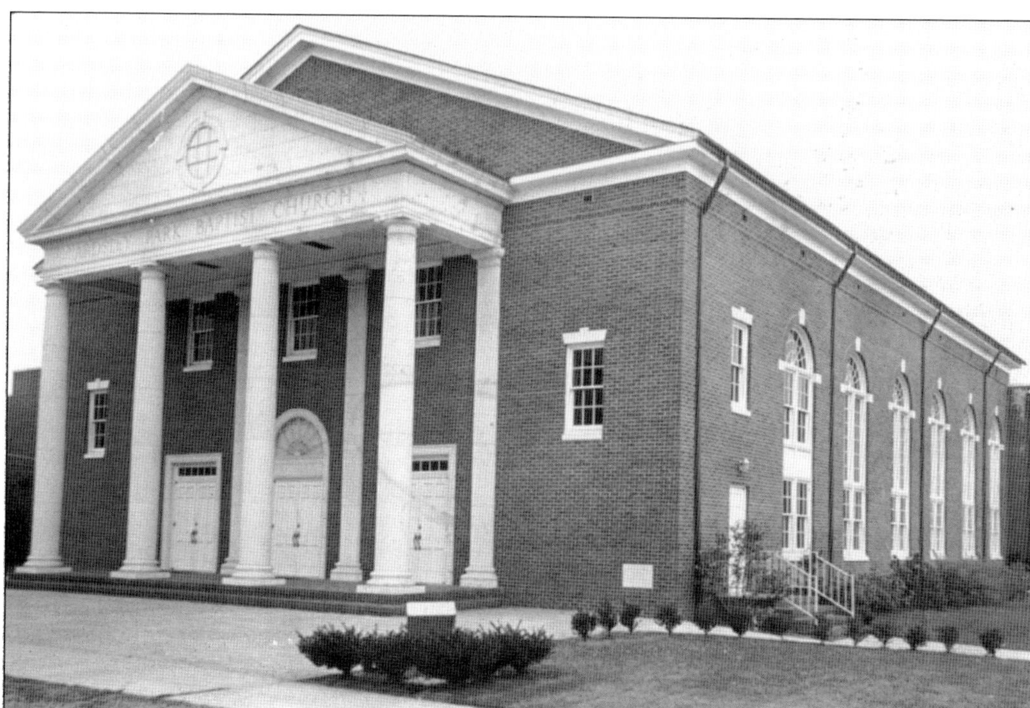

A third Ardsley Park Baptist sanctuary, facing Bull Street, was built in 1963.

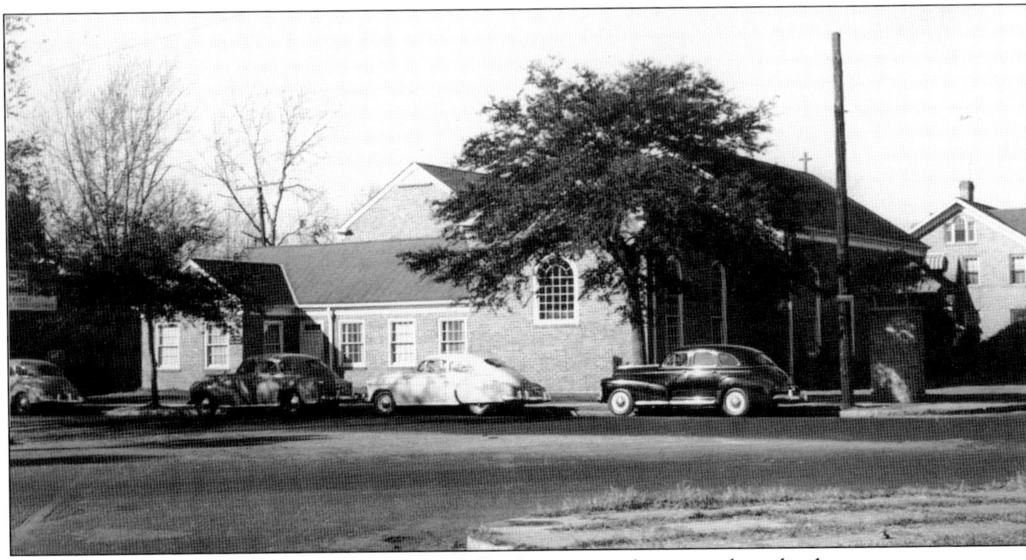

St. Michael's Episcopal Church was originally downtown but members built a new sanctuary at Washington and Waters Avenues in 1940.

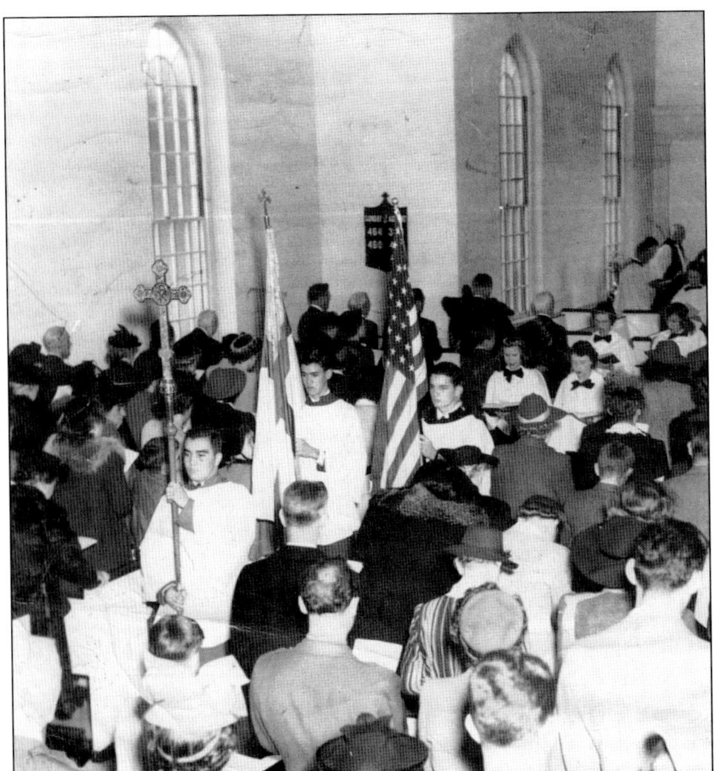

This photograph was taken during the 1940s dedication service at St. Michael's.

Six

Schools

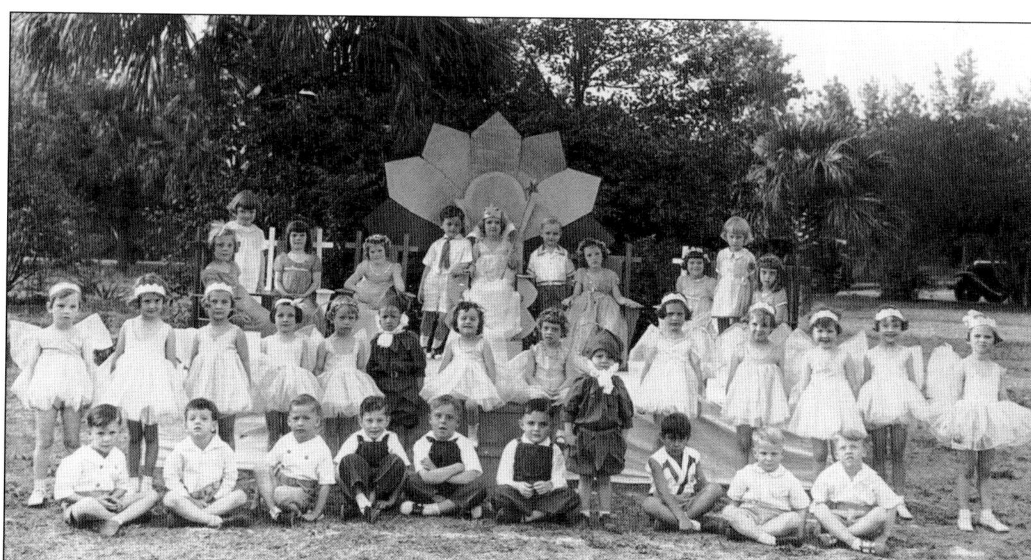

First-grade pupils at 49th Street Elementary School (renamed Charles Ellis Elementary School in 1935) starred in a play in 1933 and were photographed in Tiedeman Park at Atlantic Avenue and East 46th Street. The elf standing in the front row is Harvey Morgan, now a retired physician. The school opened in 1929 and is the oldest continuously operating school in the city.

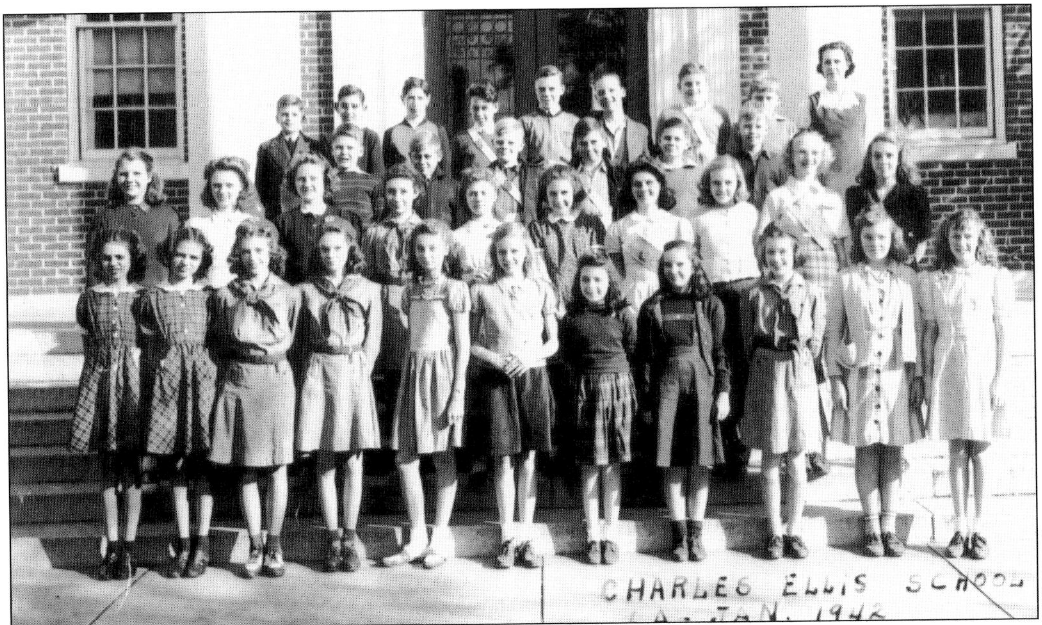

Sixth graders at Charles Ellis School had their class picture taken in front of the school in 1942. From left to right are (first row) Naomi Brown, Ruth Brown, Dot Stegin, Patty Harris, Marilyn Richmond, Nan Garis, Renee Steinberg, unidentified, Eva ?, and two unidentified children; (second row) three unidentified children, Marilyn Sickle, Mary Carter, Elizabeth Ellis, and four unidentified children; (third row) two unidentified children, James Dewberry, unidentified, Bill Campbell, and unidentified; (back row) Albert Weis, Martin Karpf, unidentified, Marvin Lesser, three unidentified children, Merritt Dixon, and the unidentified teacher.

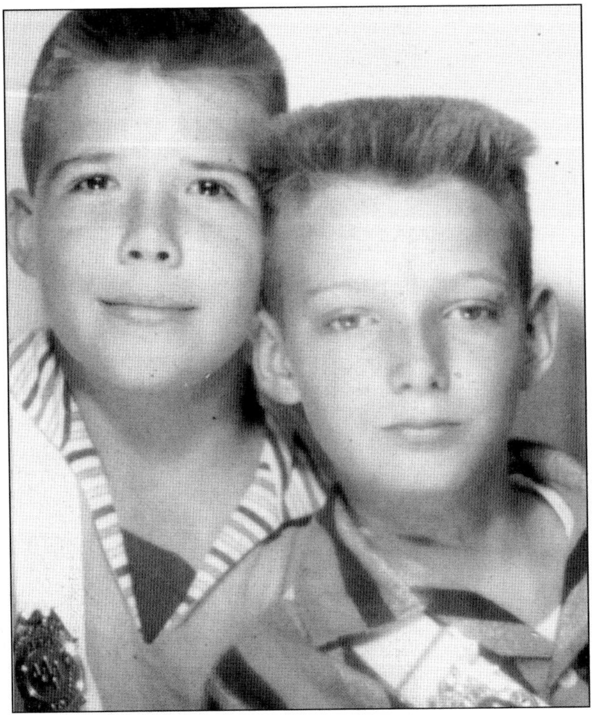

Being a patrol boy at Charles Ellis was an honor for students like Bill Ellis and Ricky Belford.

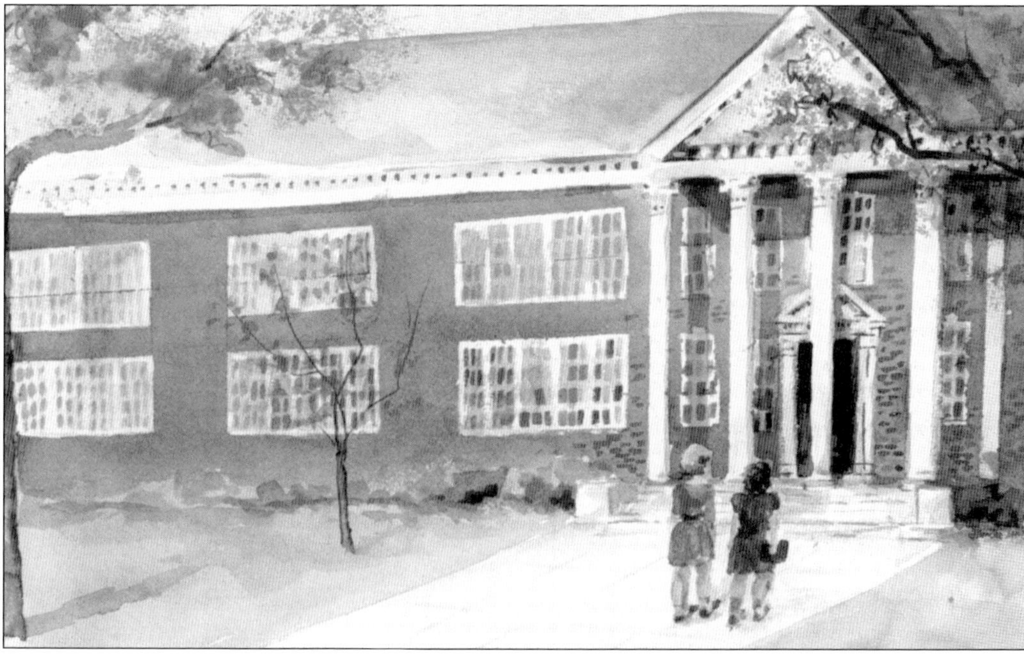

Artist Frances Dunaway Mills, who attended Charles Ellis in the 1940s, sketched the school for the book *'Memories So Fair' Savannah's Charles Ellis School*, published in 1999.

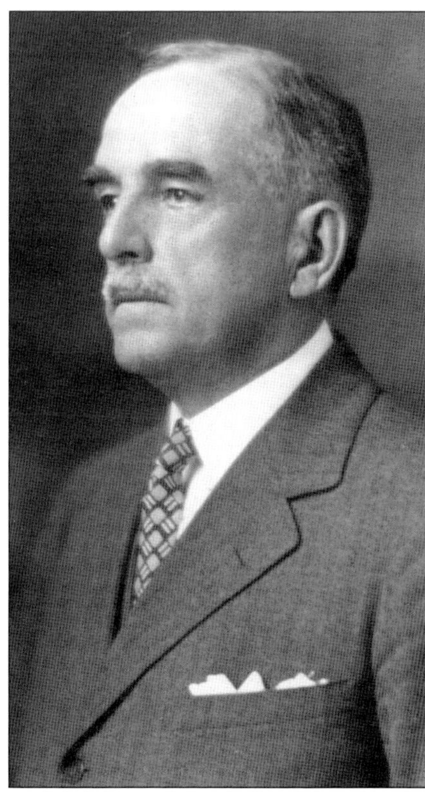

Prominent businessman Charles Ellis was a longtime member of the Savannah-Chatham Board of Education and served as board president. In 1935 49th Street School was renamed for Ellis. Today it is the only public Montessori school in Georgia.

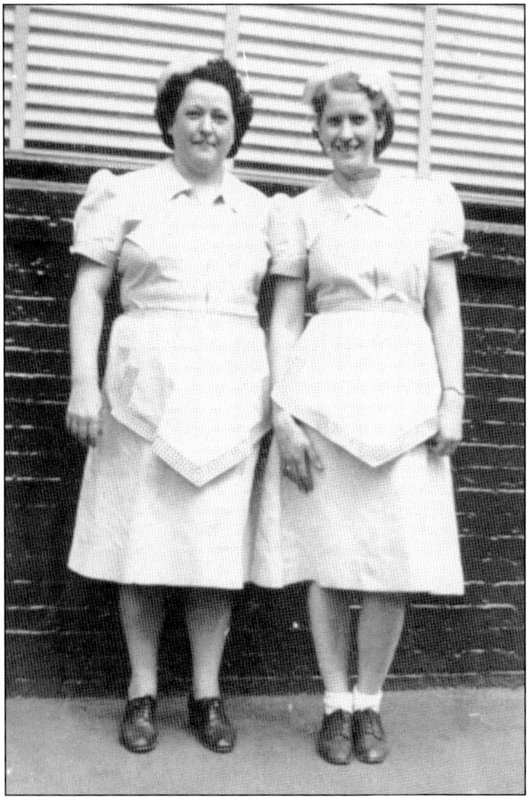

Evelyn Miles was lunchroom director at Charles Ellis for decades. She is seen, at right, with an unidentified colleague.

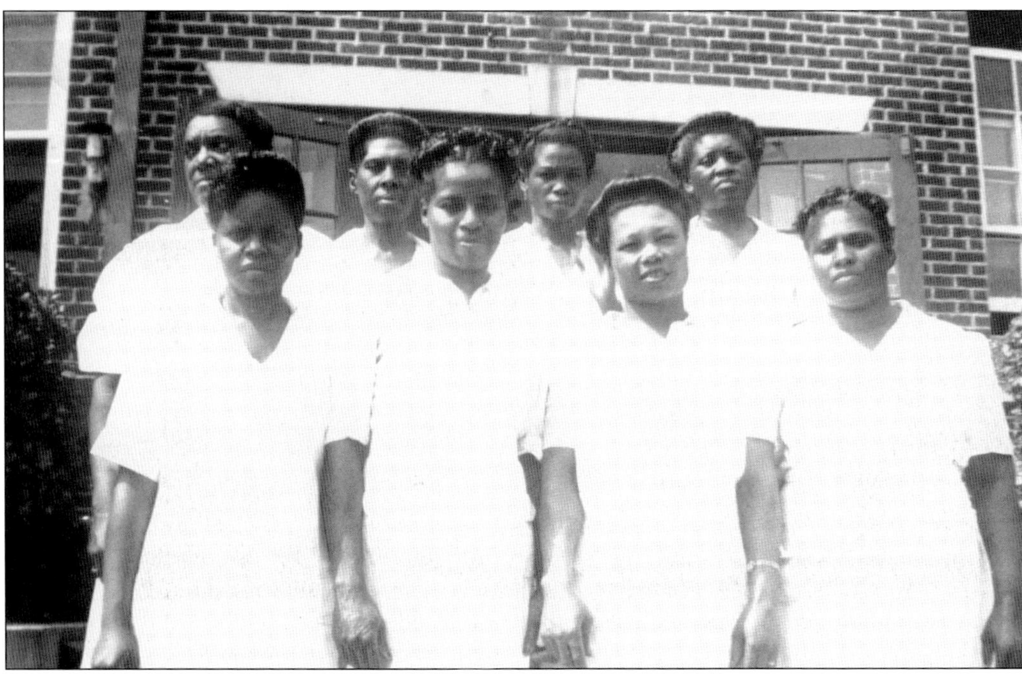

The lunch crew at Charles Ellis was well known for making delicious cinnamon rolls, brownies, and yeast rolls.

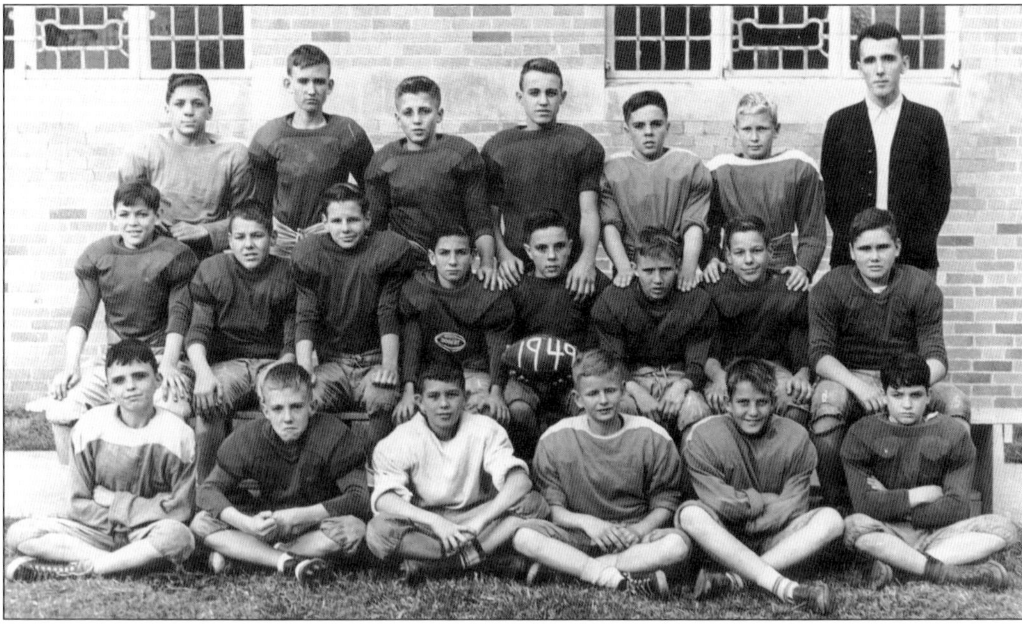

The Blessed Sacrament School football team snagged the Parochial League championship in 1949. Pictured, from left to right, are (front row) Joseph Duchesne, Jimmy Collins, Leonard Herb, Jimmy Mayes, Jimmy Burke, and Phil Simpson; (middle row) Bobby Blakewood, Jason Williams, Paul Fleming, Bob Everett, John Halligan (captain), John Thompson, Corey Williams, and Billy Cocke; (back row) Danny Mahany, Tommy Mahoney, Jerry O'Connor, Jimmy Curry (alternate captain), George Halligan, Louis Waldhour, and Johnny McCracken (coach). Absent from the picture is John Cocke. (Courtesy of Catholic Diocese Archives.)

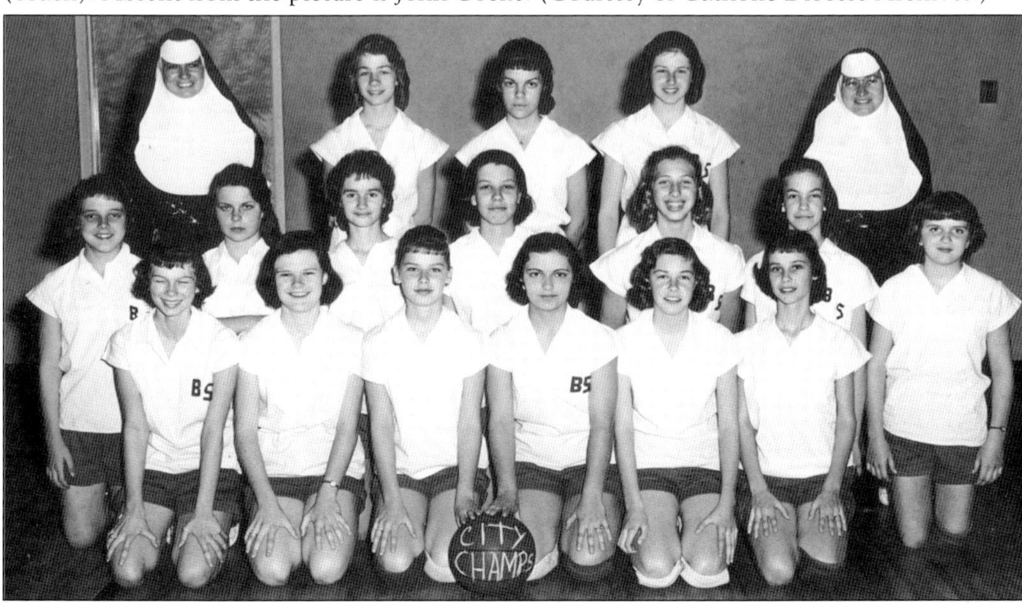

Blessed Sacrament School was established in 1939 with 68 students. Members of the 1959 girls basketball team are shown with their coaches, (back row, left) Sister Mary Mercedes Sullivan (Religious Sisters of Mercy) and (back row, right) Sister Mary Jogues Smith (Religious Sisters of Mercy). (Courtesy of Catholic Diocese Archives.)

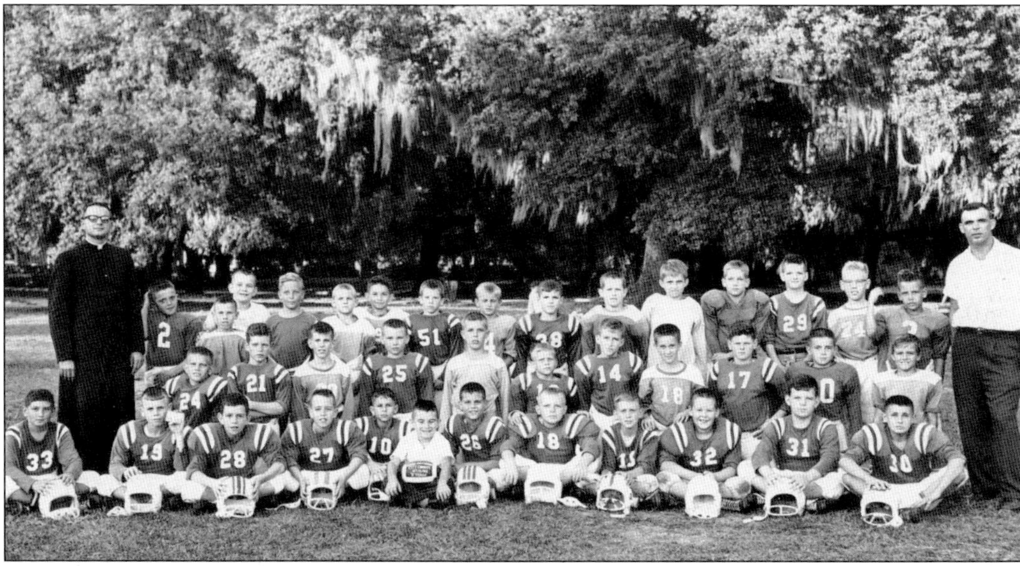

Blessed Sacrament's 1962 B-team football team walked away with the city championship. Pictured from left to right are (front row) George Abelson, Al Powers, Joe Herb, Johnny Power, Chip Robertson, unidentified, Pat Tuttle, Craig Scott, Jimmy Griffin, Kit Parker, Alan ?, and Donald Carbonell; (middle row) ? Brady, Johnny Mulligan, Martin Corcoran, unidentified, Steve Corshack, Earl Hagan, Harry Haslam, two unidentified, Frank Koncul, and Steven South; (back row) Rev. George James, Joe Koncul, John Powers, Albert Oetgen, Bobby Lamb, unidentified, Tommy Fall, Chuck Best, Jack Harmon, Mike Foran, Mike Curran, Vincent Grevemberg, Steve Kelleher, Bobby Adams, Tommy Sanders, Dennis Kelly, and unidentified. (Courtesy of Catholic Diocese Archives.)

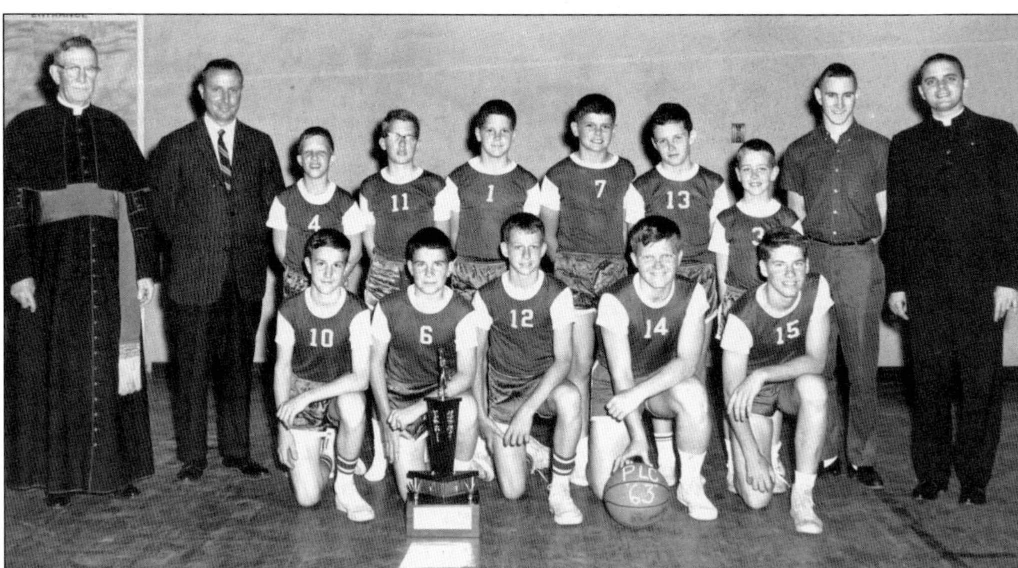

Blessed Sacrament's 1963 boys basketball team won the Parochial School League Championship (Courtesy Catholic Diocese Archives.).

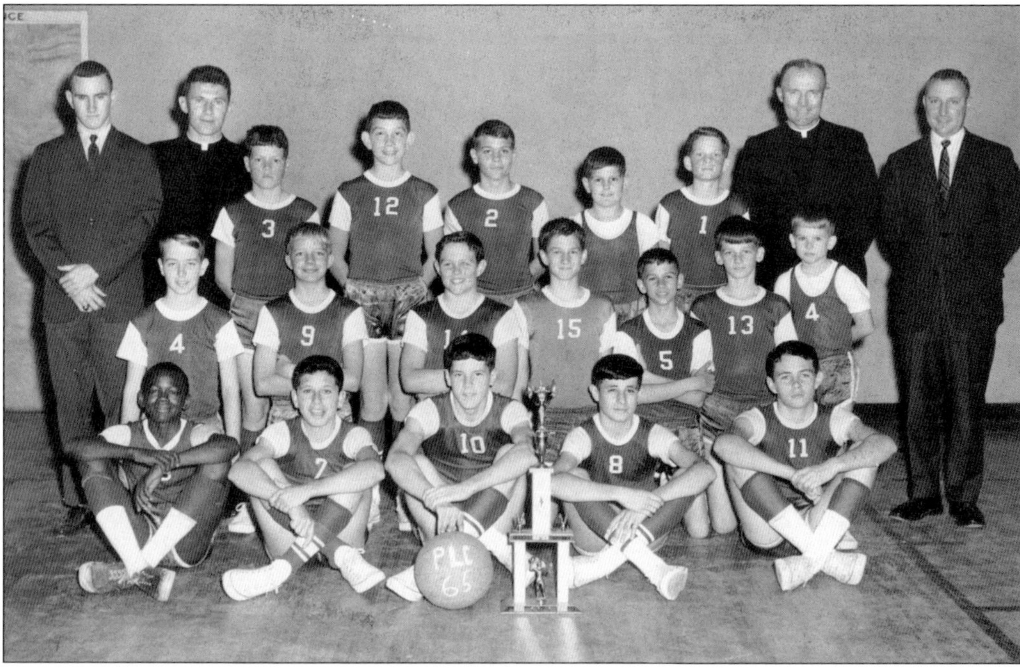

The members of Blessed Sacrament's 1965 basketball team are pictured, from left to right, as follows: (front row) Benjy Gadson, Joe Mathews, Joey Shearouse, Donald Carbonell, and David Cusick; (middle row) Johnny Power, Jimmy Keating, Pete Cusick, Buzz Crider, Chip Robertson, Joe Joyce, and Timmy Robertson; (back row) Mike Brady, Rev. ? Keane, John Mulligan, Joe Herb, Pat Tuttle, Eddie Whelan, John Lyons, Rev. Andrew J. McDonald, and Leon Behr. (Courtesy of Catholic Diocese Archives.)

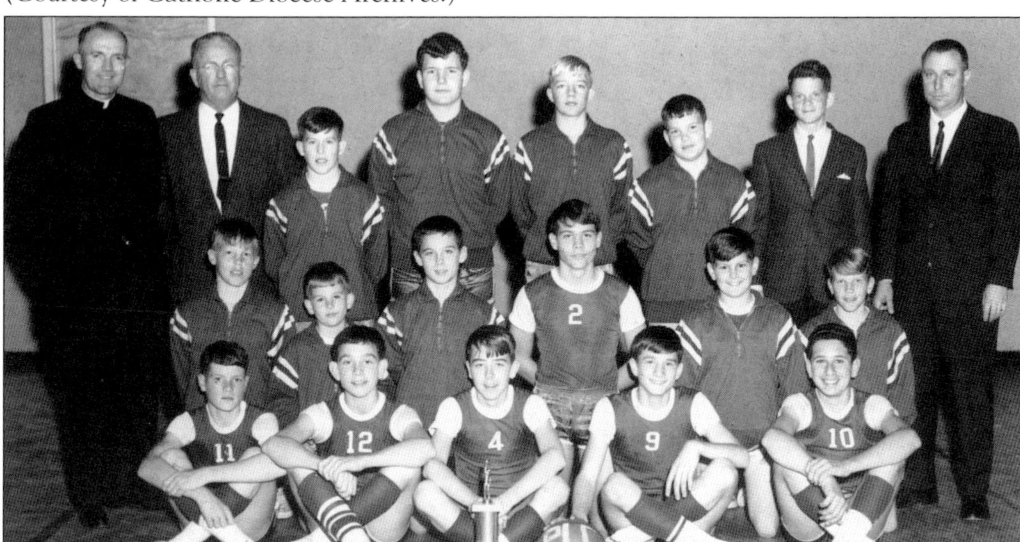

Members of Blessed Sacrament's 1966 basketball team are pictured, from left to right, as follows: (front row) John Mulligan, Joe Herb, Johnny Power, Buzz Crider, and Joe Mathews; (middle row) Bubba Williams, unidentified, Jimmy Coleman, unidentified, Eddie Whelan, and Earl Hagen; (back row) Michael Curran, unidentified, Jimmy Keating, Albert Oetgen, and John Lyons. (Courtesy of Catholic Diocese Archives.)

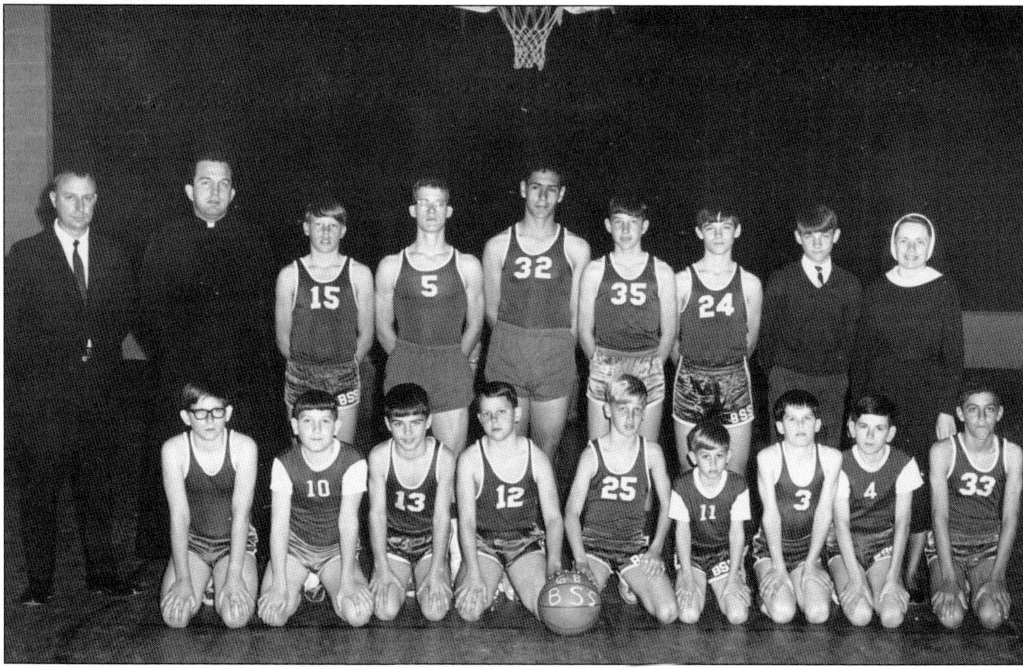

Blessed Sacrament's 1968 basketball team included players like Joe and David lamb, Tony Abbott, Jimmy Coleman, and Bubba Williams.. (Courtesy of Catholic Diocese Archives.)

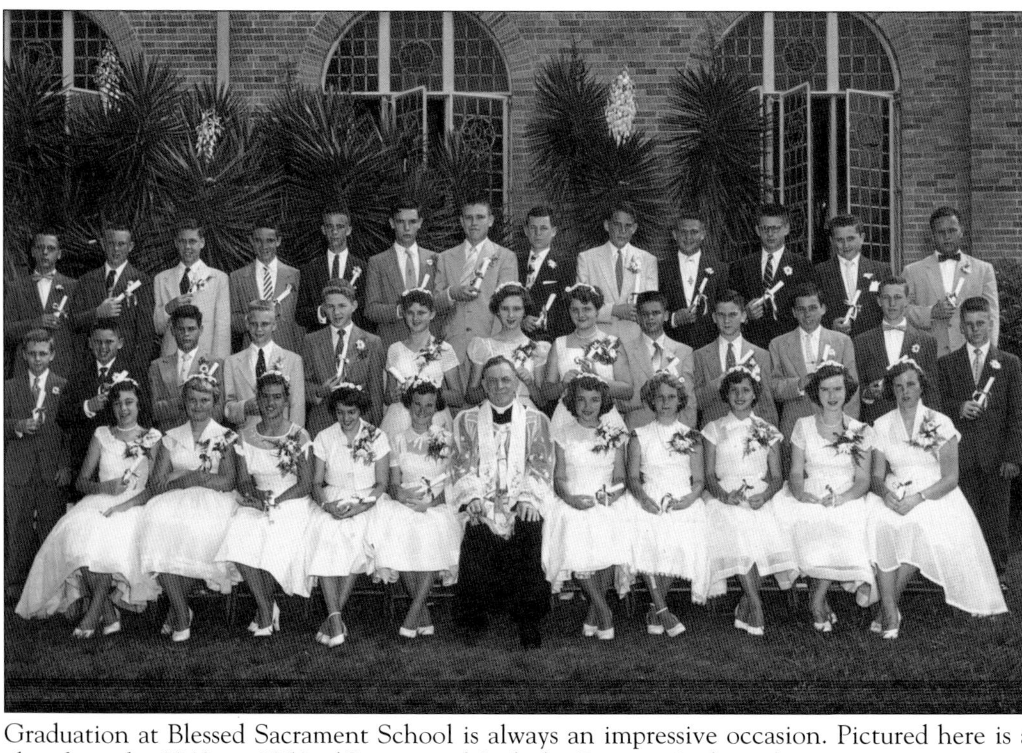

Graduation at Blessed Sacrament School is always an impressive occasion. Pictured here is a class from the 1940s or 1950s. (Courtesy of Catholic Diocese Archives.)

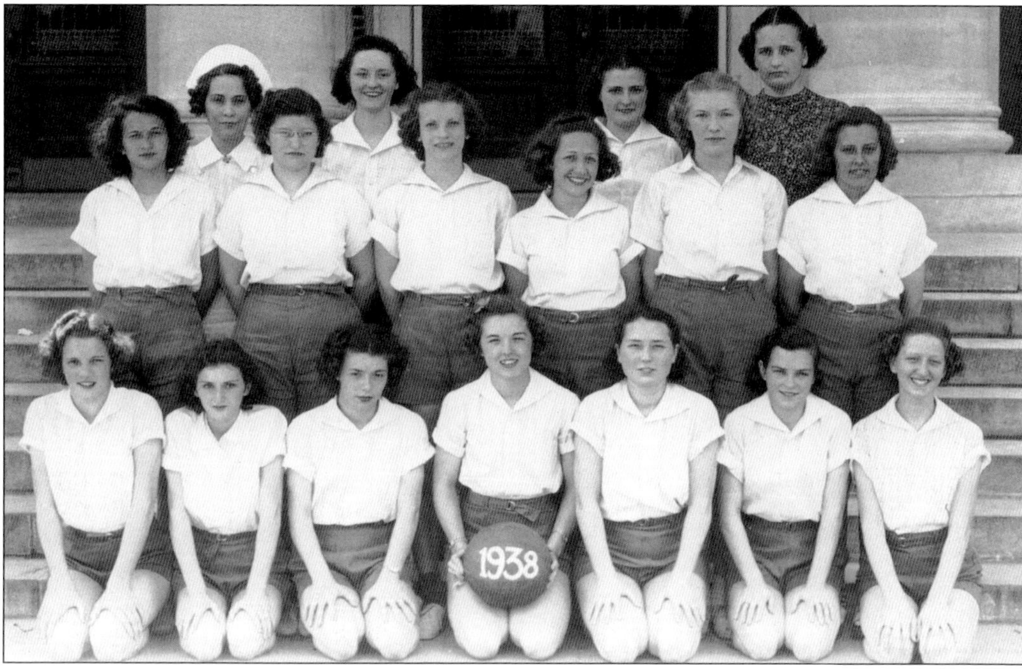

The class of 1938 was the first to graduate from the new Savannah High School built on the site of what was to be a deluxe hotel on 47th Street (Washington Avenue). The girls basketball team, only the second in the history of the school, included, from left to right, (front row) Juanita Lariscy, Mary Vandivere, Pat Horne, Beverly McFarland (captain), Louise Cheely, Ann Hadley, and Louise Sledge; (middle row) Mary Holms, Sarah Tomlin, Mary McPeters, Nellie Zipperer, Beulah Frisbee, and Elsa Schweizer; (back row) Mrs. Ida Harvey (school nurse), Ira Lee Futch, Dorothy Chestnut, and Miss Mabel Bryant (coach).

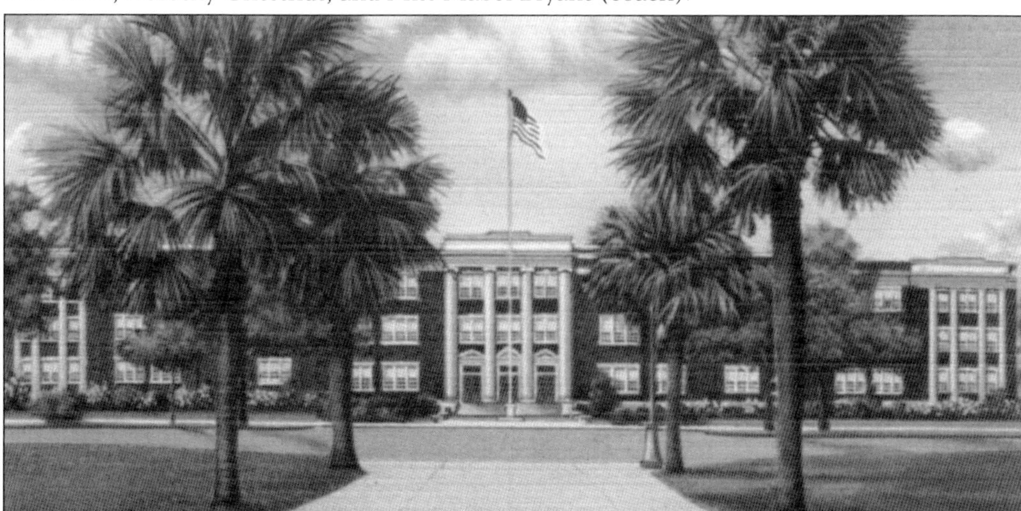

This vintage postcard shows Savannah High School, which relocated to Pennsylvania Avenue in the late 1990s. This building now is home to the Savannah Arts Academy. When it was built, with Work Projects Administration funds, the structure was the largest high school in the state and included 1,524,200 bricks and 12,800 square yards of blackboard. John Varnedoe was the first principal in the new building, which was dedicated on June 15, 1937.

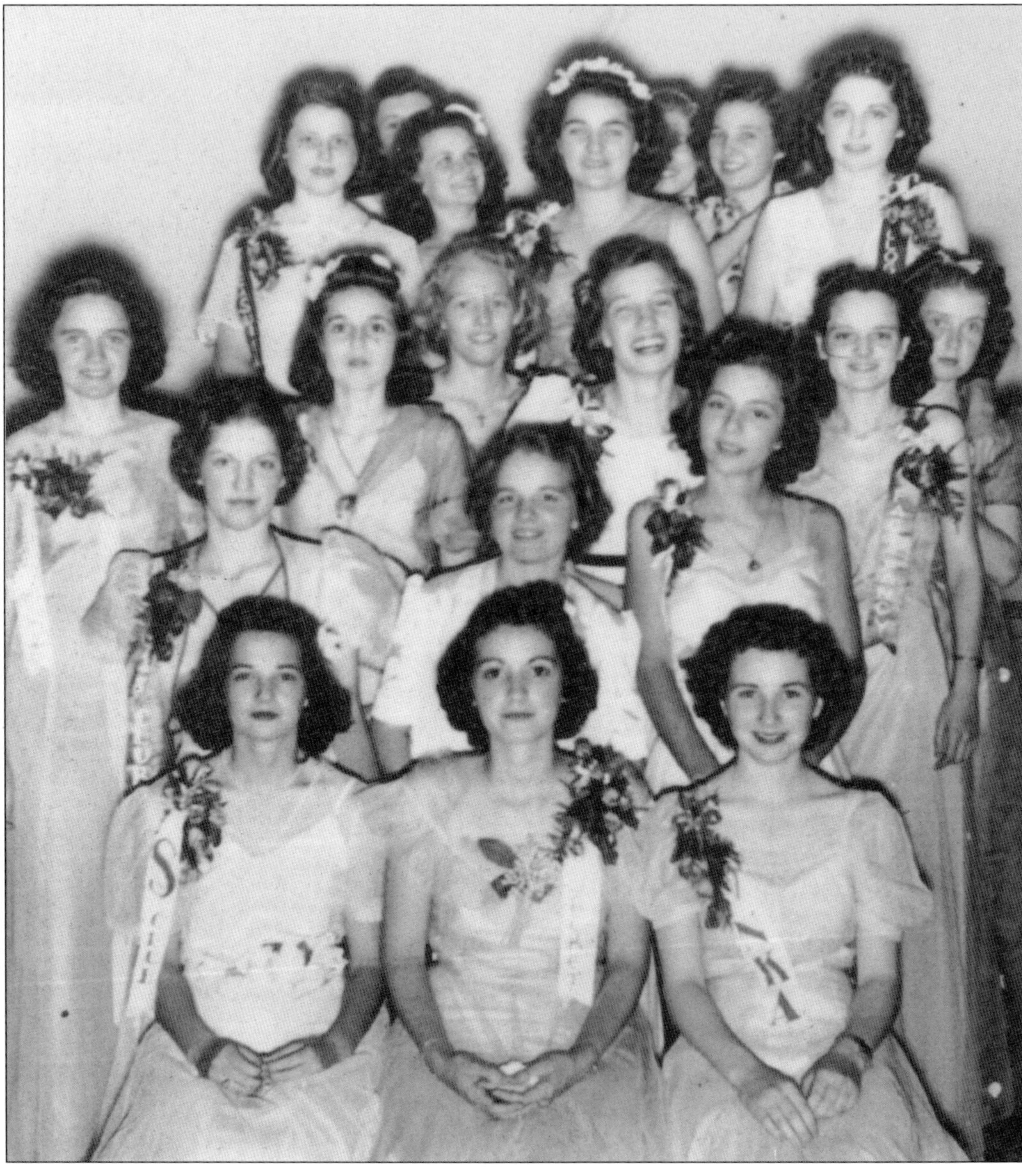

Contestants in the first Miss Savannah High in the new building included, from left to right, the following: (front row) Patty Johnson, Vivan Dupuy (elected queen), and Dorothy Newton; (second row) unidentified, Katherine Smallbones, and Frances Gnann; (third row) Elizabeth Ogletree, Beth Solana, Betty Peters, Dorothy Floyd, Lillian Anderson, and Edna Sheppard; (fourth row) Anita Fennell, Lucille Guerrard, Mae Howard, and Marilyn Mecks; (back row) Elinor Stiles, Lenora Atkinson, and Jean Saussy.

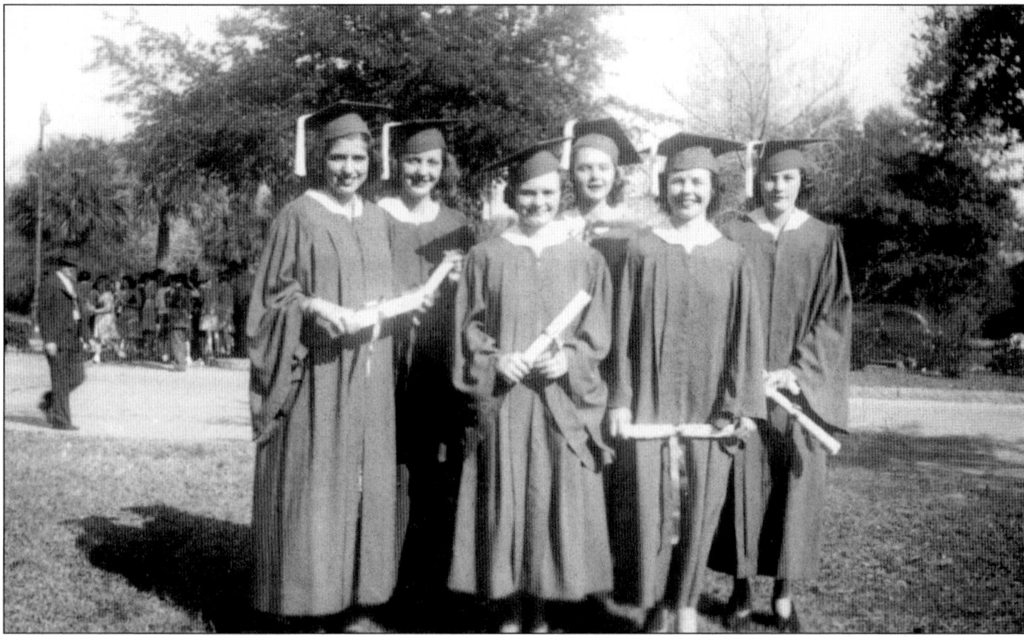

A group of graduates from Savannah's High's Class of 1943 celebrate after graduation.

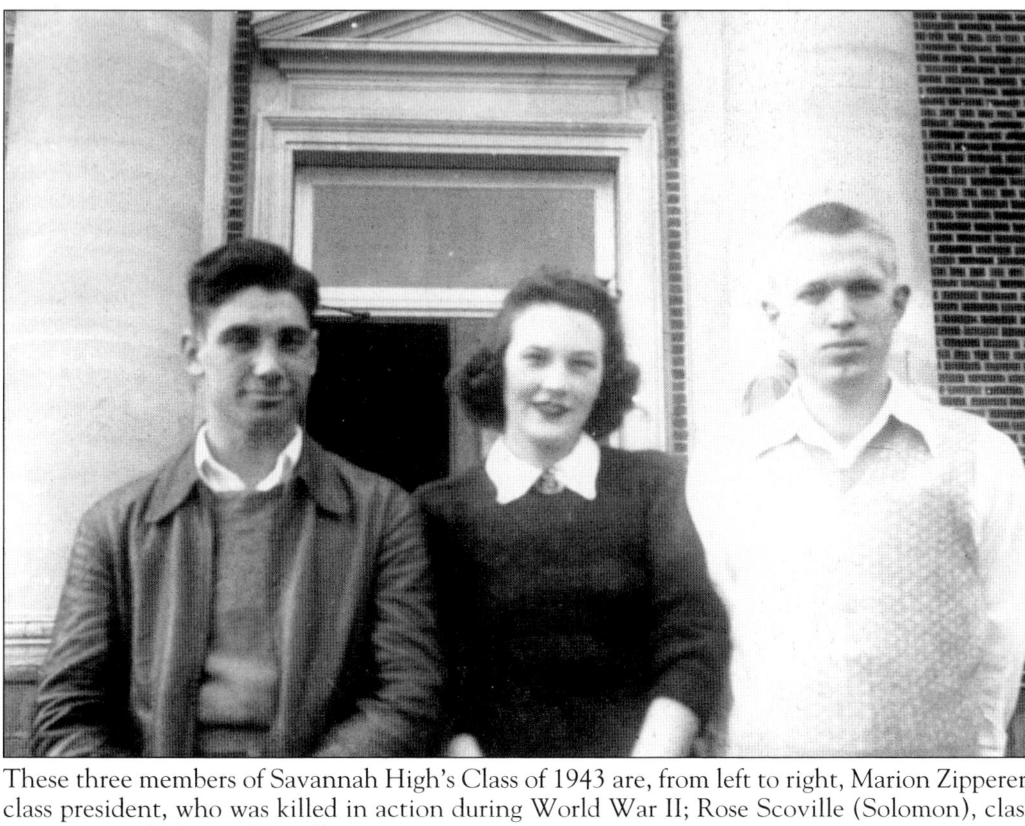

These three members of Savannah High's Class of 1943 are, from left to right, Marion Zipperer, class president, who was killed in action during World War II; Rose Scoville (Solomon), class secretary; and Vernon Russell.

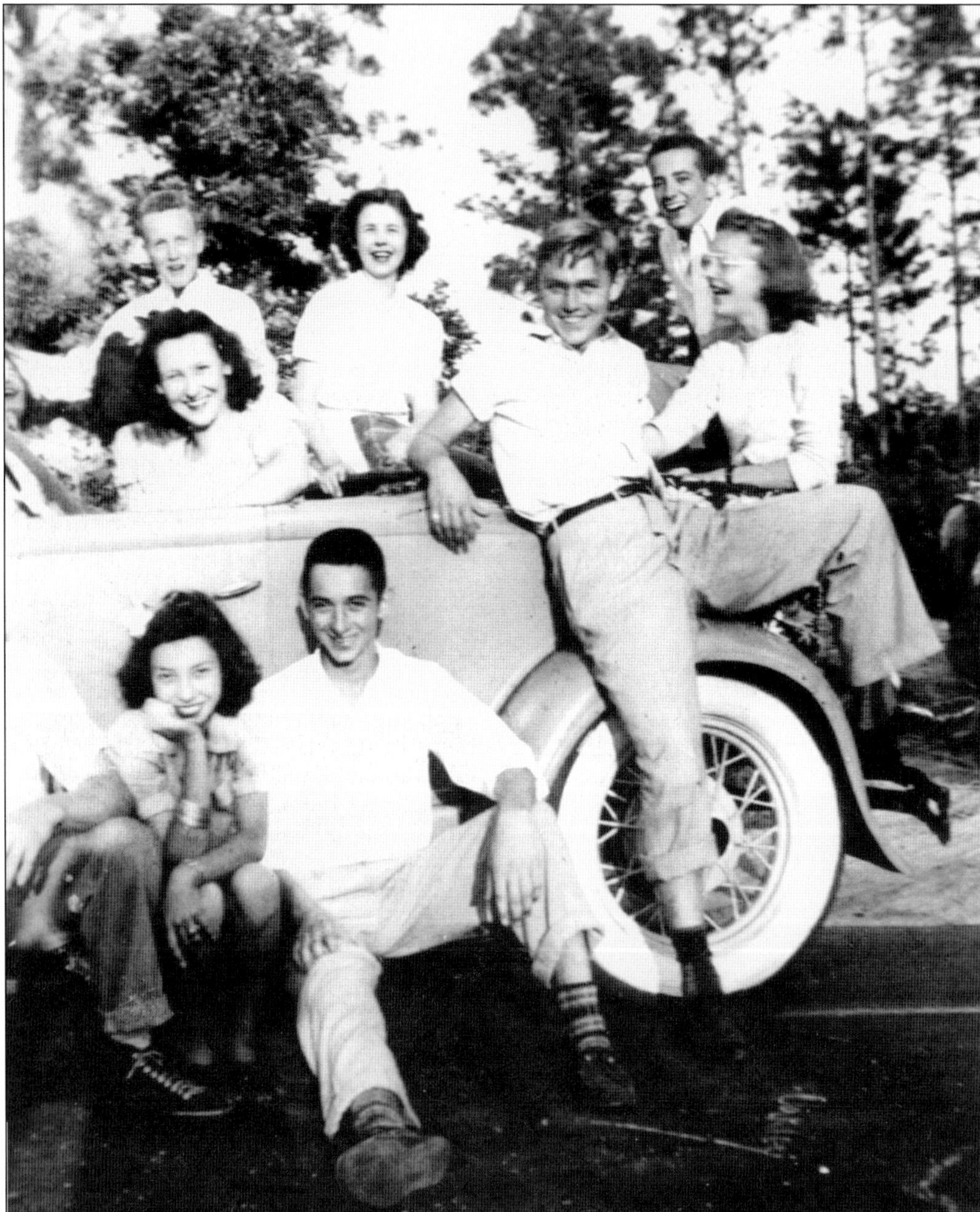

Seemingly without a care in the world members of Savannah High School's Class of 1943 celebrate the end of the year with a picnic.

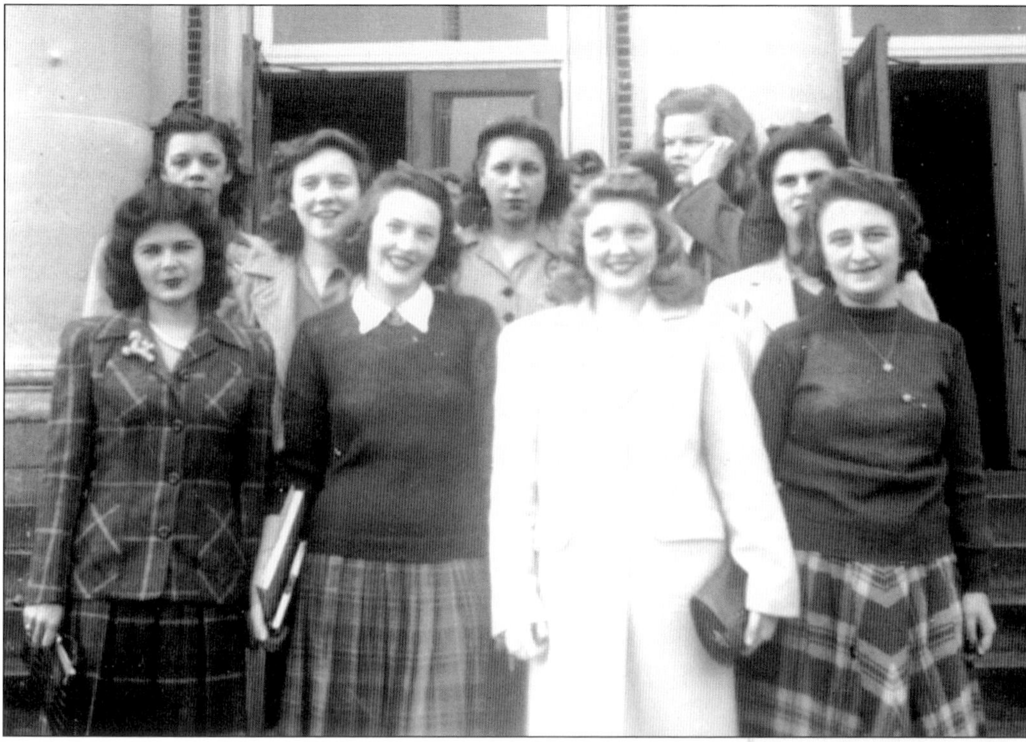

Members of the Class of 1943 stand on the 49th Street steps at the school.

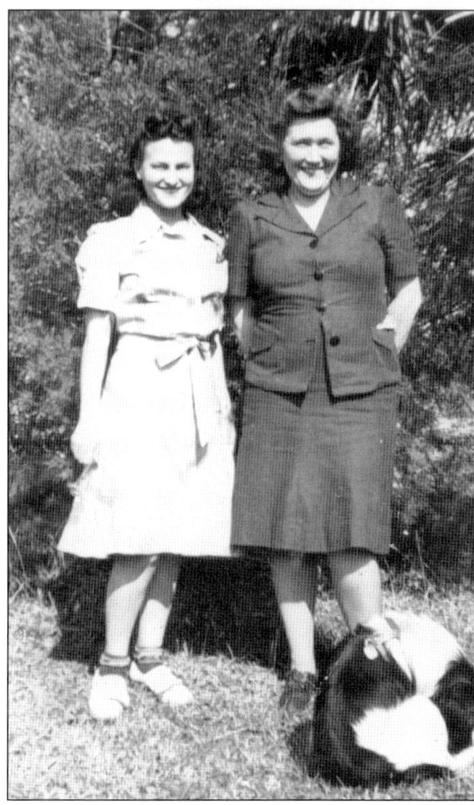

The camera captures two Savannah High School friends (and a busy pooch).

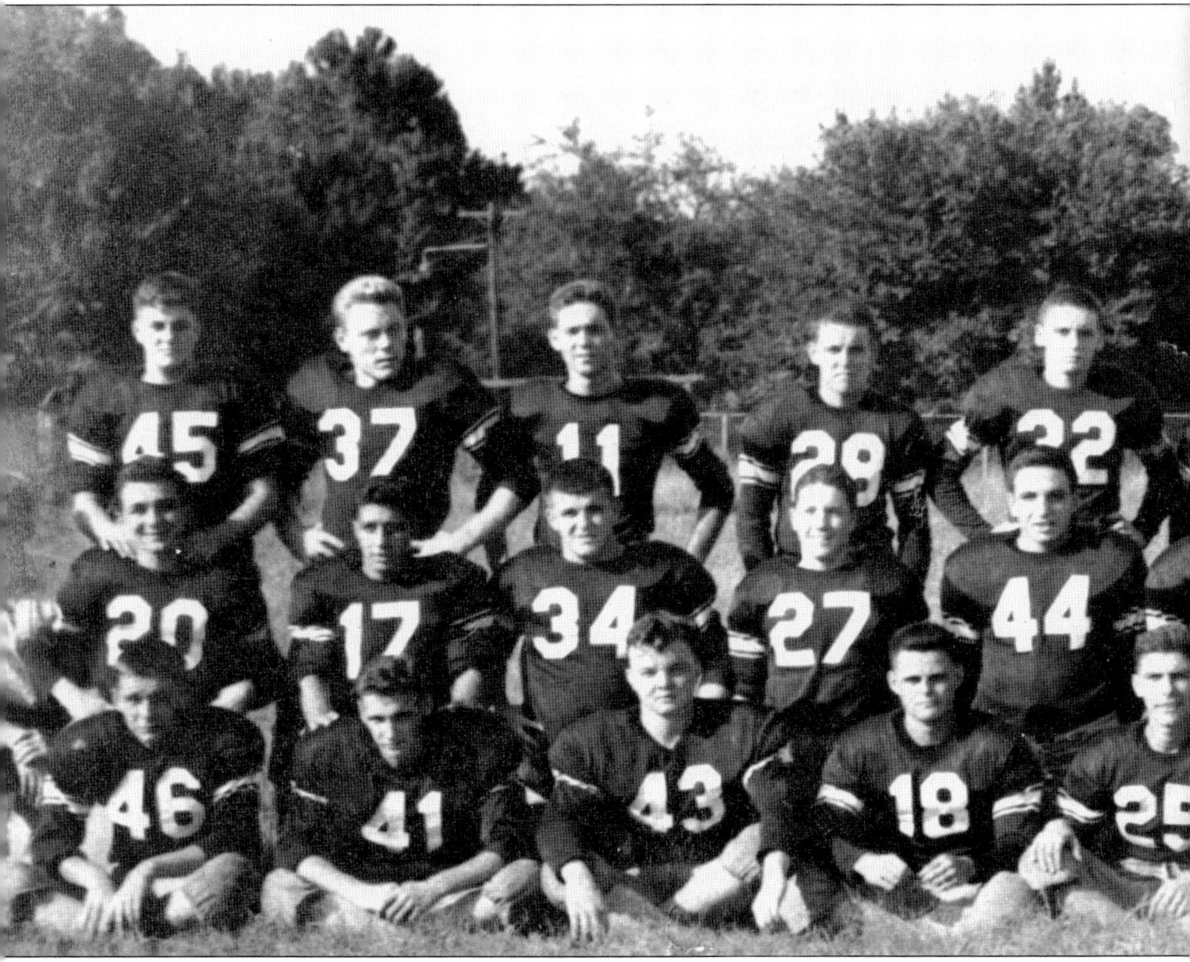

Football has always been a tradition at Savannah High School, and this picture depicts the .

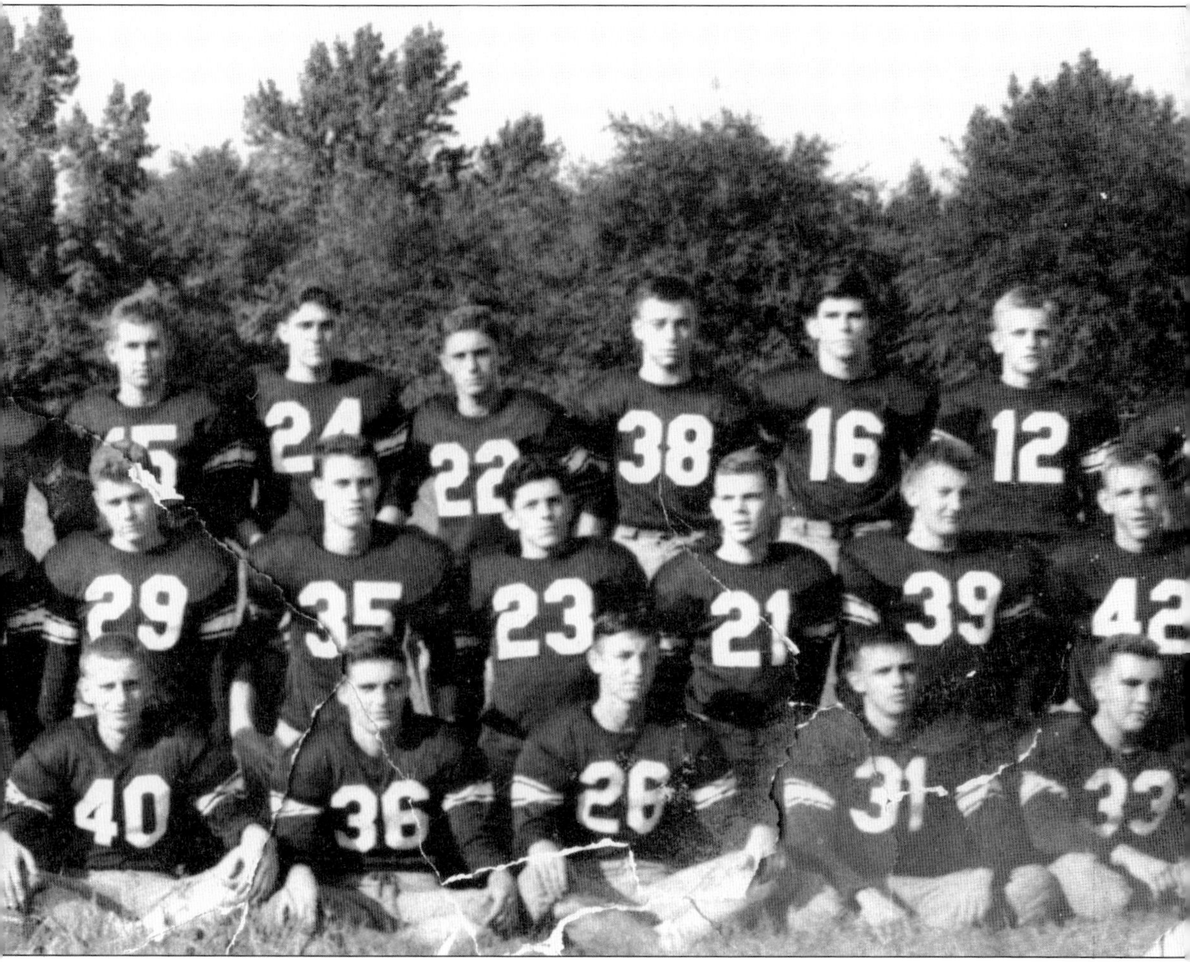

1945 squad.

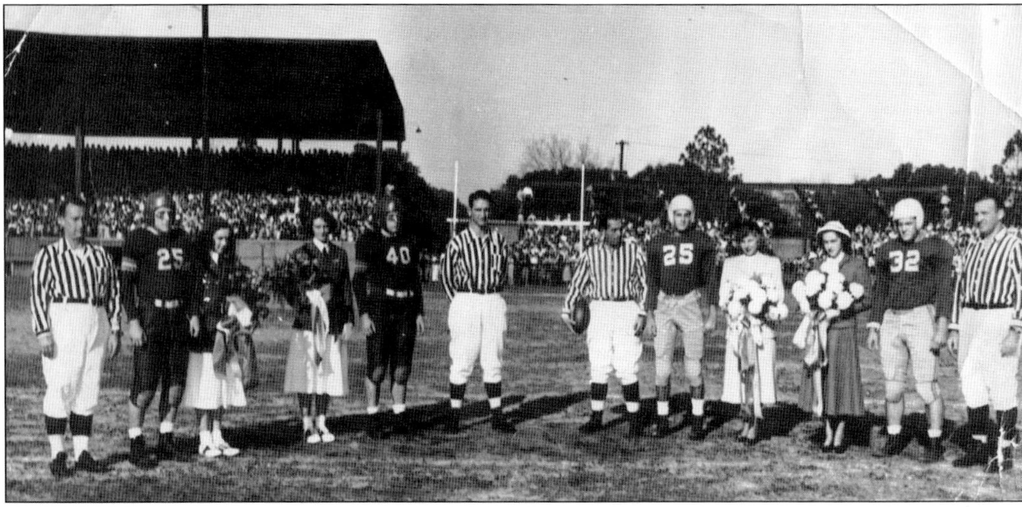

For years the Savannah High School homecoming football game was played against Benedictine Military School on Thanksgiving Day at Grayson Stadium in Daffin Park. During halftime players and their sponsors gathered for the crowning of the homecoming queen.

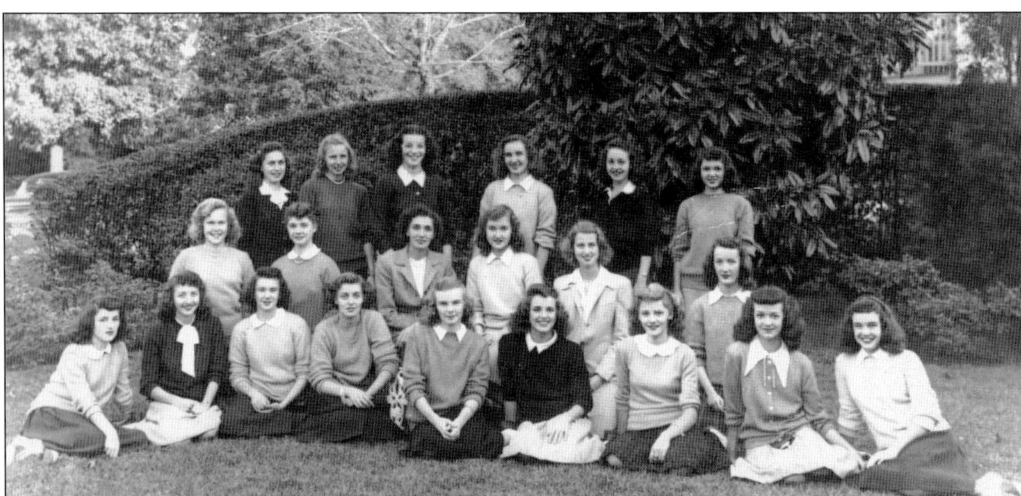

Quis Qui sorority was established as Savannah High School in the 1920s. This 1940s photo includes, from left to right, (front row) Dottie Cason, Claire Tharin, Ann Guerard, Nancy McIver, Jo McGill, Dot Stegin, Ann Ott, Joyce Russom, and Jean Hudson; (second row) Courtney Knight, Mary Carter, Mrs. ? LeHardy. Hidegard Bergen, Jean LeHardy, and Catherine Hale; (back row) Josephine Keeter, Nan Garis, Ann McCaskill, Ruthie Bright, Jane Wooten, and Gerry Sieg.

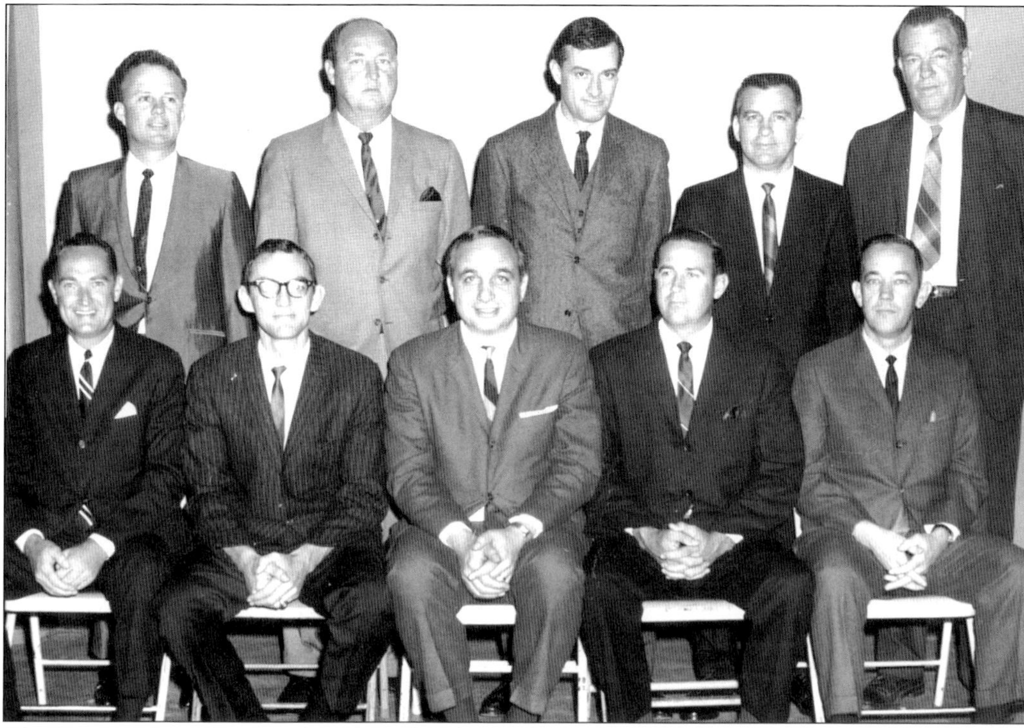

The Savannah High 1949 championship basketball team reunited in 1966 for this photograph. From left to right are (front row) Bill Wood, Jack Owens, John Rousakis, Bill Campbell, and C.M. Adams; (back row) Buddy Saluda, Bogie Bryant, Ben Cunningham, Tom Ridgeway, and Coach Chick Shiver.

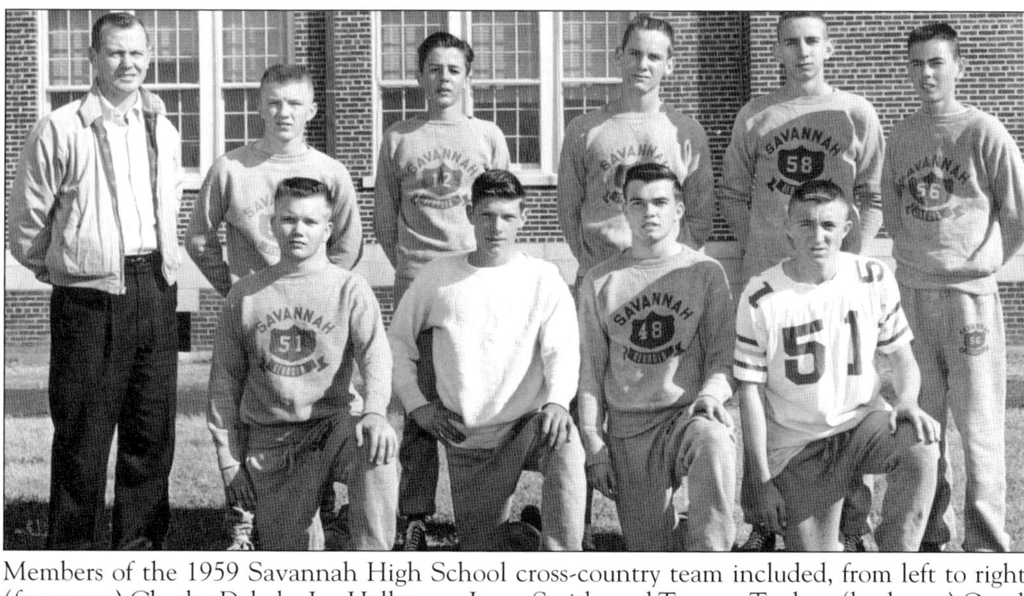

Members of the 1959 Savannah High School cross-country team included, from left to right, (front row) Charles Debele, Jay Hellstrom, Larry Smith, and Tommy Tucker; (back row) Coach Bubba Atwood, Paul Elder, Dan Atkinson, Edward Lamb, Carl Flatham, and Melvin Thomas. Team members not shown were David Abercrombie, Tommy Boon, George Rivers, Murray Clayton, and Carl Blair.

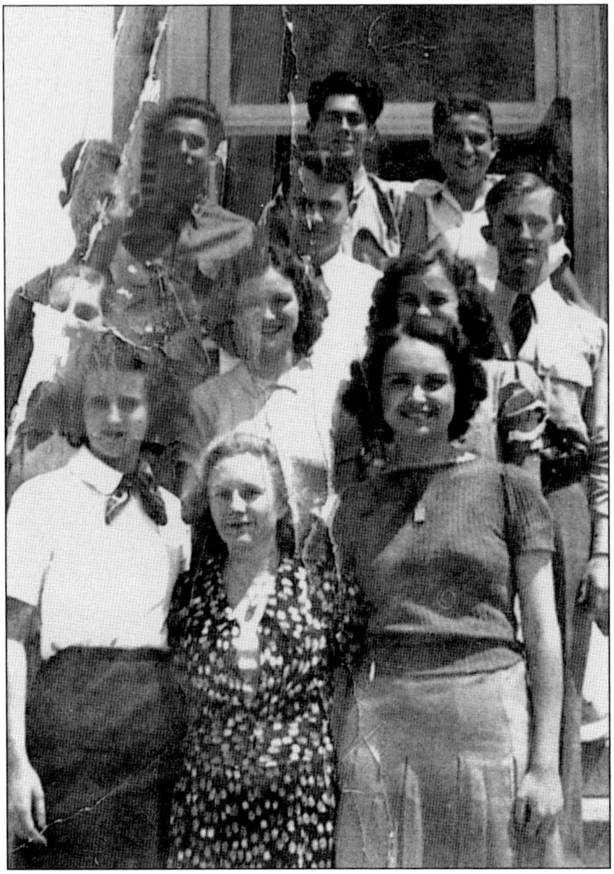

Until the 1950s Commercial High School shared space at Savannah High School. Overcrowding, however, necessitated a move to the former Richard Arnold School. The members of Commercial's Curtain Club, a dramatic group, seen here included Marian Hendry (Lynes) in the polka-dotted dress. The four men standing in the back row are, from left to right, Ralph Miles, Tom Payne, Rufus Burkhalter, and Jimmy Cronk. The drama club was directed by Mrs. Stacy Keach.

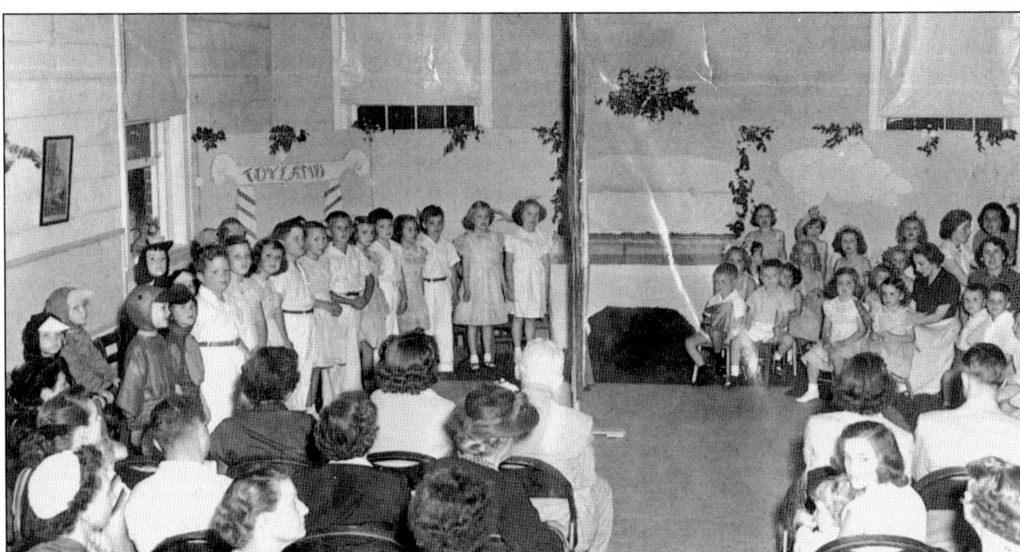

St. Michael's Episcopal Church operated a preschool and primary school in the 1940s and 1950s. This play was presented for parents and friends around 1950.

Seven

Old Fashioned Fun

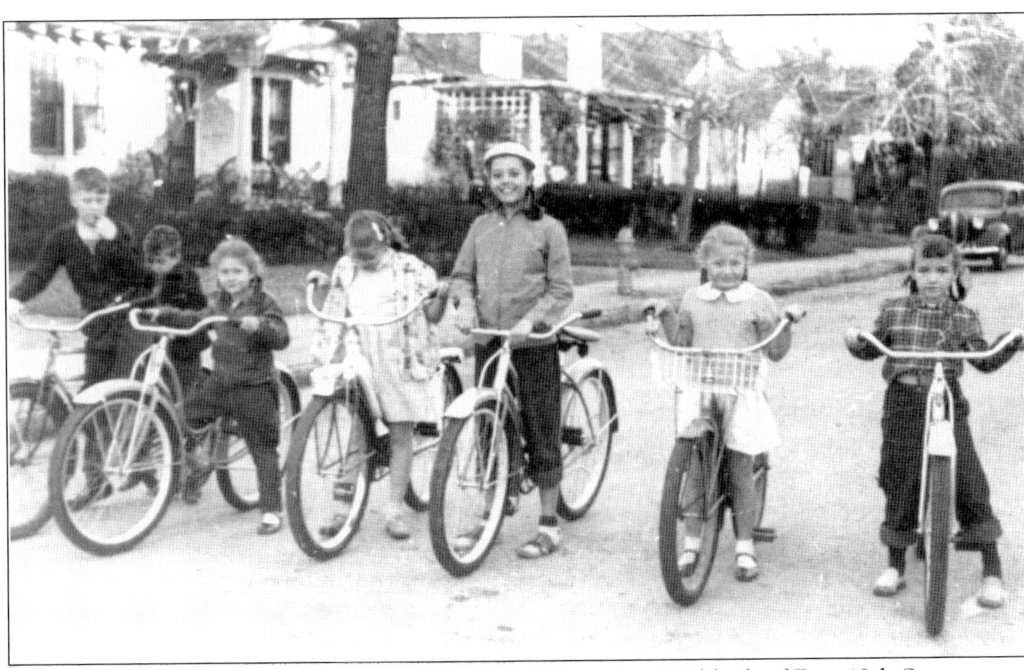

This bicycle brigade was photographed in the 1940s in the 700 block of East 48th Street.

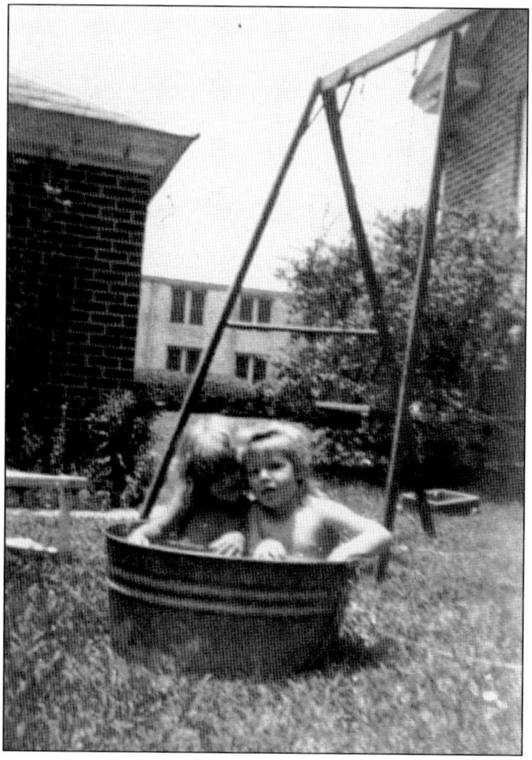

In the good ole days, children found many ways to have fun. On a summer day in 1945 Suzanne Sterne (Shier) and Melinda Whalley (Burke) cooled off in a washtub in the backyard of the Burke home at East 46th and Paulsen Streets. In the background is First Presbyterian Church.

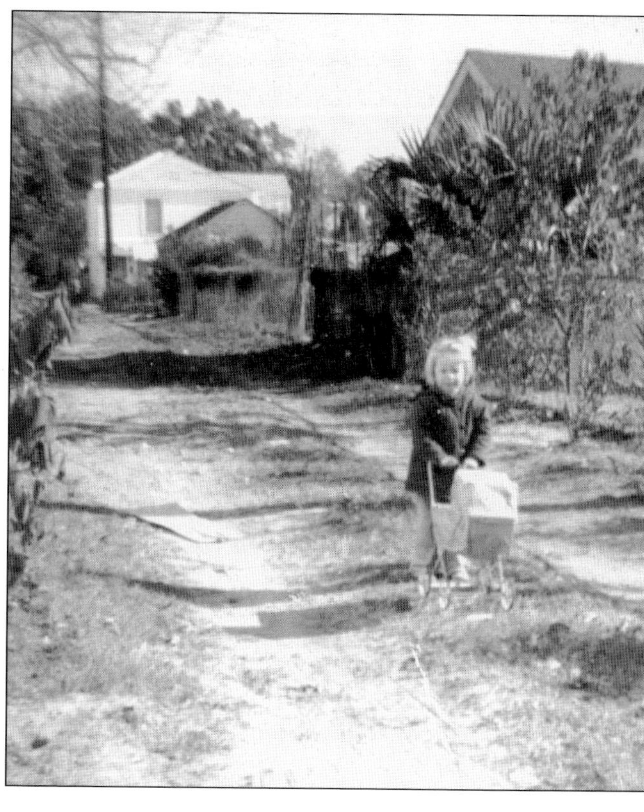

This little girl, photographed in the late 1950s, took her doll for a stroll down one of the neighborhood lanes.

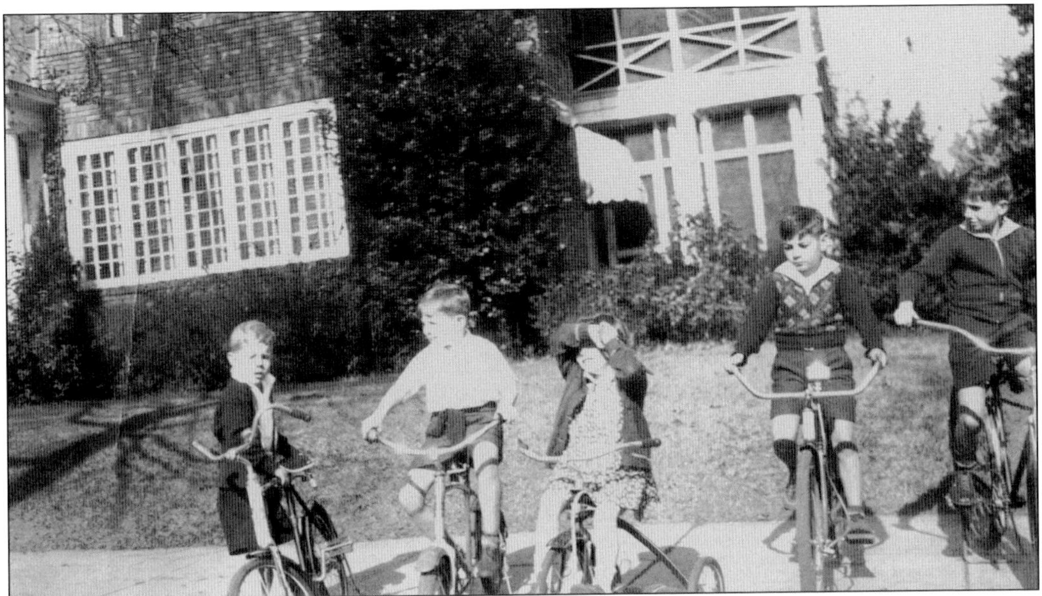

Boys and girls on bikes interrupted an afternoon adventure long enough to have their picture snapped by a proud mother.

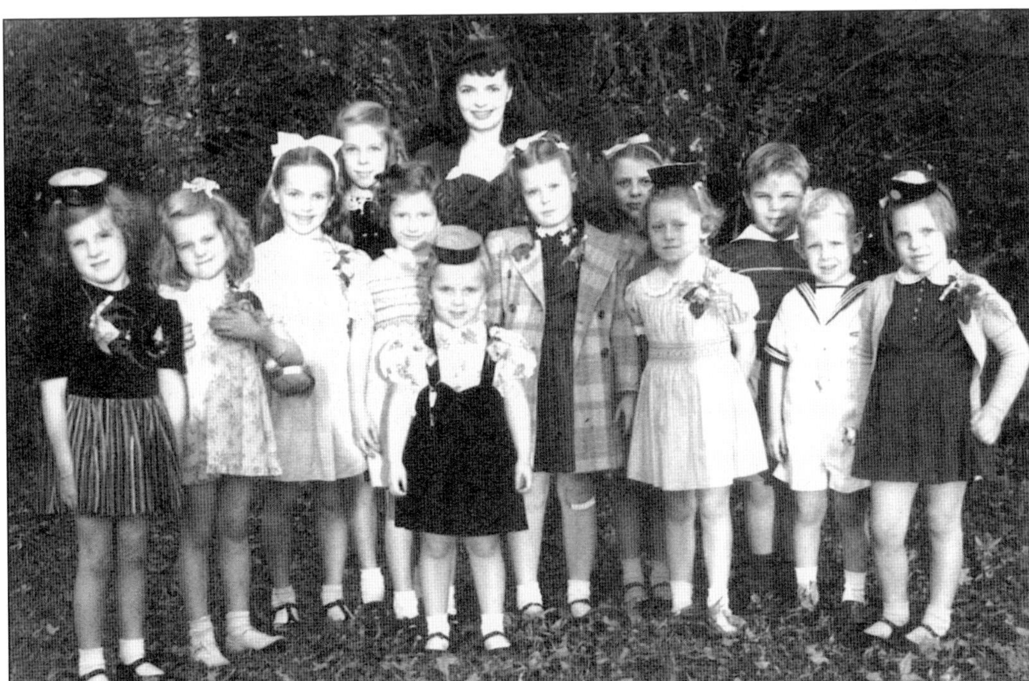

Sandra Wells celebrated her seventh birthday in 1943 with a party at her home in the 700 block of East 48th Street. Guests included, from left to right, Elaine Jones, Karen Davis, Sandra Wells, Sally Schofield, Lorraine Wells, Dottie Clark, Mary Ann Rourke, Jeanne Demmond, Sandra Shearouse, Billie Proctor, Harris Lewis, Sonny Morrison, and Kay Shearouse.

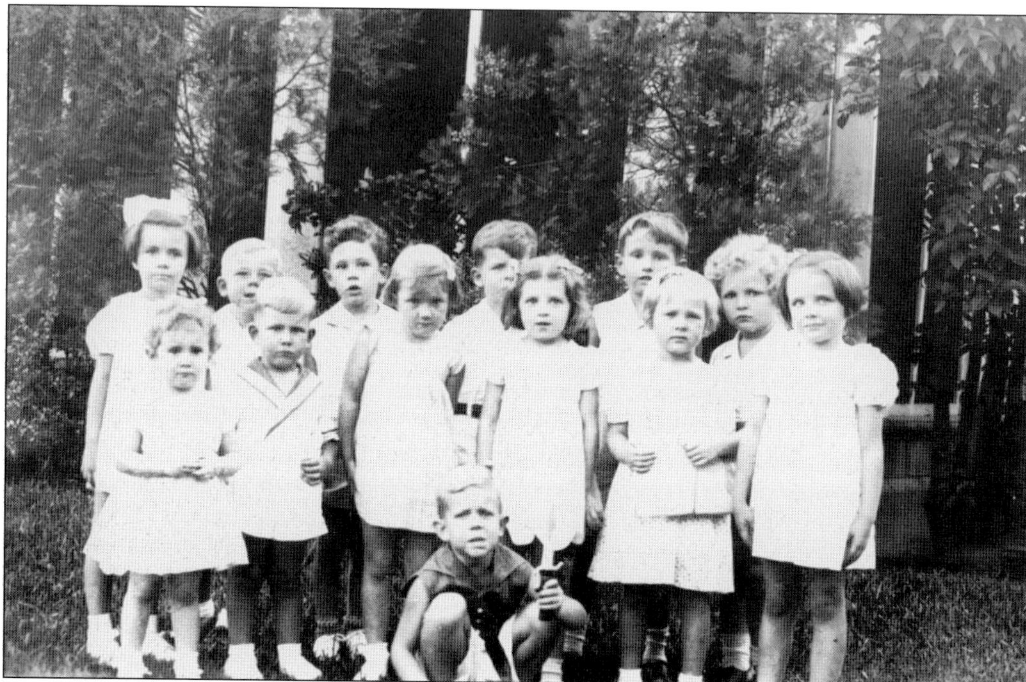

Deb Maner, front, invited neighborhood pals to his birthday party at his East 45th Street home. Guests included Susie Hill, Gratz Myers, Carl Espy, Betty Roberts, T.A. Bryson, Wilene Clark, Kenneth Roberts, Dickie Royce, and Beth Neville.

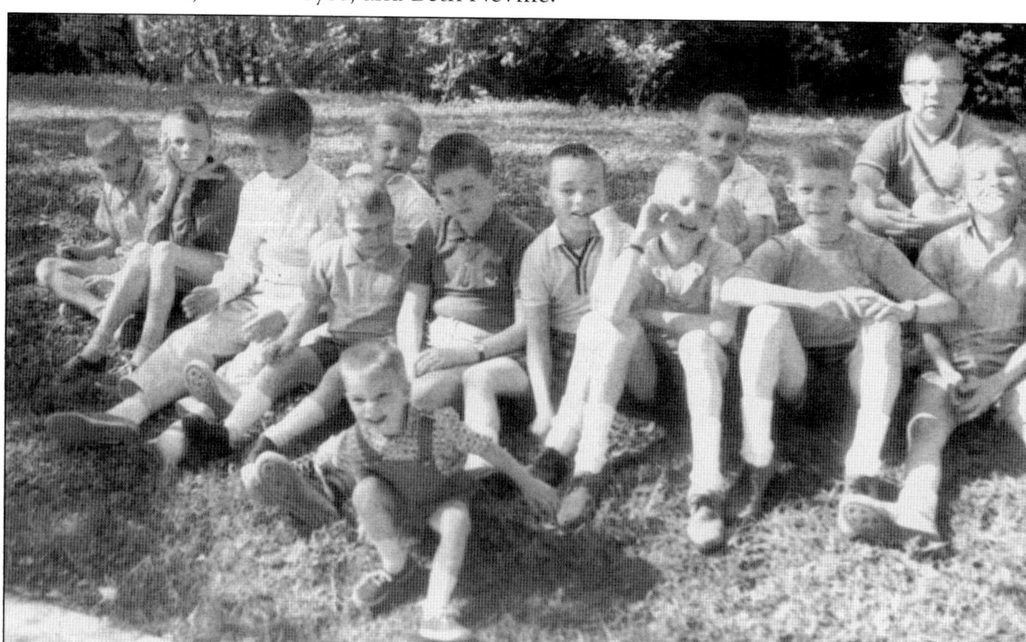

Chums who lived around East 49th and 50th Streets in 1963 gathered for this casual photograph. From left to right are, (front row) John Compton, (middle row) Kelly Compton, Henry Clay, John Cope, unidentified, Frank Arden, Kurt Schwalbe, Kim Abbott, Tony Abbott, and Chip Compton; (back row) Jimmy Hungerpiller, Chuck Henderson, and Hugh D'Anna.

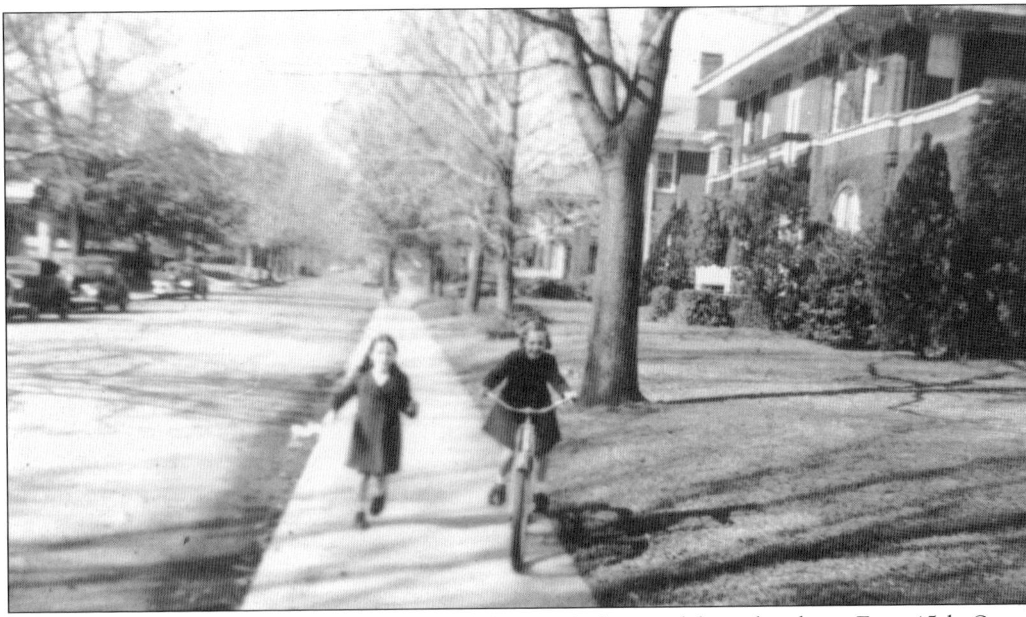

Suzie Hill (Williams) and Betty Carswell (Morris) skip and bicycle along East 45th Street in 1940.

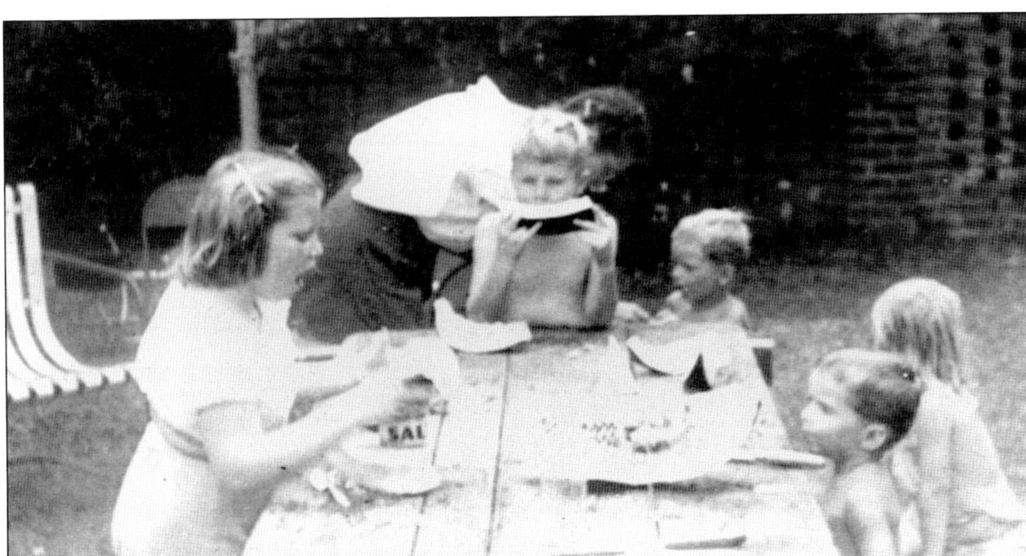

A summer's day, a cool watermelon, and a group of hungry children are the ingredients in a recipe for happiness. This appreciative crowd, photographed in the early 1950s, included, from left to right, Barbie Little, Martha Belford (leaning over) helping Ricky Belford; two unidentified children, and Lee Belford.

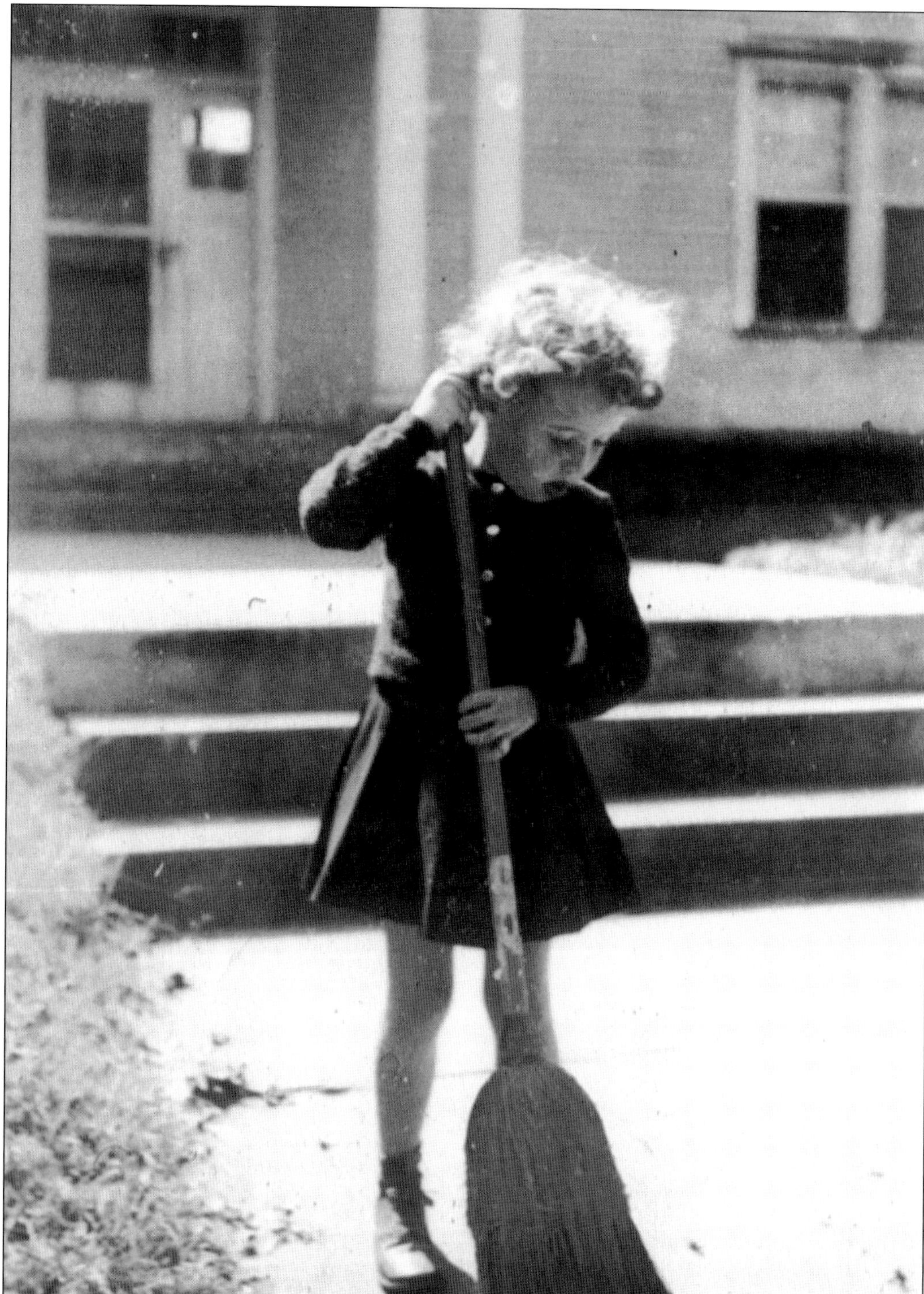

In the 1940s sweeping the sidewalk brought much pleasure to this little girl on East 51st Street as long as she didn't step on a crack and break her mother's back, as the old children's rhyme warns.

Eight

RECREATION

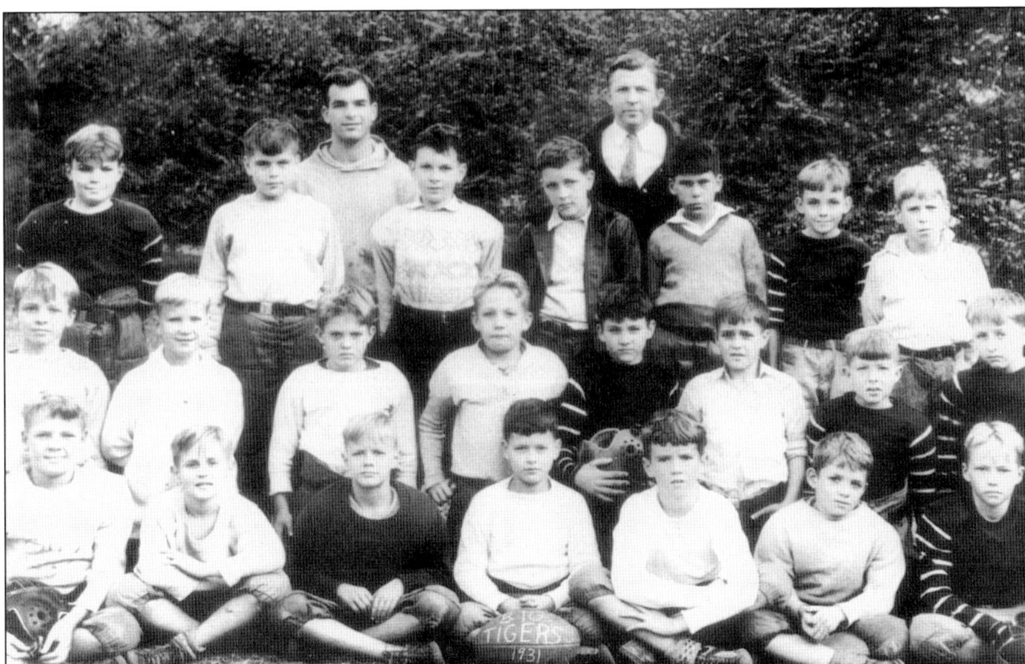

Nearby Daffin Park was where many neighborhood boys practiced football for the Tiger Club. In this 1931 photograph are, from left to right, (front row) Raymond Demere, Willie Robertson, Buck Benton, Henry Garwes, Sam Ross, Marcus Baker, and Charlie Golson; (middle row) Jack Myers, Billy Winburn, Frank McIntire, Dick Fuller, Tommy Gilbert, Lewis Mills, Mickey Logan, and Shelby Myrick; (back row) Bodie Wort, Pat Patton, Morton Haas, Johnny Adams, Lionel Drew, Moultrie Lee, and Schley Knight, Assistant Coach ? Tuttle, and Coach Fred Garis.

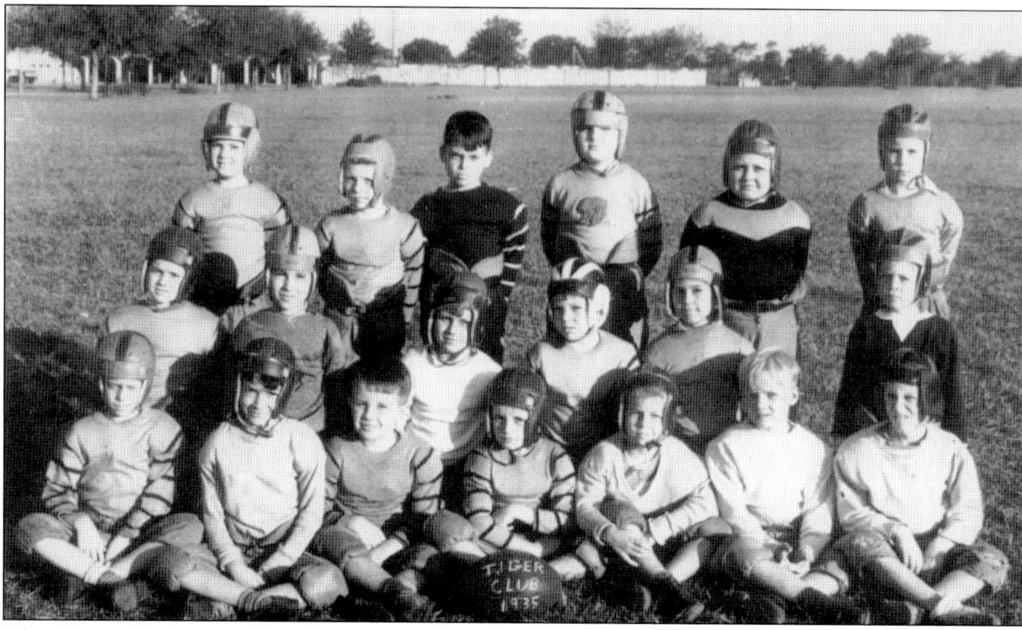

The Tiger Club was officially organized in 1933 by R.M. Demere with a membership of 30 boys and Fred Garis as director. The mission statement explained that "games in the club are a means of teaching sportsmanship, a desire to win and learning to play with others." Members of the 1935 Tigers are pictured, from left to right, as follows: (front row) Sam Cann, Henry Levy, Charles Jarrell, Edward Brennan, Gordon Jones, Charles Demere, and Sammy Coons; (middle row) Joe Logan, Frank Bryson, Richard Shaw, Frank Peeples, Bruce Sams, and Jimmy Hancock; (back row) David Johnson, Billy Rankin, David Bryson, Alec McDonald, P.J. Thomas, and Brian Brown.

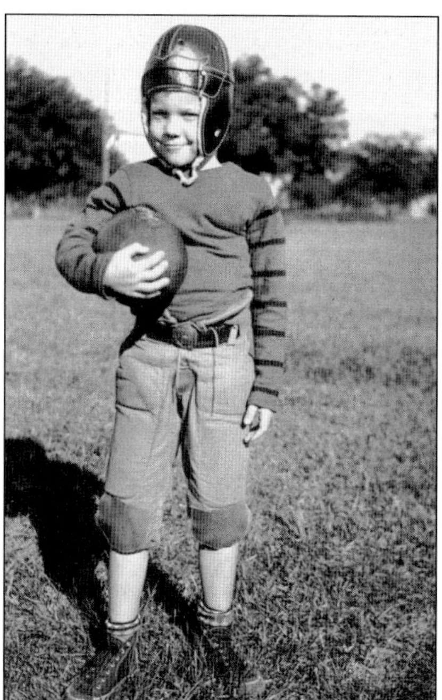

Tigers came in all sizes, including a little Deb Maner who played in the 1930s.

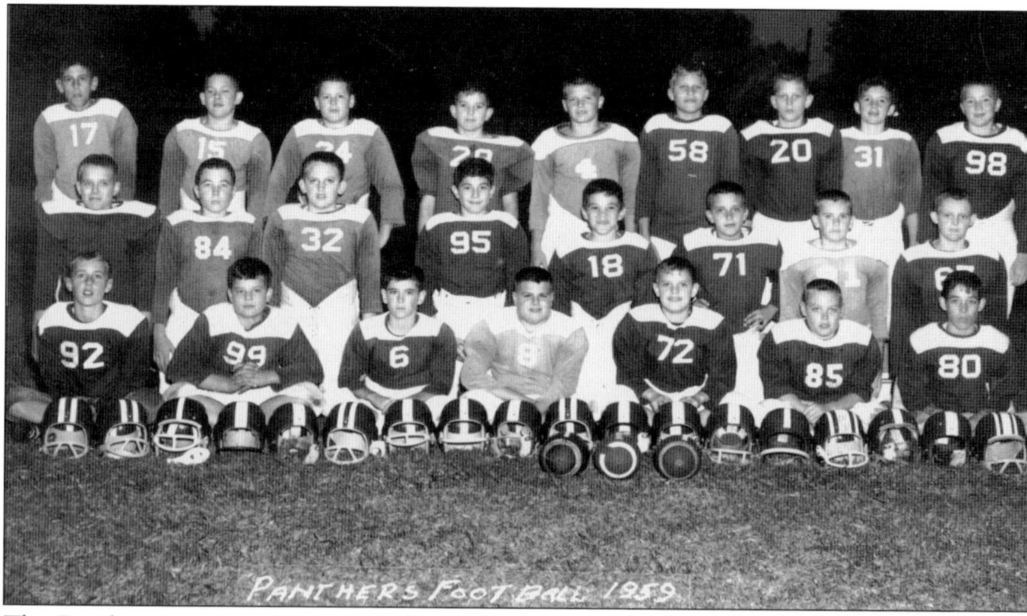

The Panthers were another group of boys who practiced in Daffin Park, under the direction of Coach Tom Moore. The 1959 team included, from left to right, (front row) Carl Weeks, unidentified, Bill Burroughs, two unidentified boys, Johnny Lientz, and Joe Inglesby; (middle row) unidentified, David Carter, Cliff McCurry, Johnny Mamalakis, Tooty Aliotta, Tim Nugent, Hollis Puckett, and Charlie Jordan; (back row) Dicky Myers, Bill Perry, unidentified, Tommy Douglas, Raddy Zittrouer, Gary Allen, Bubba Victor, Gay Mayfield, and Bobby Havens.

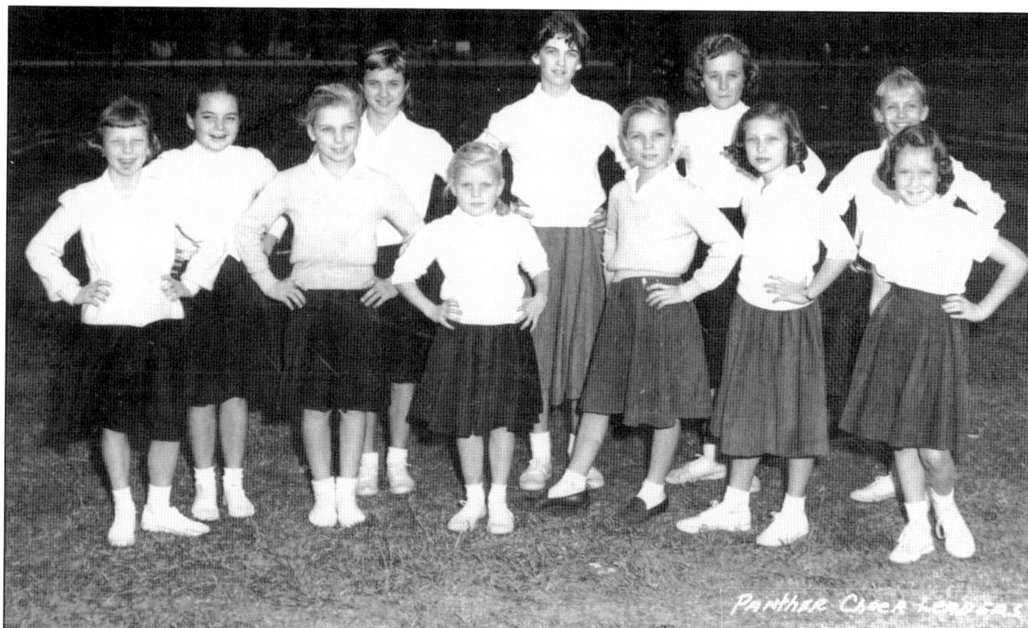

Neighborhood girls got into the act by being Panthers cheerleaders. From left to right are (front row) unidentified, Jean Powers, Patty Daniels, Jane Powers, Carolyn Reiser, and unidentified; (back row) Julia Hodges, Diane Bailey, Diane Jackson, Jenell Rogers, and Terry Densley.

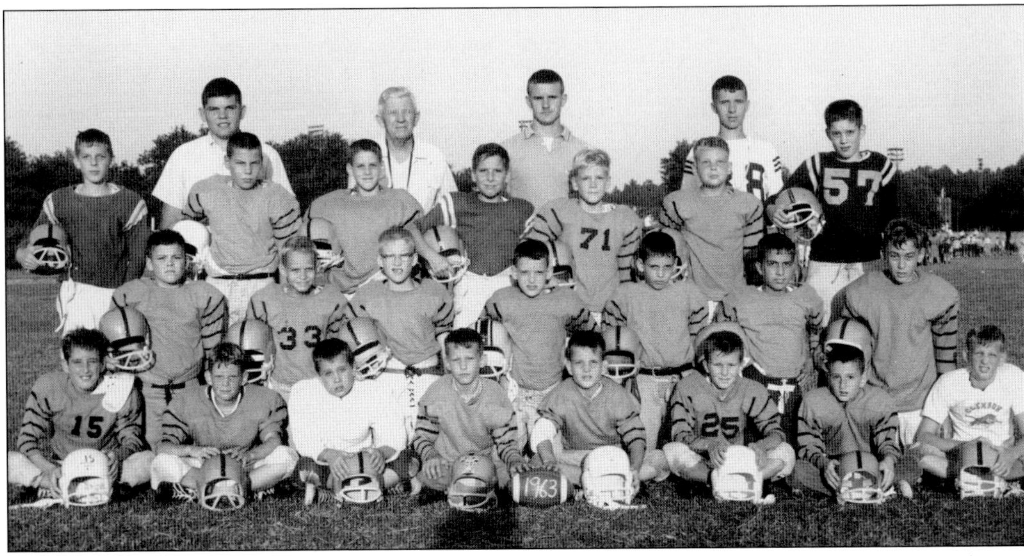

The Tigers were still going strong in 1963 when these boys played. From left to right are (front row) Bill Hopkins, John Lyons, unidentified, Corky Ormond, George Oelschig, Billy Bradley, unidentified, and Andy Calhoun; (second row) two unidentified boys, John Boykin, unidentified, Harvey Gilbert, Shep Bryson, and David Hendrix; (third row) David Dickey, Frank Streiff, three unidentified boys, ? McIntosh, and Charles Dailey; (back row) unidentified, Fred Garis, and two unidentified boys.

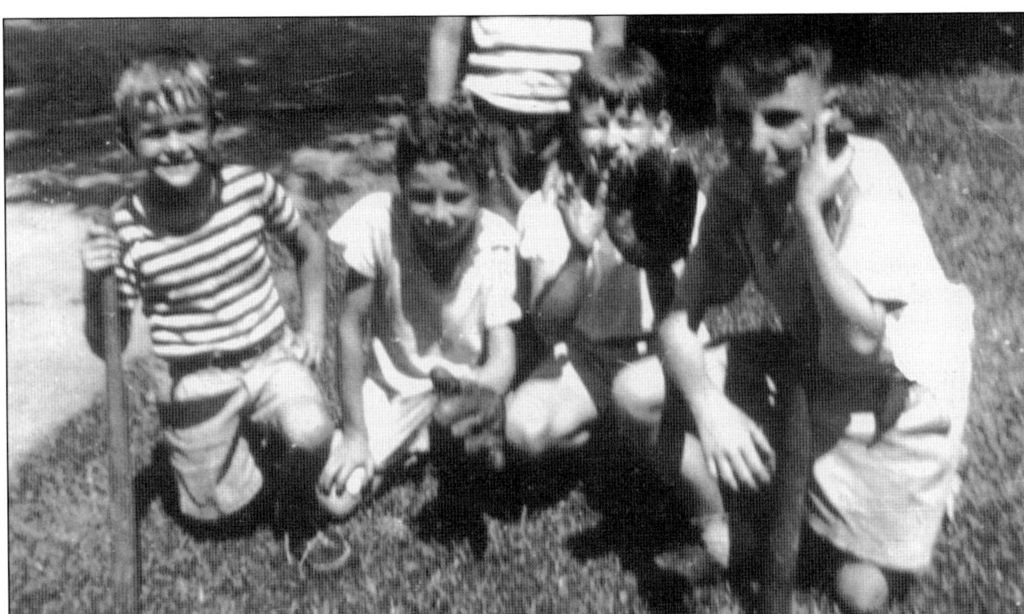

Preparing for a game of catch or baseball in the 1930s are, from left to right, Billy Murphy, Ken Palmer, Harvey Morgan, and Gene McCracken.

Nine

Neighborhood Glimpses

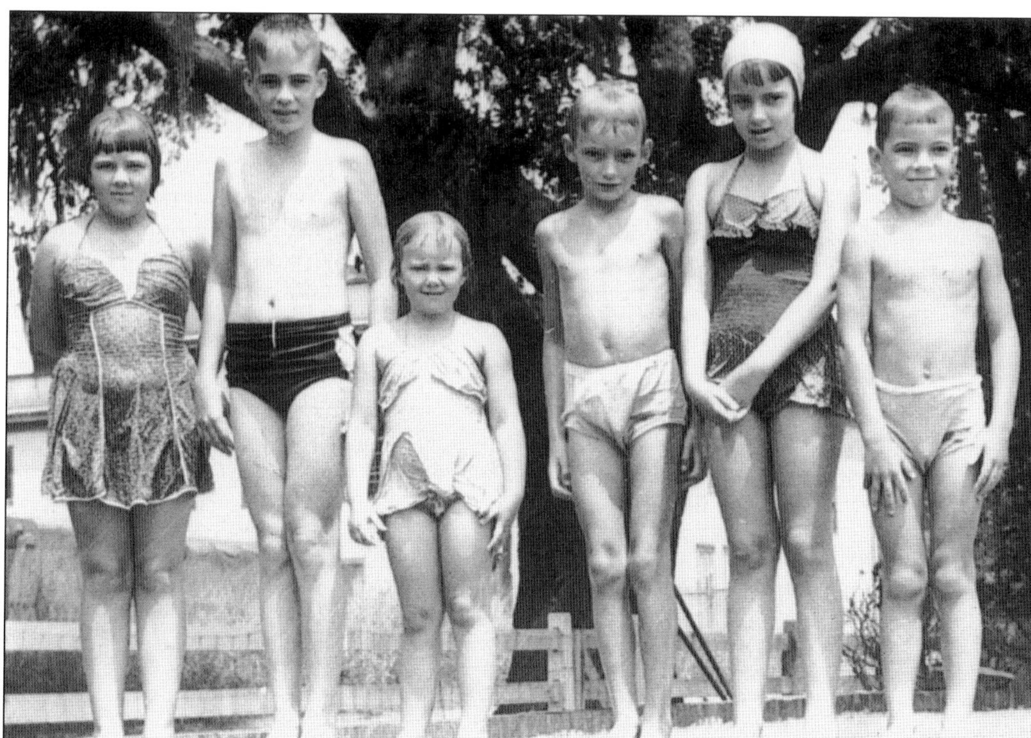

A kid was in high cotton, as they say, if he or she were lucky enough to go to a swimming pool in the 1940s and 1950s. Preparing for a dip in the 1950s are, from left to right, Lois Olsen, Bill Belford, Ann Olsen, Ricky Belford, Mary Olsen, and Lee Belford.

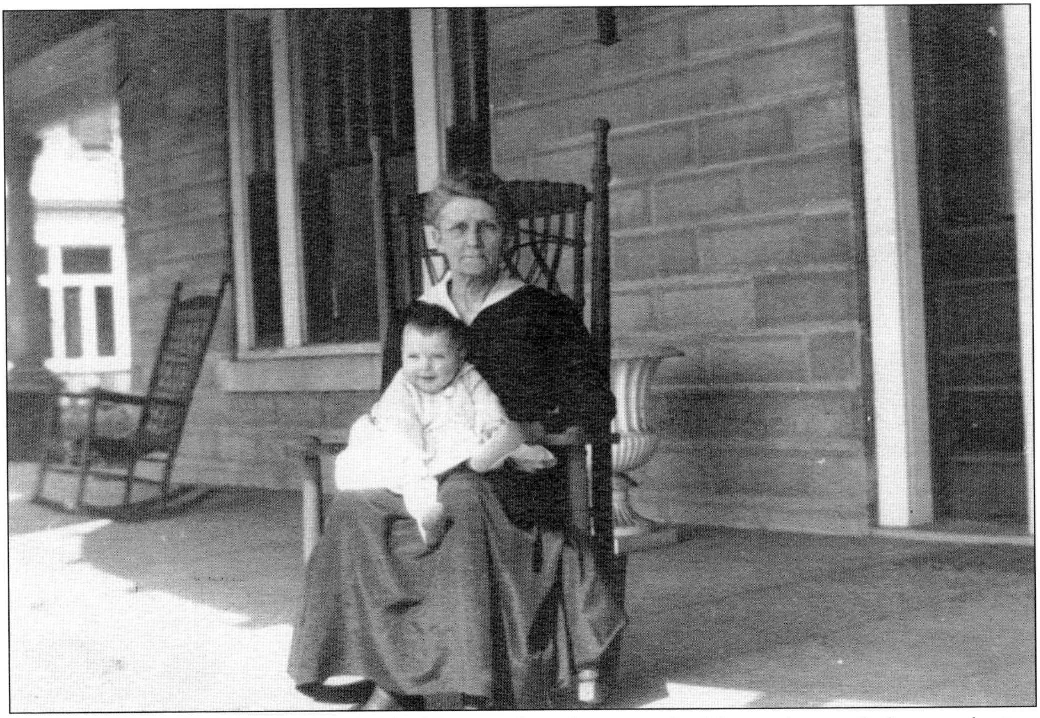

Many neighborhood homes have fabulous porches that are ideal for rocking a baby or relaxing on a swing. This photograph was taken at a Victory Drive home around 1920.

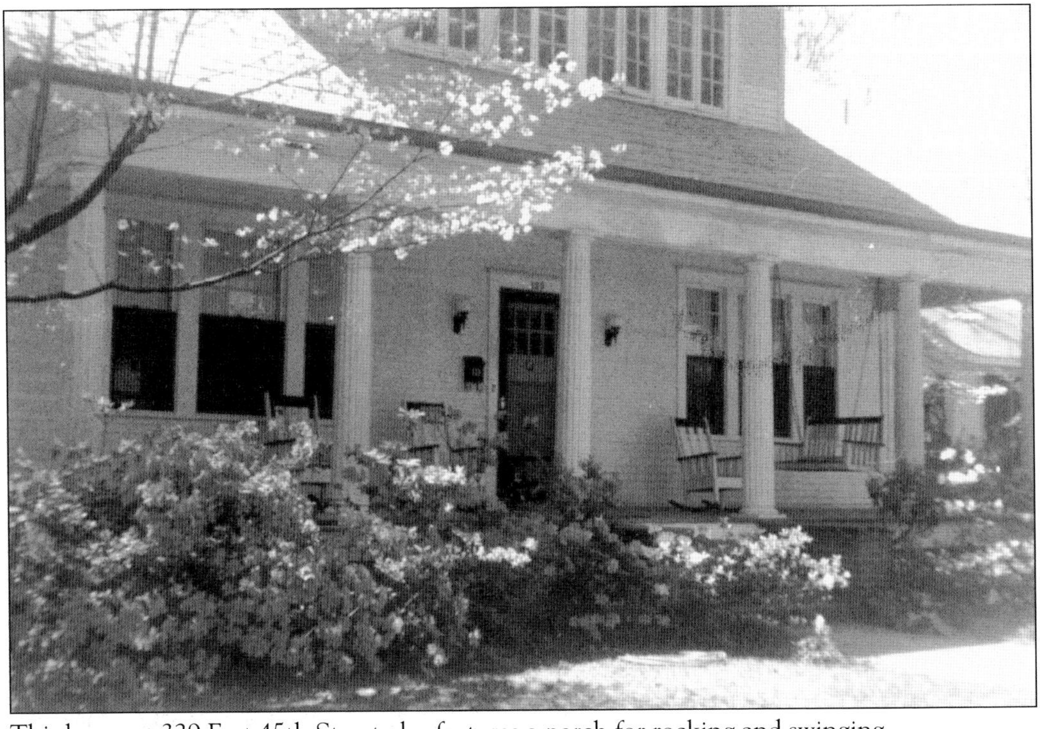

This house at 329 East 45th Street also features a porch for rocking and swinging.

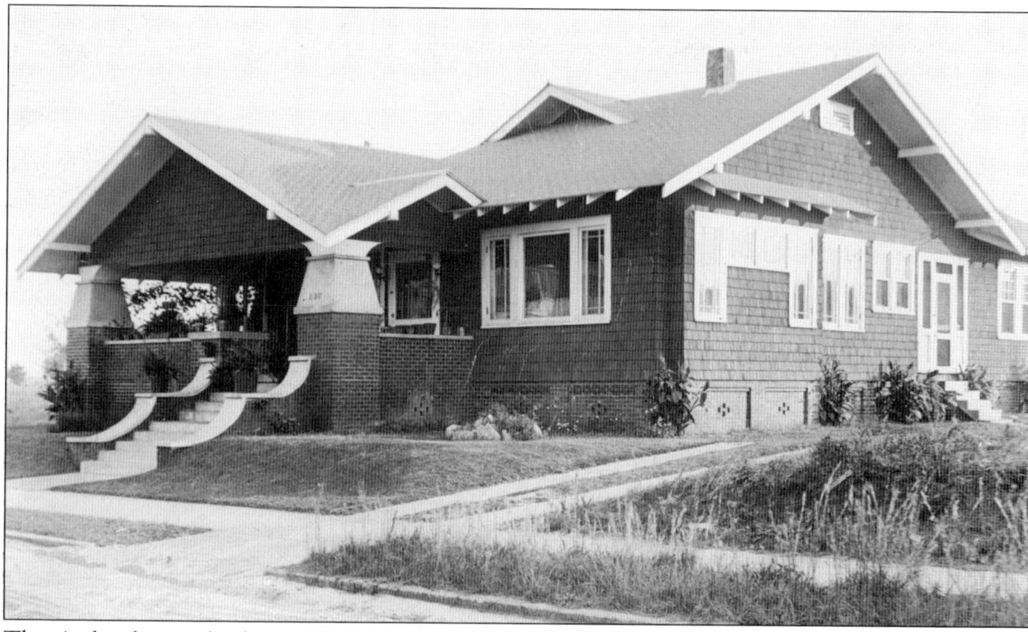

The Arden home, built in 1920 at 49th and Habersham Streets, is a wonderful example of Arts and Crafts–style architecture. Frank Arden has lived in the house all his life.

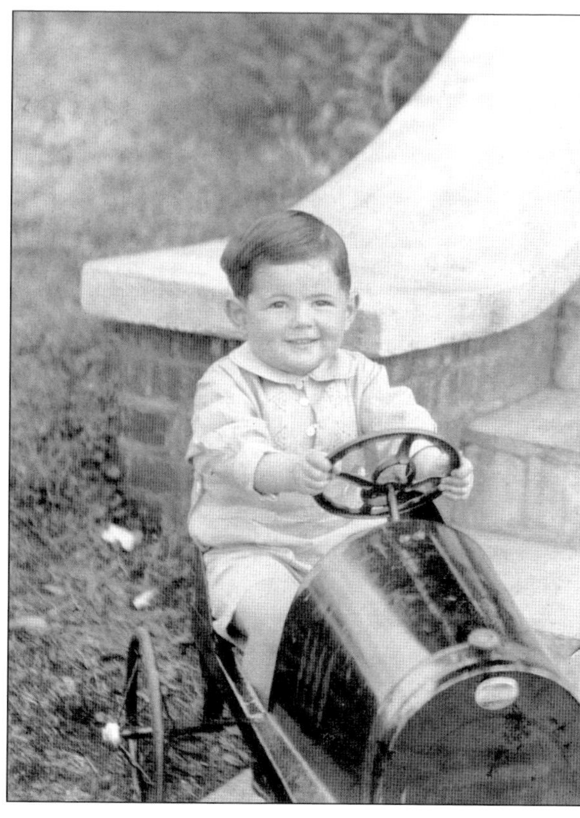

Frank Arden, who was two years old in 1926, enjoys his toy car.

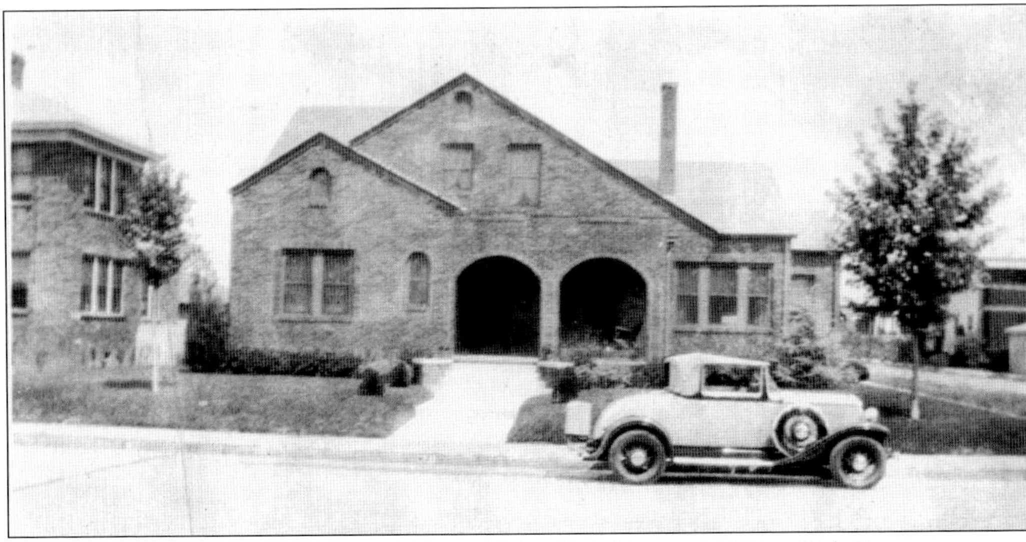

For many years this was the home of Mr. and Mrs. C.A. Bart at 434 East 50th Street.

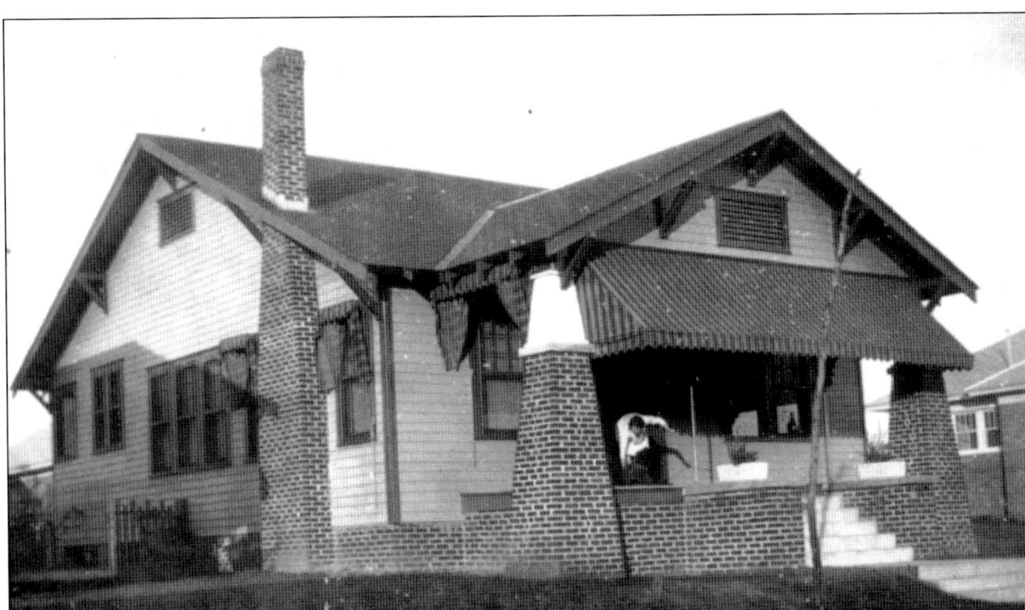

For many years this was the home of Mr. and Mrs. C.A. Bart at 434 East 50th Street.

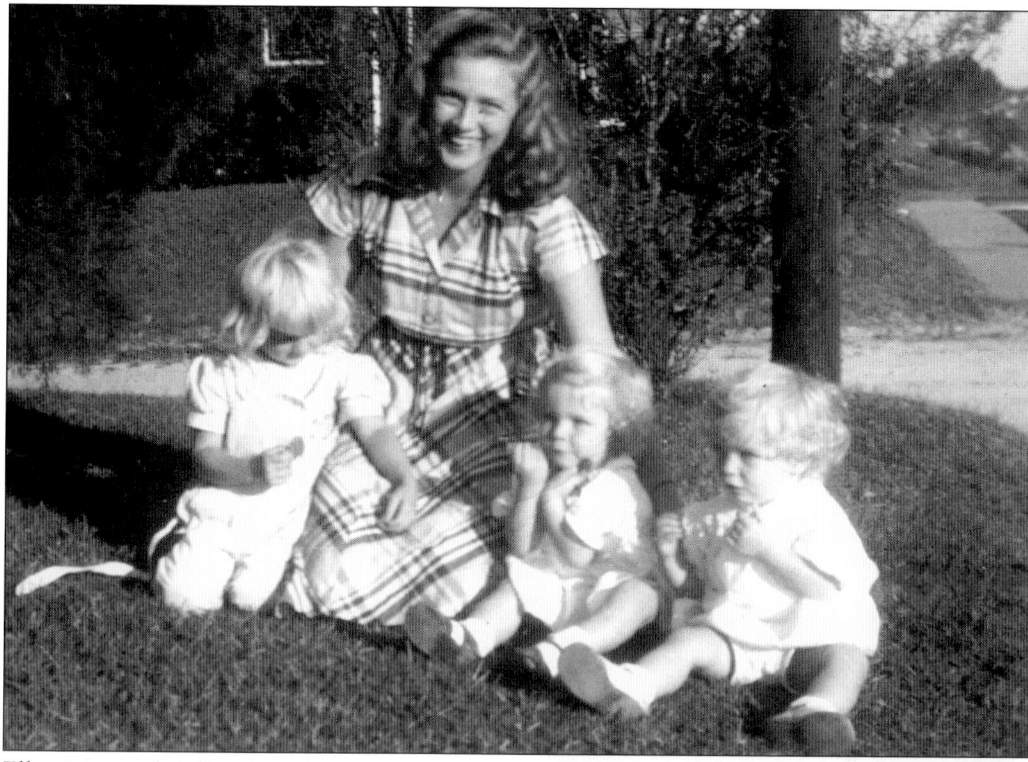

Ellen Martin (Mallory) tends to Nancy Powers (Chapman) and twins Jean Powers (Sparks) and Jane Powers (Sparks) in the late 1940s.

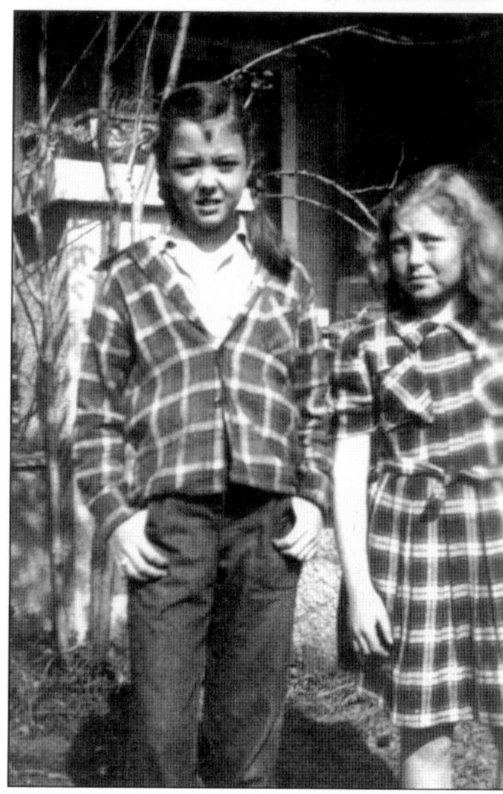

Lucie Butler and Billie Proctor look pretty in plaid in 1947.

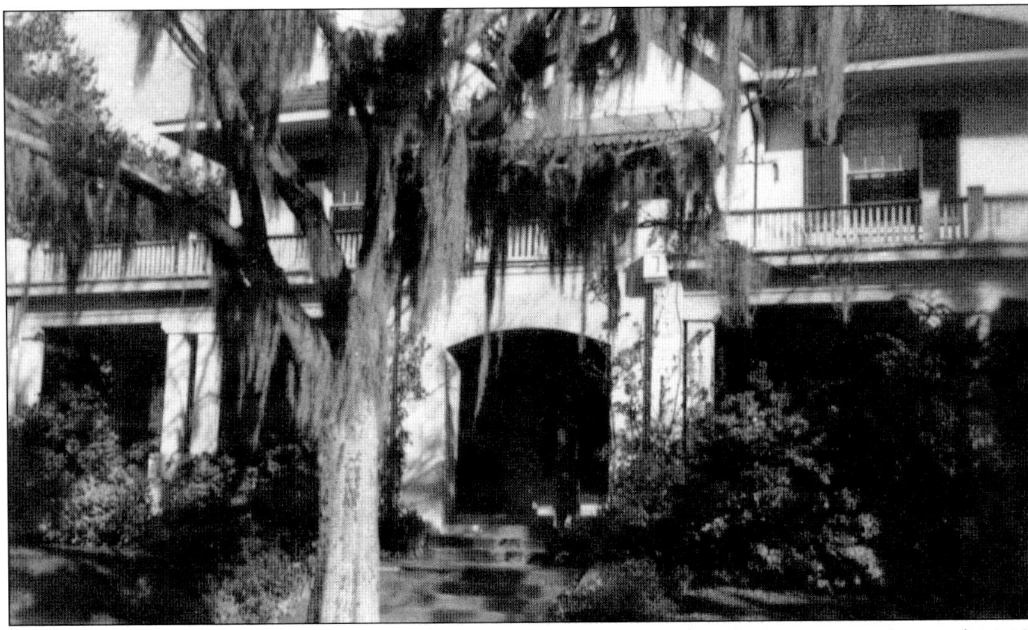

The home at 102 East 44th Street was built for the Ehrlich family between 1911 and 1912. Witcover was the architect and the A.A. Artley Company was the contractor. The design combines elements of mission and Spanish Revival styles.

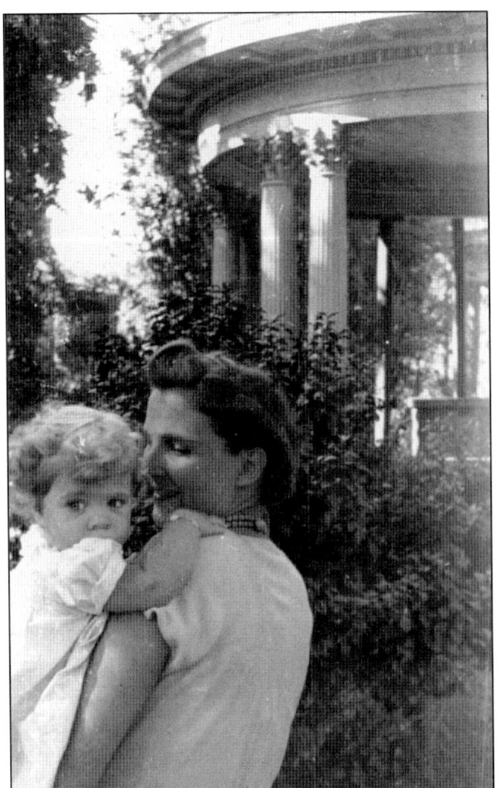

This photo of Electa Robertson Hoffman and her baby daughter Robbie Hoffman (Culver) was taken in front of the Robertson family home at 920 Victory Drive.

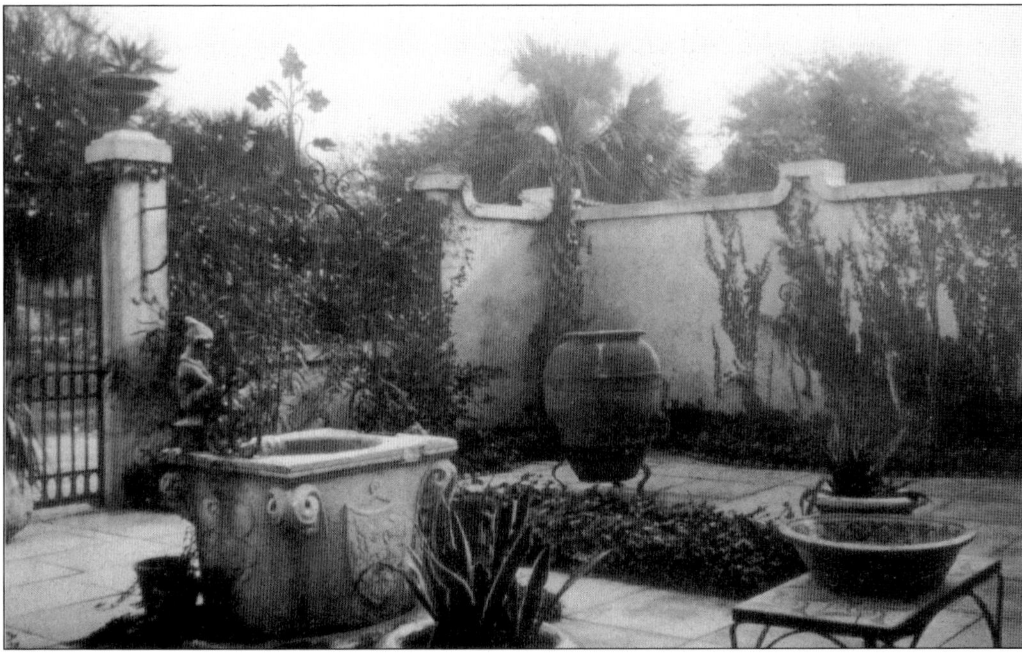

The elaborate garden at 2711 Abercorn Street includes a goldfish pond, urns, and decorative ironwork.

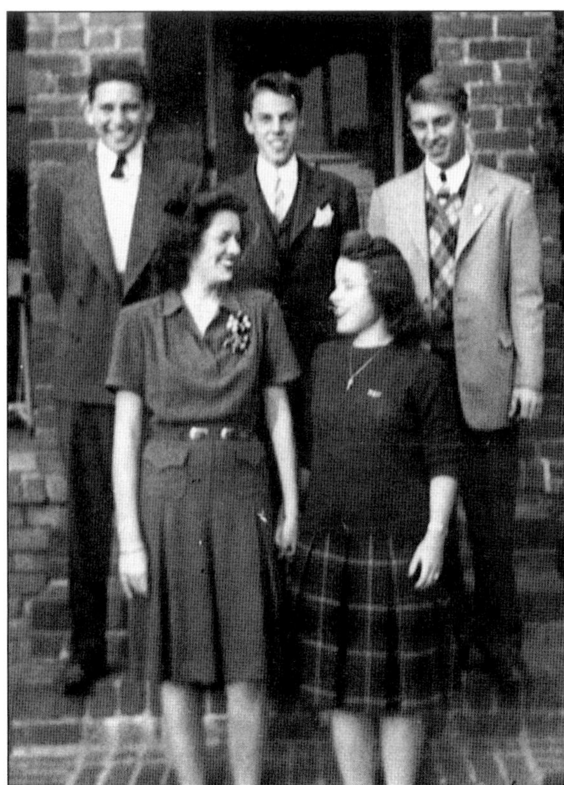

High school pals posed for this photograph in the early 1940s. From left to right are (front row) Betty Johnson and Jean Hanson; (back row) Melvin Berlin, Paul Strickland, and Ray Rehm.

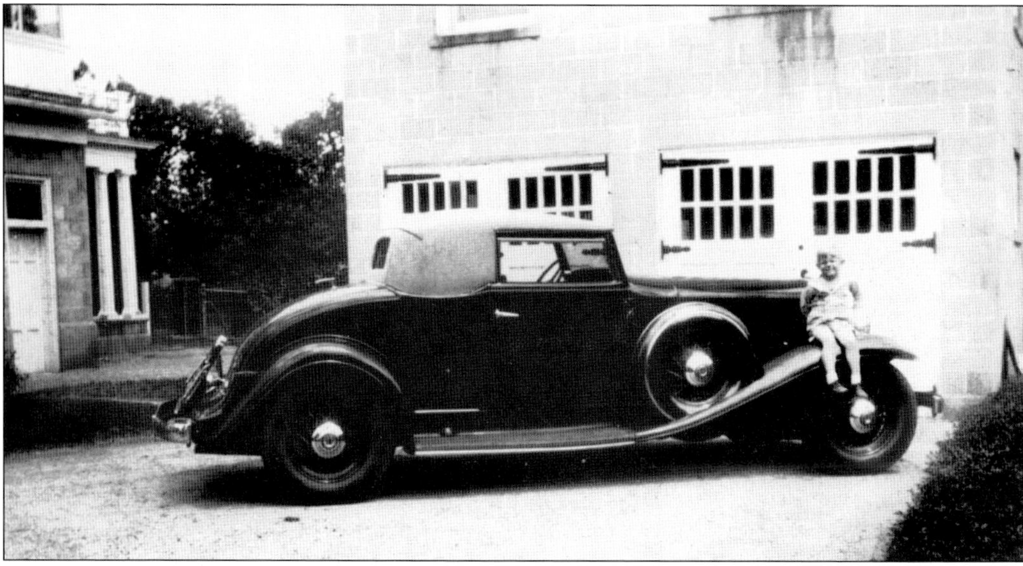

Deb Maner sits on his father's Packard behind the Maner home at 101 East 45th Street. This home is one of many in the neighborhoods that have carriage houses, which once were used as servants' quarters.

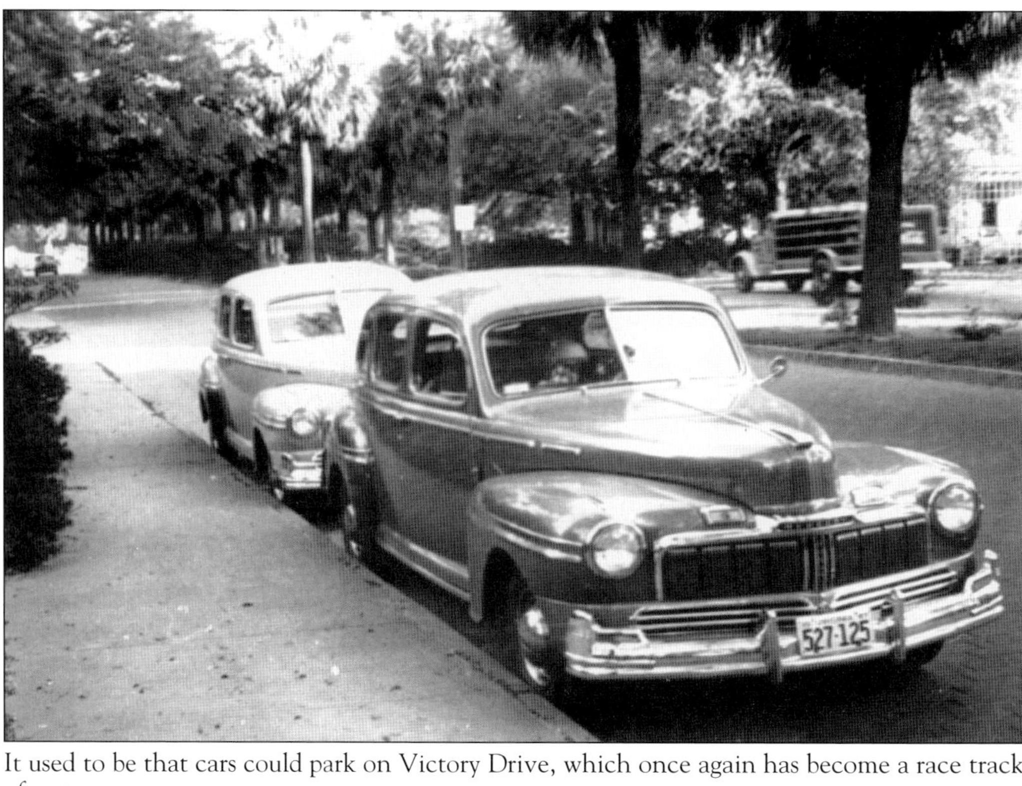

It used to be that cars could park on Victory Drive, which once again has become a race track, of sorts.

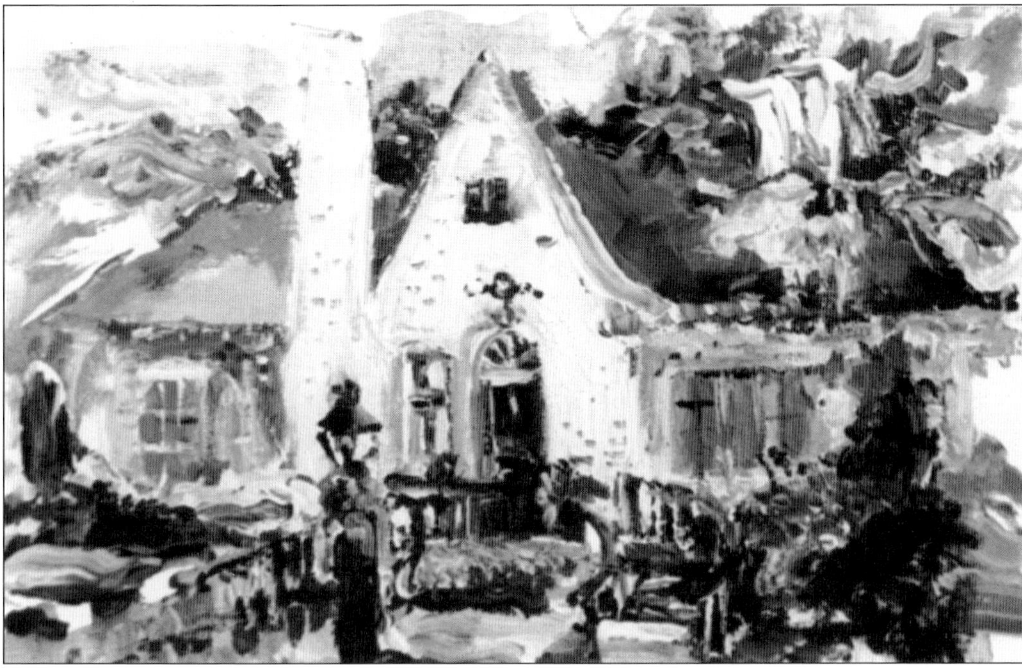

Neighborhood homes have often been the subject of artists' work. Sharon Sasseen painted this picture of her East 50th Street home while she was a student at the University of Georgia.

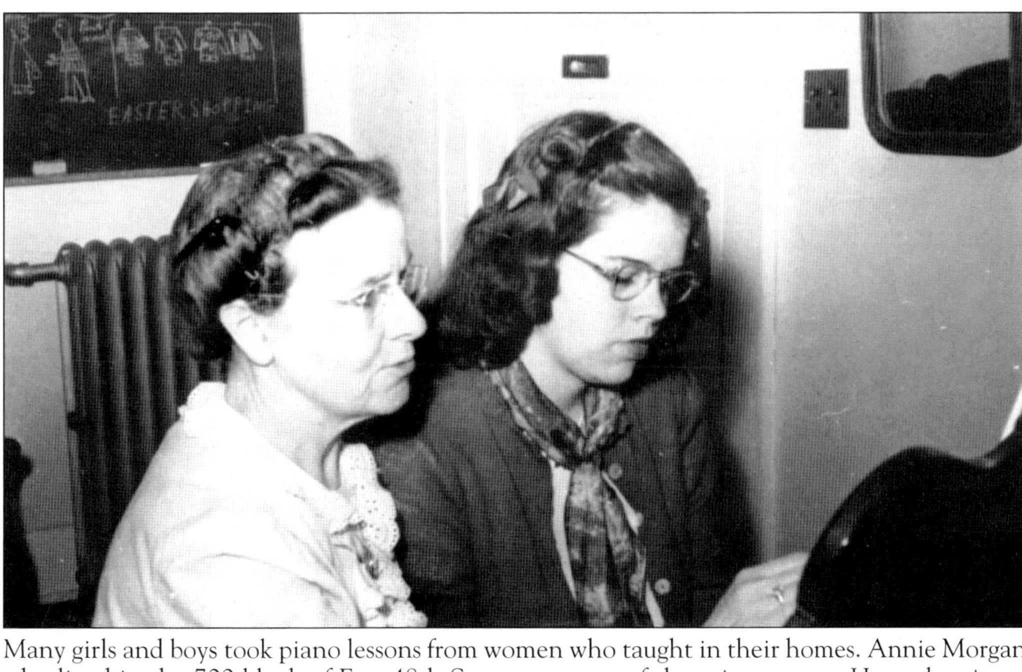

Many girls and boys took piano lessons from women who taught in their homes. Annie Morgan, who lived in the 700 block of East 48th Street, was one of those instructors. Here, she gives a lesson to Ethel McCurry (Burriss).

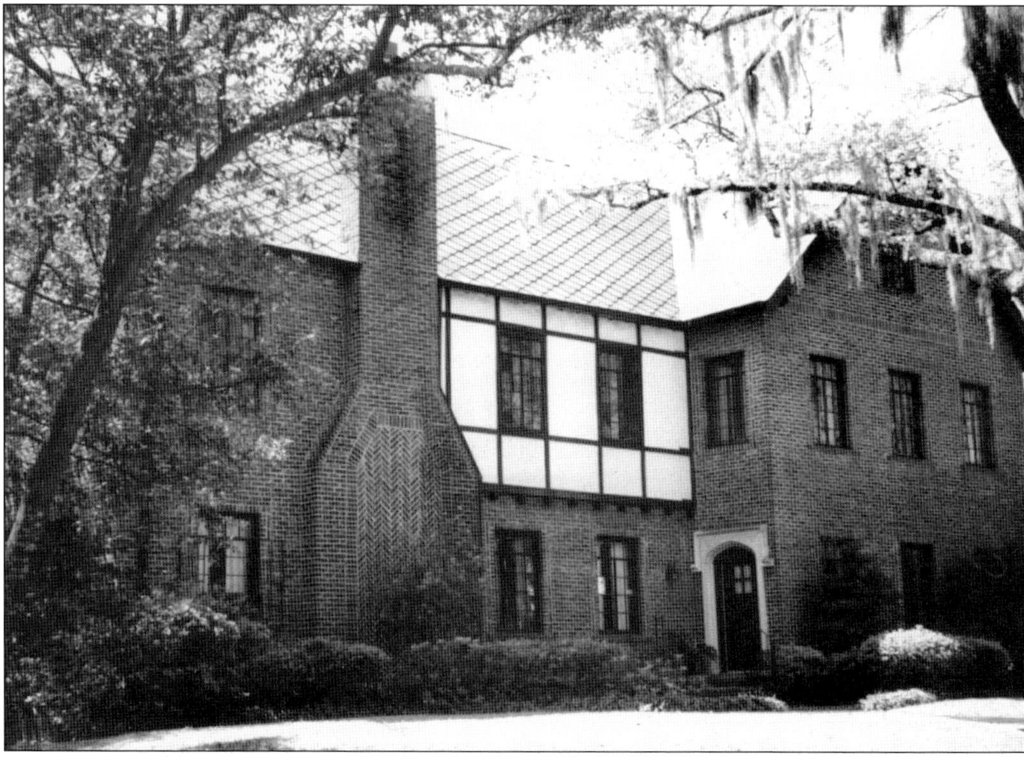

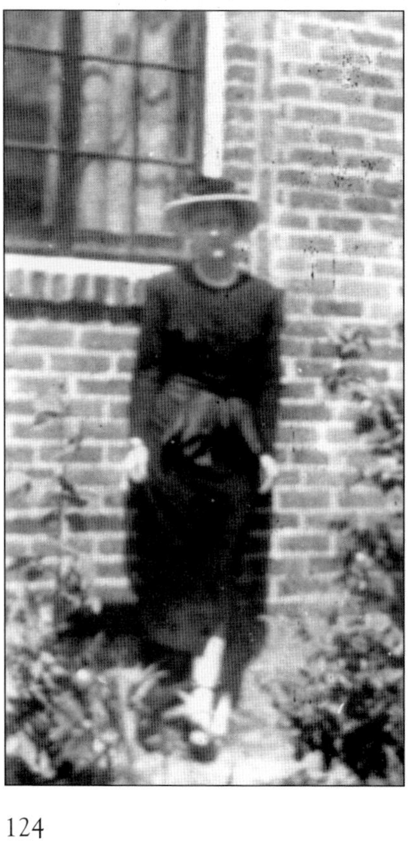

The brick Tudor Revival home at 27 East 49th Street was built in 1926 for W.H. Fry. It was later purchased by the Bernstein family and then by Dr. R. Lester Neville whose family owned it from 1943 until 1991.

Sara Neville poses on the side of her East 49th Street home.

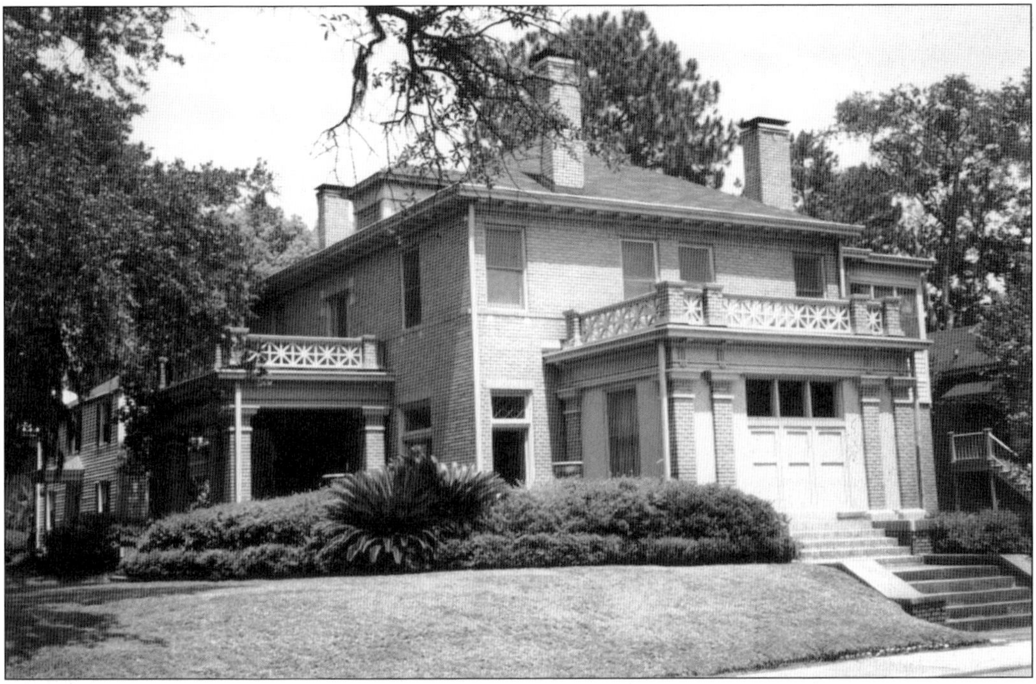

This home at 538 East Victory Drive was built for Judge Beverly Evans in 1920.

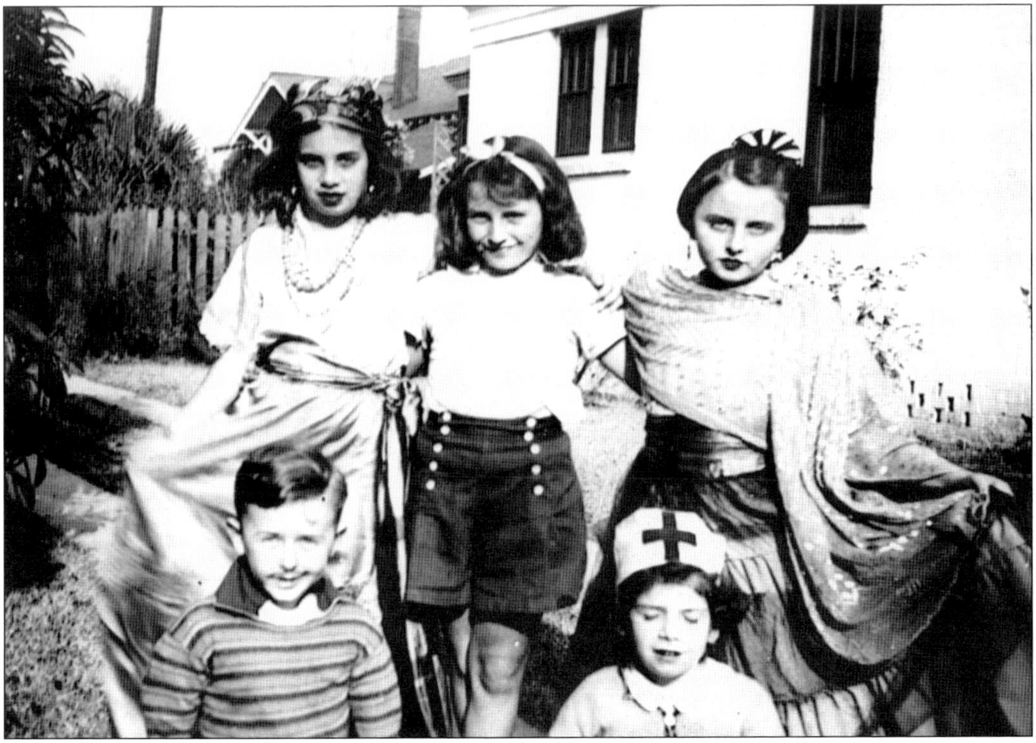

Dress-up was another way to have fun. Pictured here, from left to right, are (front row) Kayton Smith and Margery Guthman (Braverman); (back row) Jane Guthman (Kahn), Betty Ray Fleishel, and Bobbie Smith (Levy).

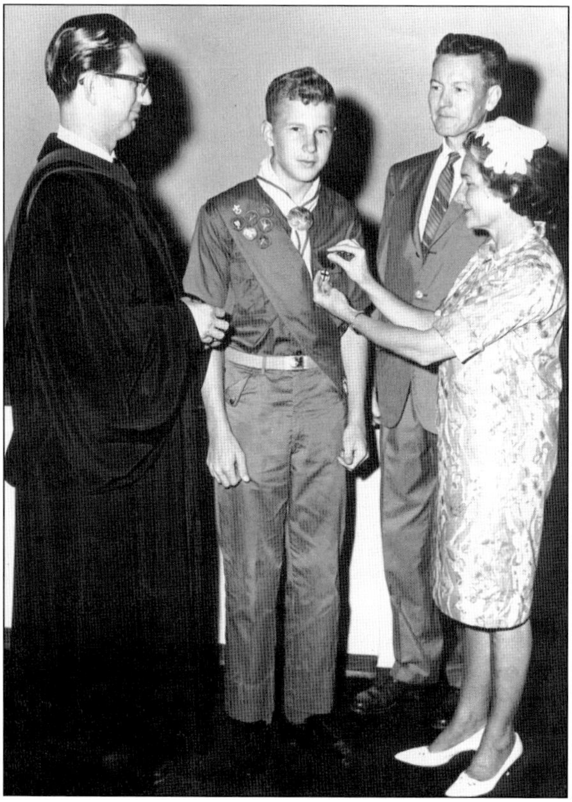

Charles Davis Jr. of First Christian Church is shown receiving the Boy Scout God and Country Award from his mother, Mrs. Helen Davis, as his father, C. Hubert Davis Sr., looks on with Rev. Robert Gill.

A 1940s-era Boy Scout troop sponsored by Ardsley Park Baptist Church included the following, pictured from left to right: (front row) unidentified, Benjamin F. Griffith, Claude Smith, Billy Summerlin, John C. Griffith, and W.L. New; (back row) Rev. W.J. Jones, Rusty Russell, Eddie Thomas, Ben Mark, Cecil Milligan, H.V. Summerlin, Harvey Rivenbark, and Marshall Morgan.

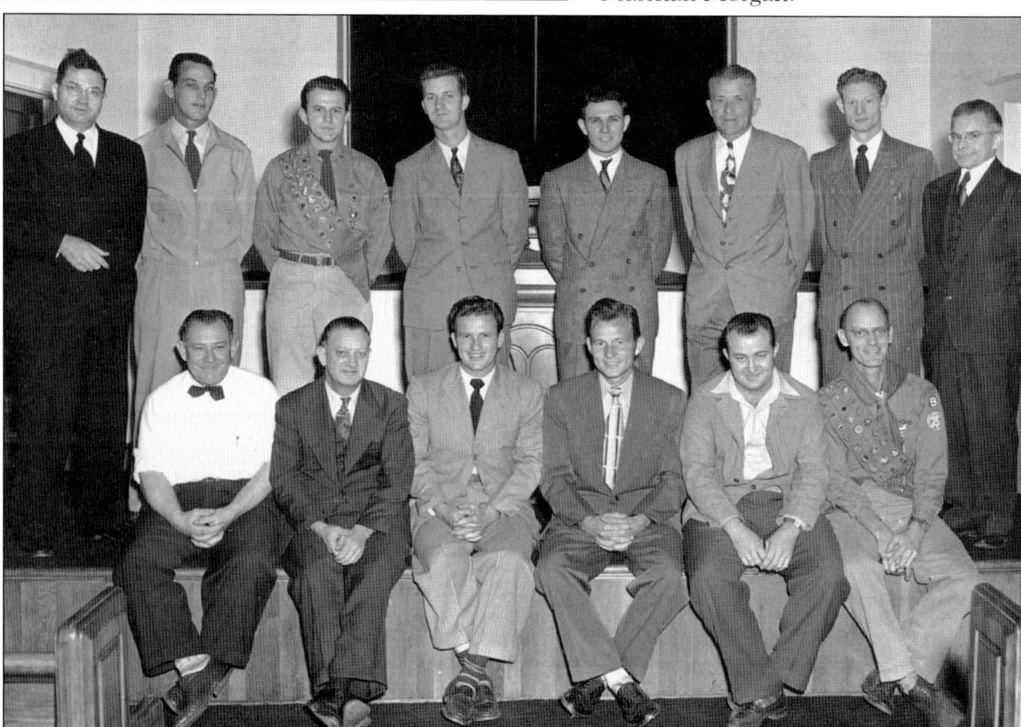

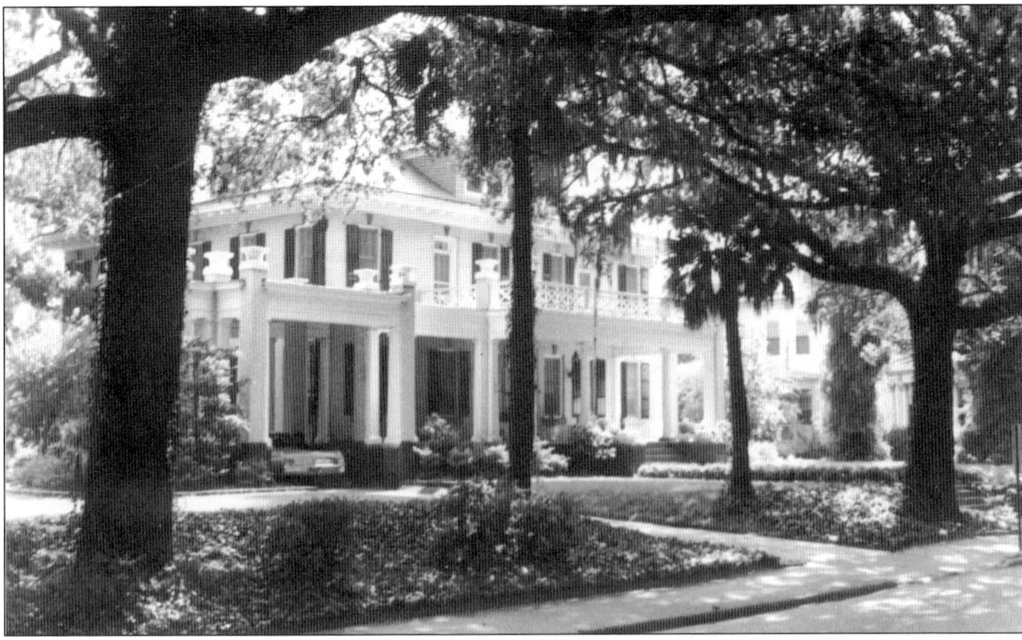

The Pearce home at 910 East Victory Drive was the first built in Chatham Crescent.

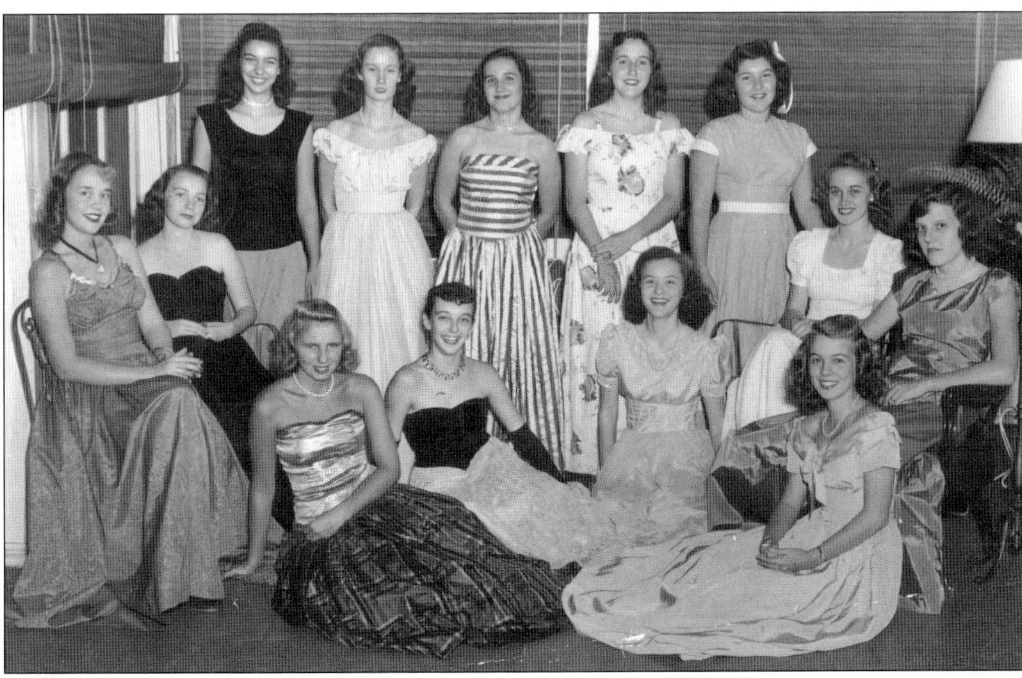

This 1940s Quis Qui photograph includes, from left to right, (on floor) two unidentified members, Nan Garis, Betty Rhodes, Ann Strozier, and Ann Morgan; (back row) unidentified, Marianna McGee, Ruthie Bright, two unidentified girls, Audrey Cammack, and unidentified.

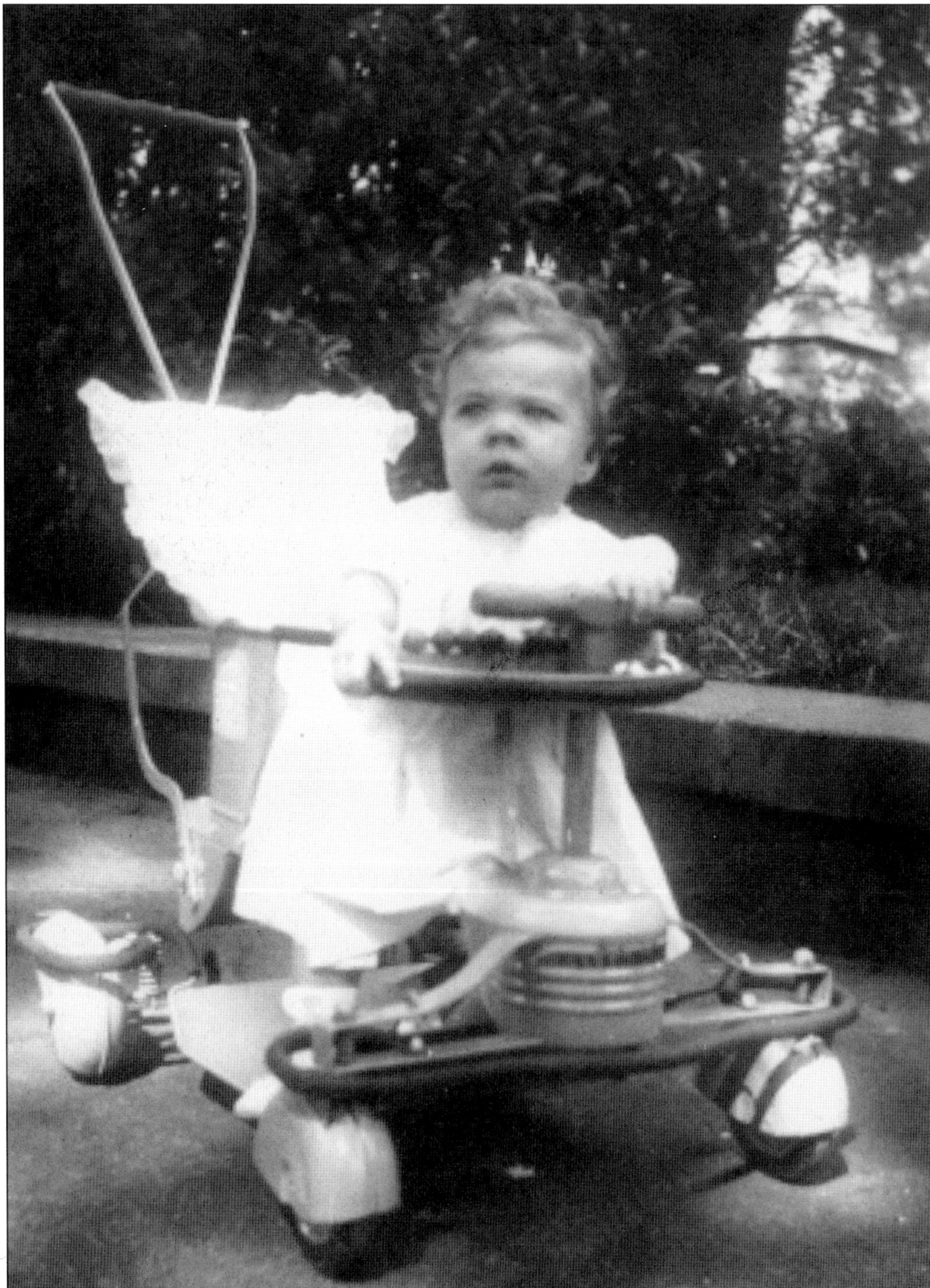

From the very beginning, life in Ardsley Park, Chatham Crescent, and Ardmore has been relaxing and fun, especially for babies like this adorable little girl who took a ride in a 1940s-era stroller.